The Industrial Revolution was a turning point in human history that affected all aspects of everyday life. Technological innovations marked a transition in manufacturing processes, leading to greater production and unprecedented standards of living.

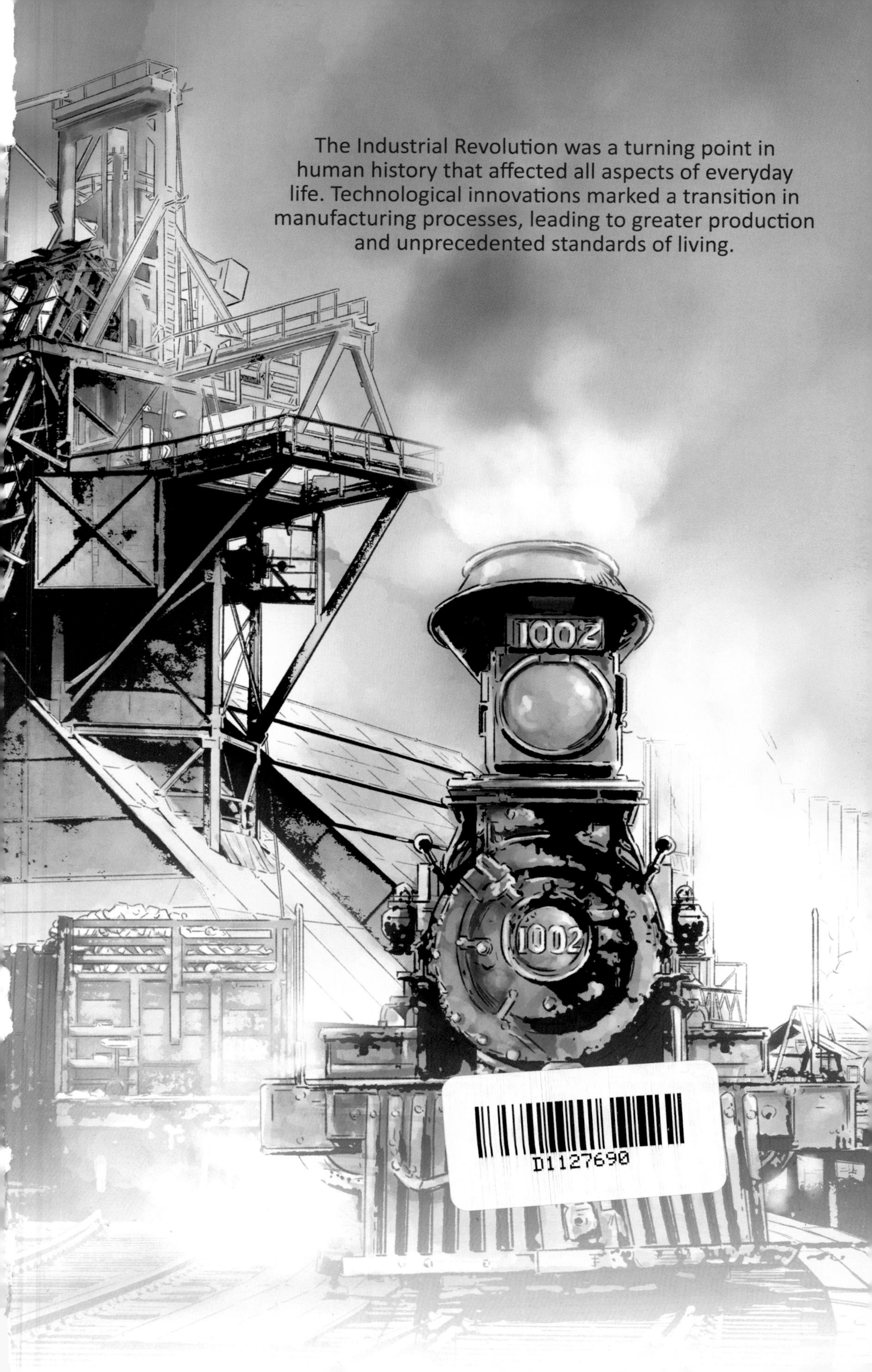

1002
1002

THE INDUSTRIAL REVOLUTION

Writer	:	Lewis Helfand
Illustrator	:	Naresh Kumar
Editor	:	Sourav Dutta
Colorists	:	Ashwani Kashyap and Parveen Kumar Singh
Letterer	:	Bhavnath Chaudhary
Graphic Designer	:	Mukesh Rawat
Cover Artists	:	Naresh Kumar, Vijay Sharma and Pradeep Sherawat

Mission Statement

To entertain and educate young minds by creating unique illustrated books that recount stories of human values, arouse curiosity in the world around us, and inspire with tales of great deeds of unforgettable people.

CAMPFIRE®

Published by Kalyani Navyug Media Pvt Ltd
101 C, Shiv House, Hari Nagar Ashram, New Delhi 110014, India
ISBN: 978-93-81182-28-4
Copyright © 2016 Kalyani Navyug Media Pvt Ltd

Printed in India

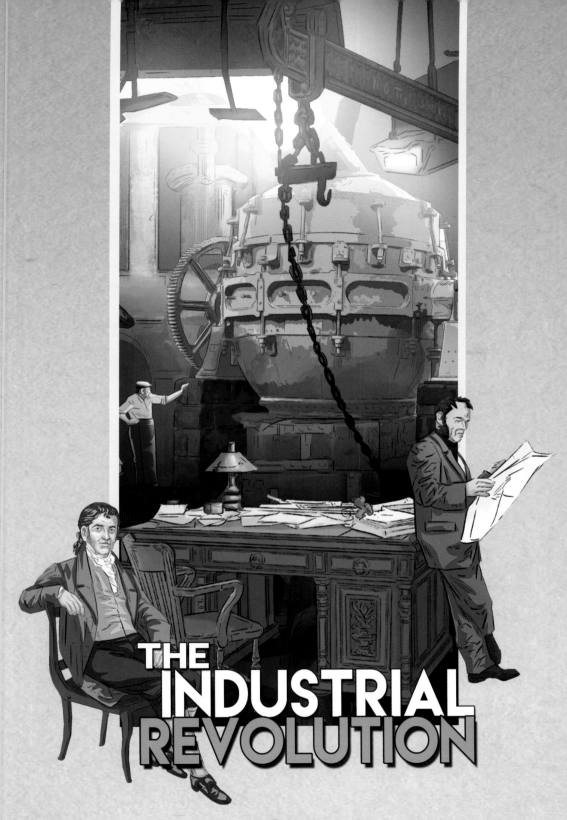

THE INDUSTRIAL REVOLUTION

CAMPFIRE®

KALYANI NAVYUG MEDIA PVT LTD

About the author

Lewis Helfand is a resident of Narberth, Pennsylvania and grew up wanting to write comic books. His journey to figure out how to do that has involved everything from studying sculpture and politics to traveling through Spain and Denmark to writing about adventure sports and sword making. He is currently merging all these diverse interests writing graphic novels for Campfire. Some of his recent titles include the award winning *Nelson Mandela: The Unconquerable Soul, Mother Teresa: Angel Of The Slums, They Changed The World: Edison-Tesla-Bell, They Changed the World: Crick & Watson* and *World War Two: Under the Shadow of the Swastika.*

About the artist

A resident of New Delhi, India, Naresh Kumar describes himself as a seeker who is continuously trying to learn as much as he can, and his art is an expression of his curiosity toward the world. A firm believer in humanity, Naresh brings an experienced hand to the drawing board, and his photo-realistic style captures the subtle emotions of his characters. His work features in a number of titles from Campfire, which include *World War Two: Against the Rising Sun, Genesis: From Creation to the Flood, Julius Caesar, Martin Luther King Jr.: Let Freedom Ring,* and *They Changed the World: Crick & Watson.*

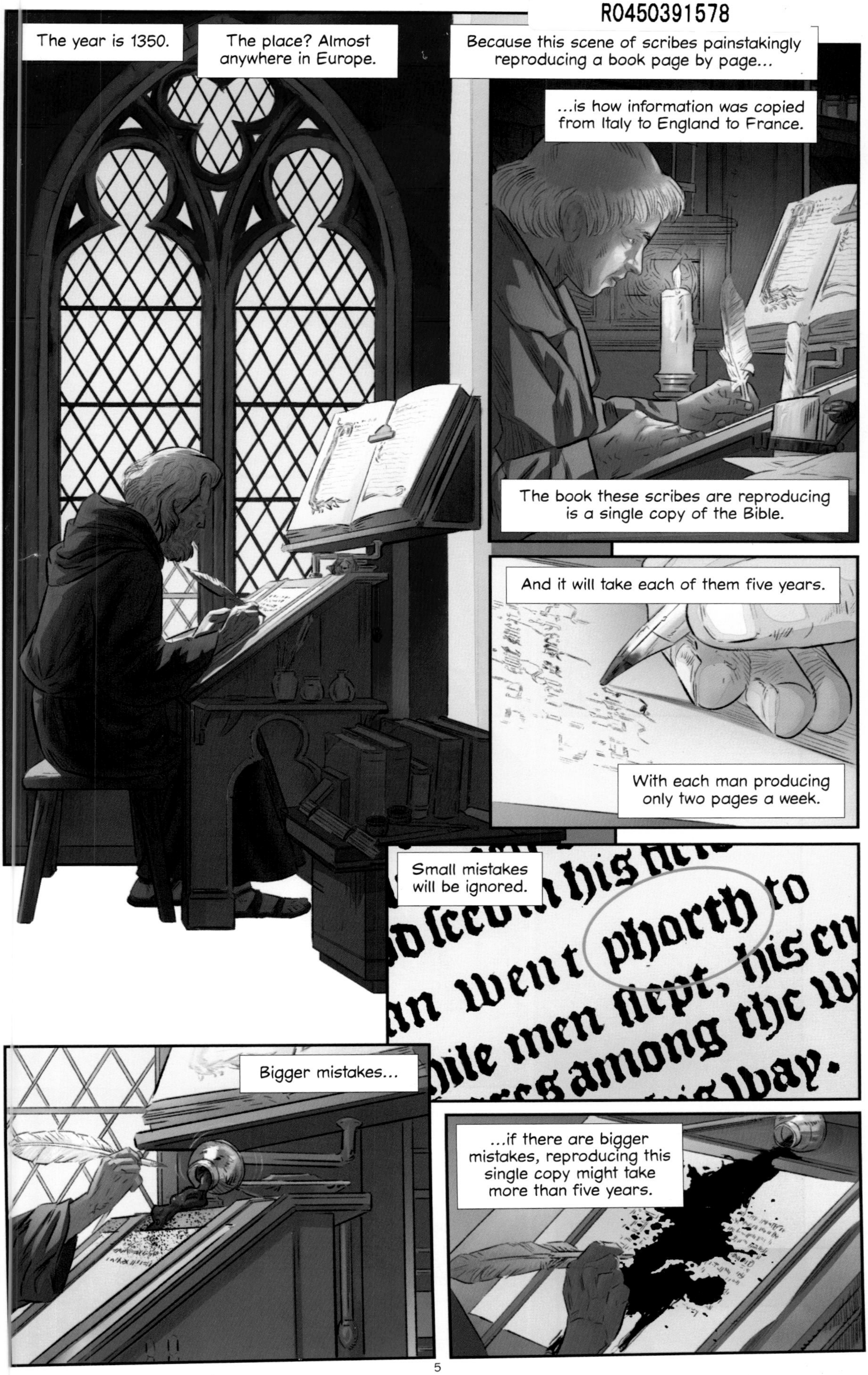
The year is 1350.
The place? Almost anywhere in Europe.
Because this scene of scribes painstakingly reproducing a book page by page...
...is how information was copied from Italy to England to France.
The book these scribes are reproducing is a single copy of the Bible.
And it will take each of them five years.
With each man producing only two pages a week.
Small mistakes will be ignored.
his
went phorth to
men slept, his
among the
way.
Bigger mistakes...
...if there are bigger mistakes, reproducing this single copy might take more than five years.

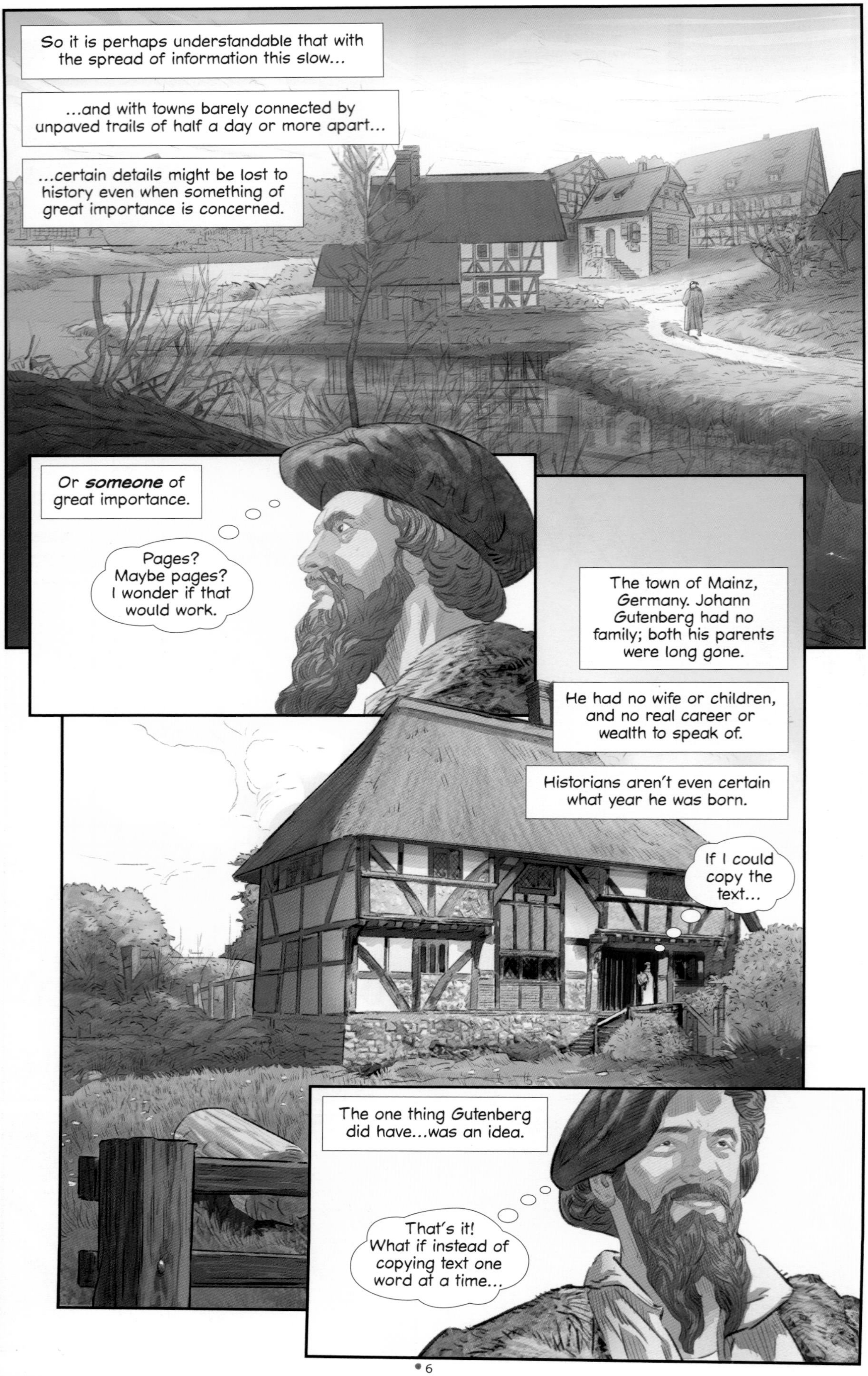

So it is perhaps understandable that with the spread of information this slow...
...and with towns barely connected by unpaved trails of half a day or more apart...
...certain details might be lost to history even when something of great importance is concerned.
Or ***someone*** of great importance.
Pages? Maybe pages? I wonder if that would work.
The town of Mainz, Germany. Johann Gutenberg had no family; both his parents were long gone.
He had no wife or children, and no real career or wealth to speak of.
Historians aren't even certain what year he was born.
If I could copy the text...
The one thing Gutenberg did have...was an idea.
That's it! What if instead of copying text one word at a time...

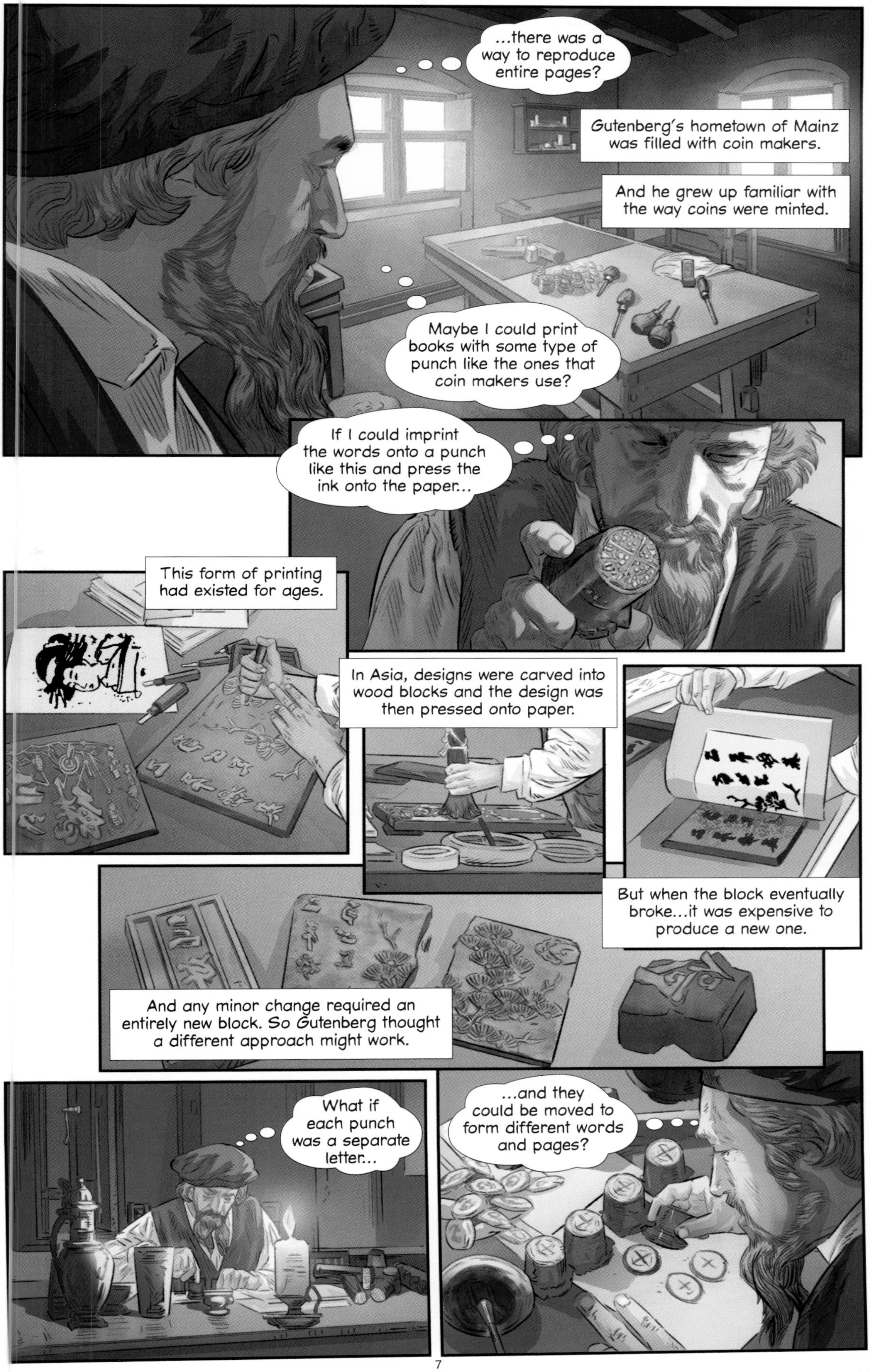
...there was a way to reproduce entire pages?
Gutenberg's hometown of Mainz was filled with coin makers.
And he grew up familiar with the way coins were minted.
Maybe I could print books with some type of punch like the ones that coin makers use?
If I could imprint the words onto a punch like this and press the ink onto the paper...
This form of printing had existed for ages.
In Asia, designs were carved into wood blocks and the design was then pressed onto paper.
But when the block eventually broke...it was expensive to produce a new one.
And any minor change required an entirely new block. So Gutenberg thought a different approach might work.
What if each punch was a separate letter...
...and they could be moved to form different words and pages?

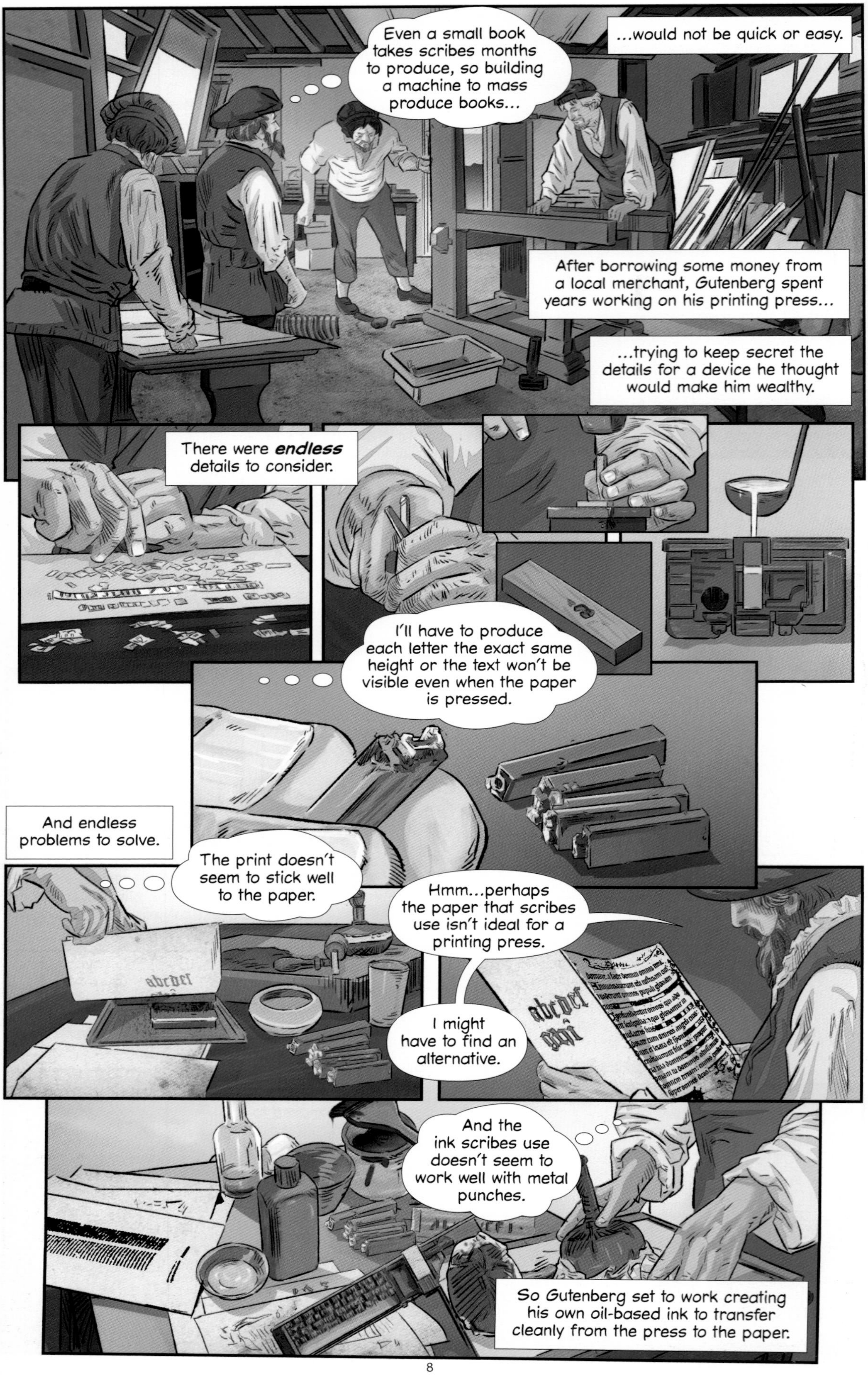
Even a small book takes scribes months to produce, so building a machine to mass produce books...
...would not be quick or easy.
After borrowing some money from a local merchant, Gutenberg spent years working on his printing press...
...trying to keep secret the details for a device he thought would make him wealthy.
There were ***endless*** details to consider.
I'll have to produce each letter the exact same height or the text won't be visible even when the paper is pressed.
And endless problems to solve.
The print doesn't seem to stick well to the paper.
Hmm...perhaps the paper that scribes use isn't ideal for a printing press.
I might have to find an alternative.
And the ink scribes use doesn't seem to work well with metal punches.
So Gutenberg set to work creating his own oil-based ink to transfer cleanly from the press to the paper.

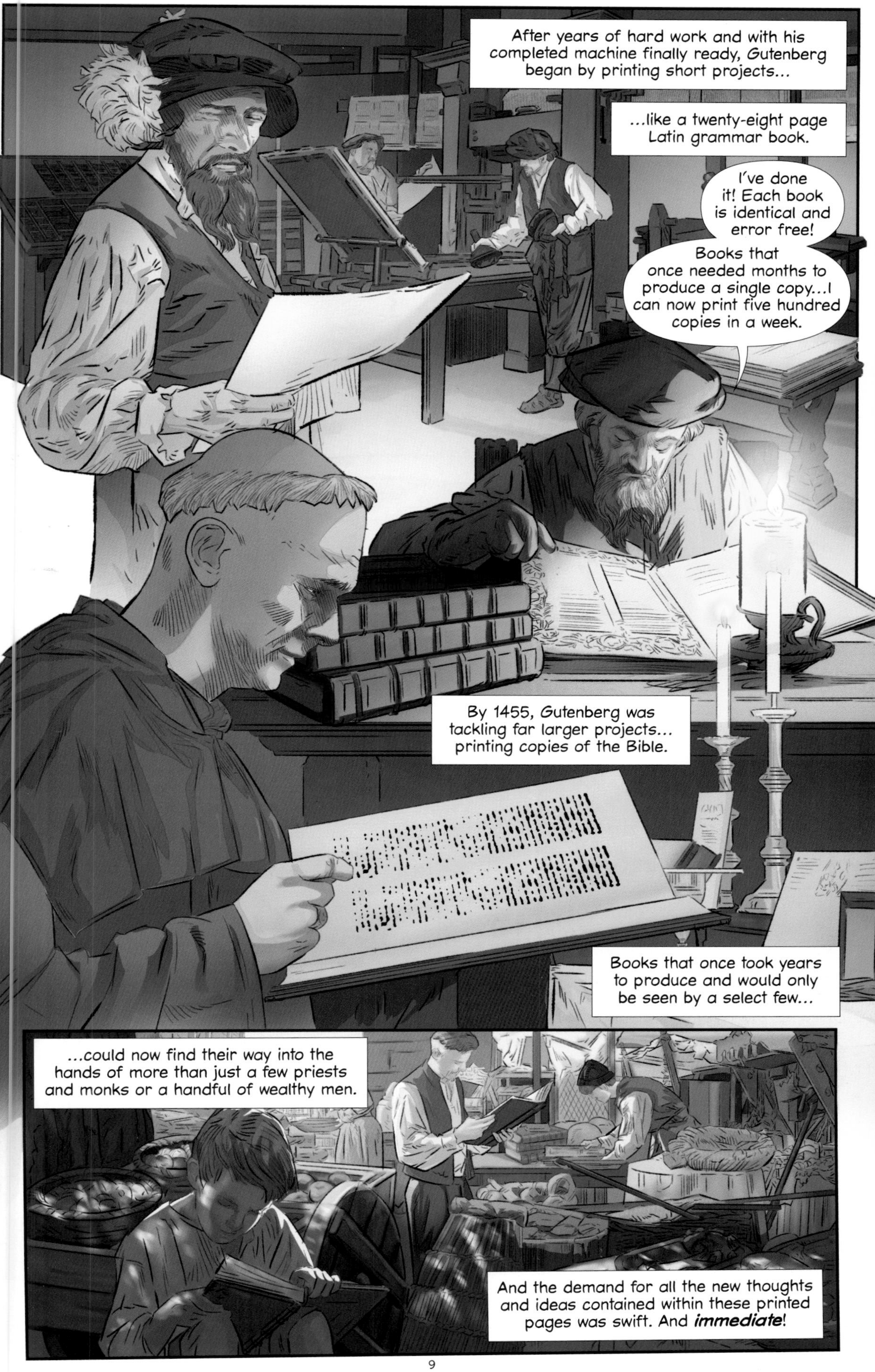
After years of hard work and with his completed machine finally ready, Gutenberg began by printing short projects...
...like a twenty-eight page Latin grammar book.
I've done it! Each book is identical and error free!
Books that once needed months to produce a single copy...I can now print five hundred copies in a week.
By 1455, Gutenberg was tackling far larger projects... printing copies of the Bible.
Books that once took years to produce and would only be seen by a select few...
...could now find their way into the hands of more than just a few priests and monks or a handful of wealthy men.
And the demand for all the new thoughts and ideas contained within these printed pages was swift. And *immediate*!

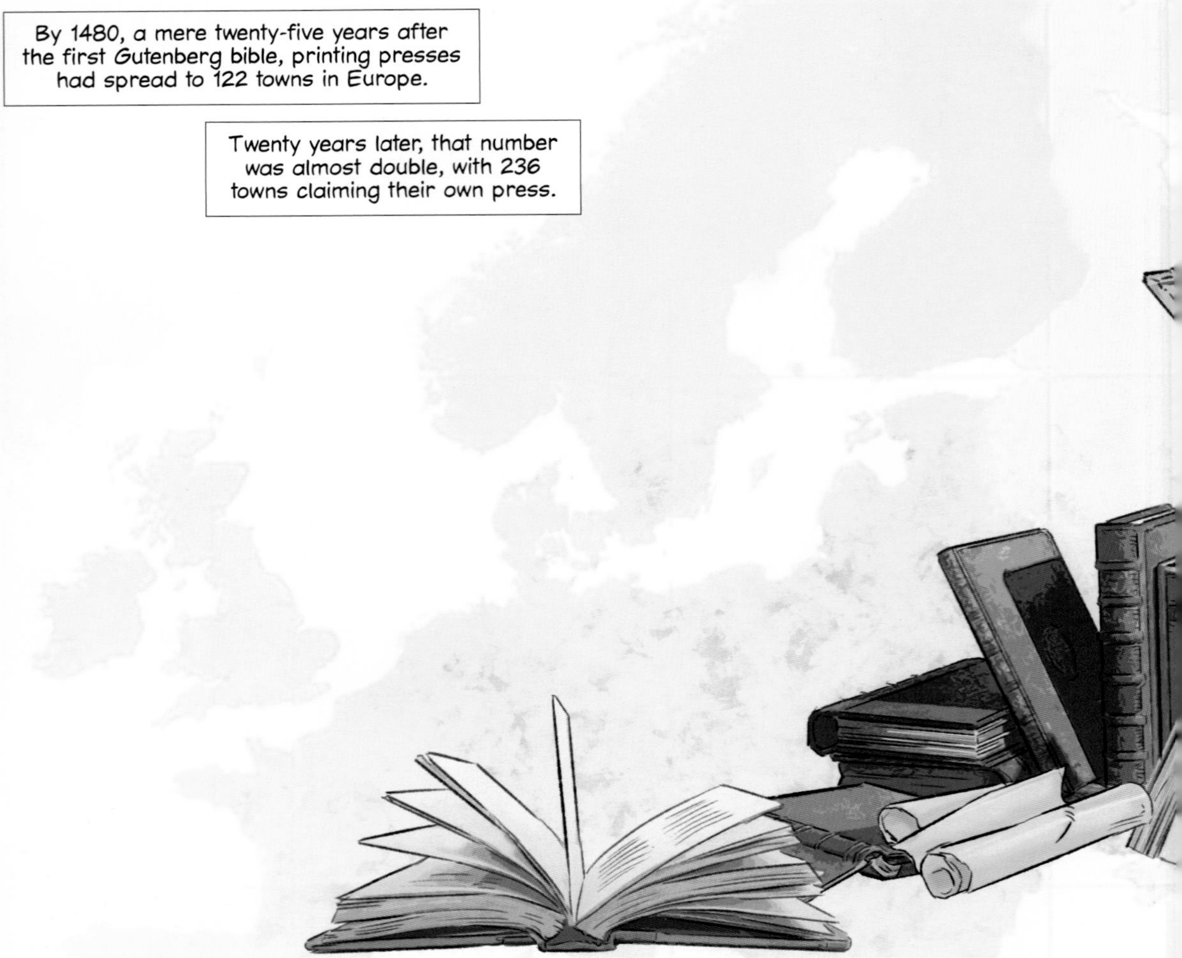
By 1480, a mere twenty-five years after the first Gutenberg bible, printing presses had spread to 122 towns in Europe.
Twenty years later, that number was almost double, with 236 towns claiming their own press.

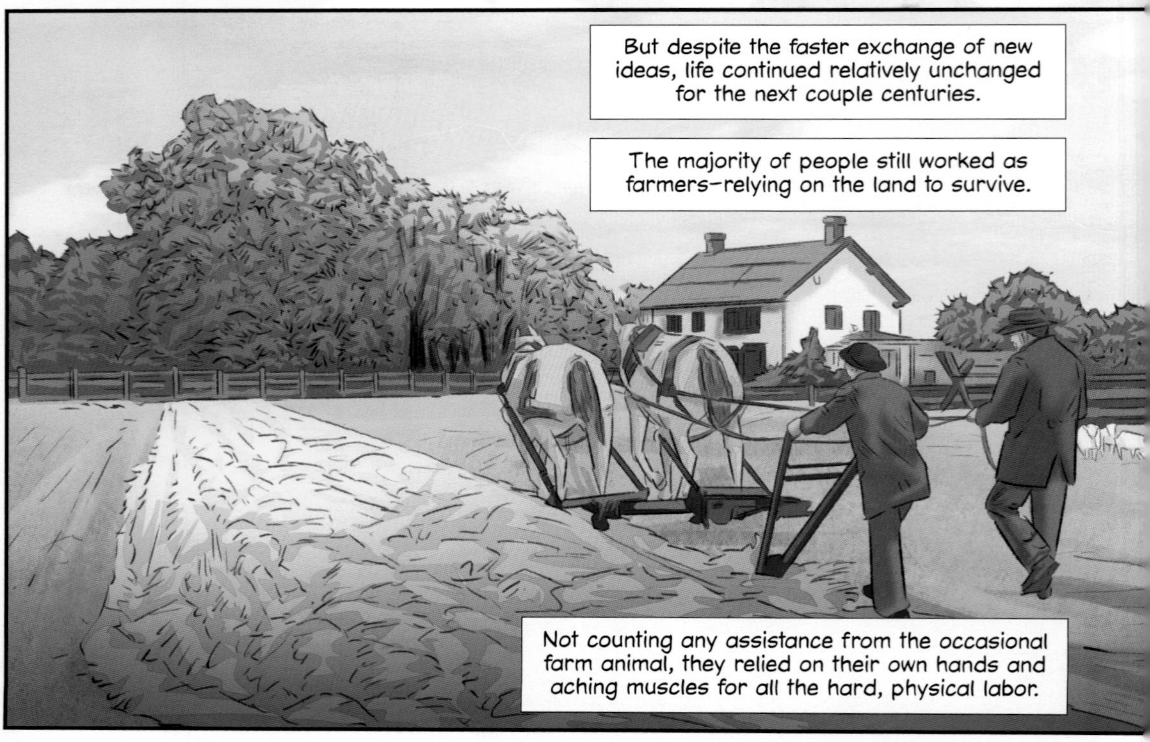
But despite the faster exchange of new ideas, life continued relatively unchanged for the next couple centuries.
The majority of people still worked as farmers—relying on the land to survive.
Not counting any assistance from the occasional farm animal, they relied on their own hands and aching muscles for all the hard, physical labor.

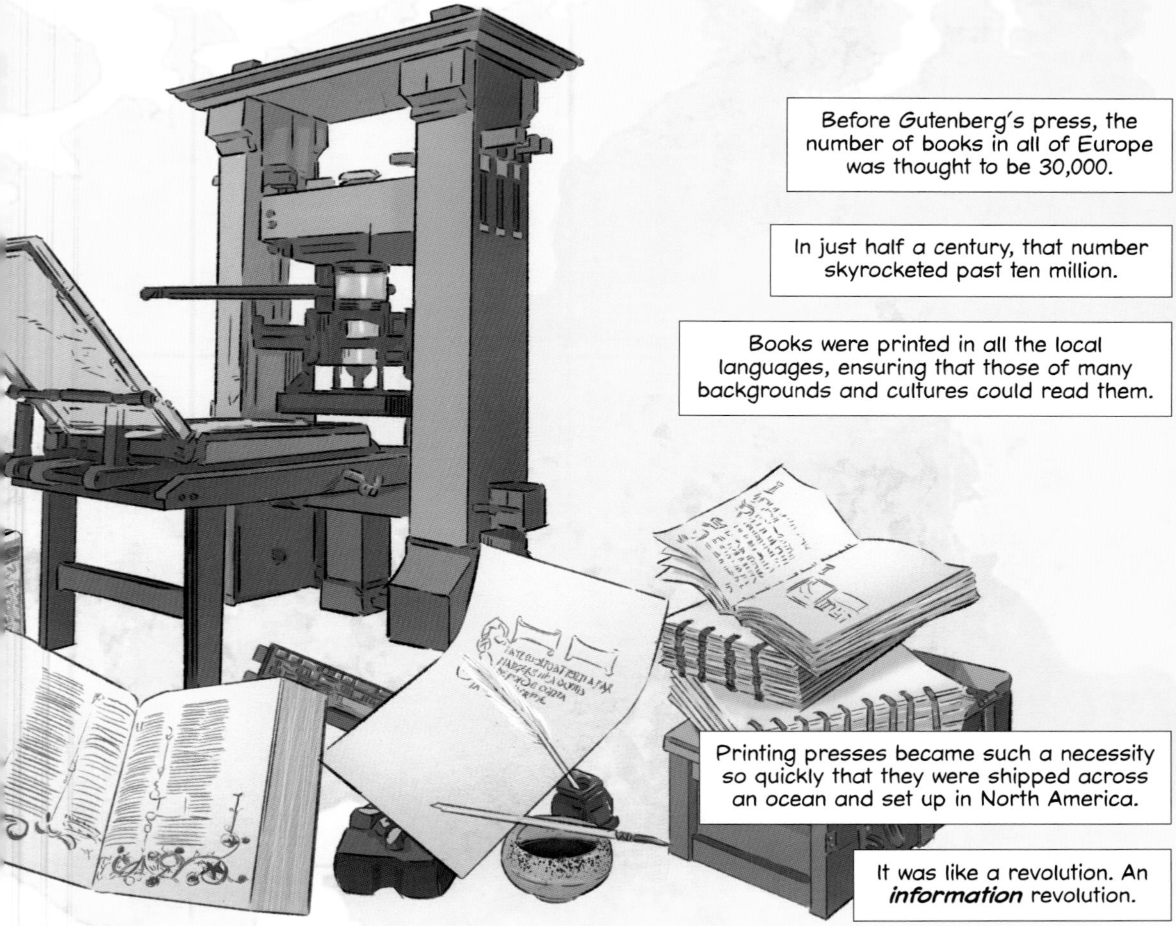
Before Gutenberg's press, the number of books in all of Europe was thought to be 30,000.
In just half a century, that number skyrocketed past ten million.
Books were printed in all the local languages, ensuring that those of many backgrounds and cultures could read them.
Printing presses became such a necessity so quickly that they were shipped across an ocean and set up in North America.
It was like a revolution. An ***information*** revolution.

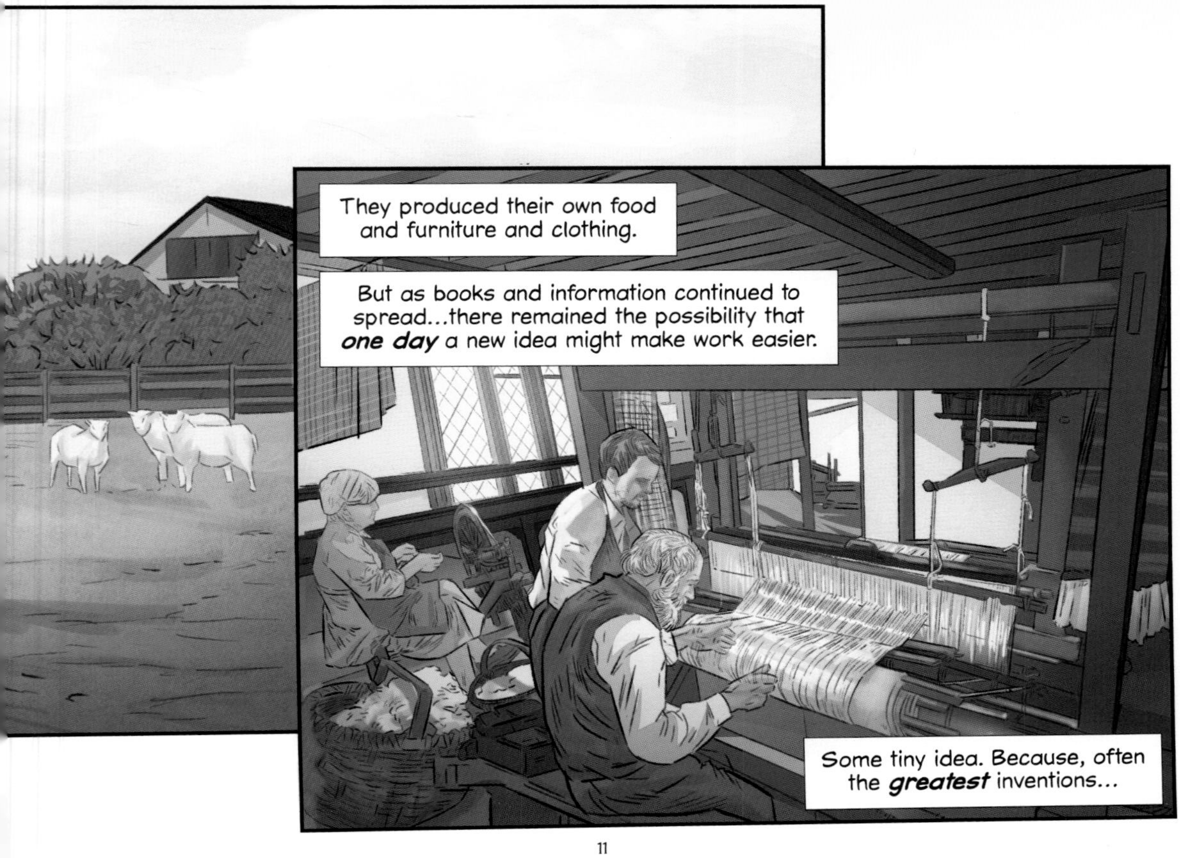
They produced their own food and furniture and clothing.
But as books and information continued to spread...there remained the possibility that ***one day*** a new idea might make work easier.
Some tiny idea. Because, often the ***greatest*** inventions...

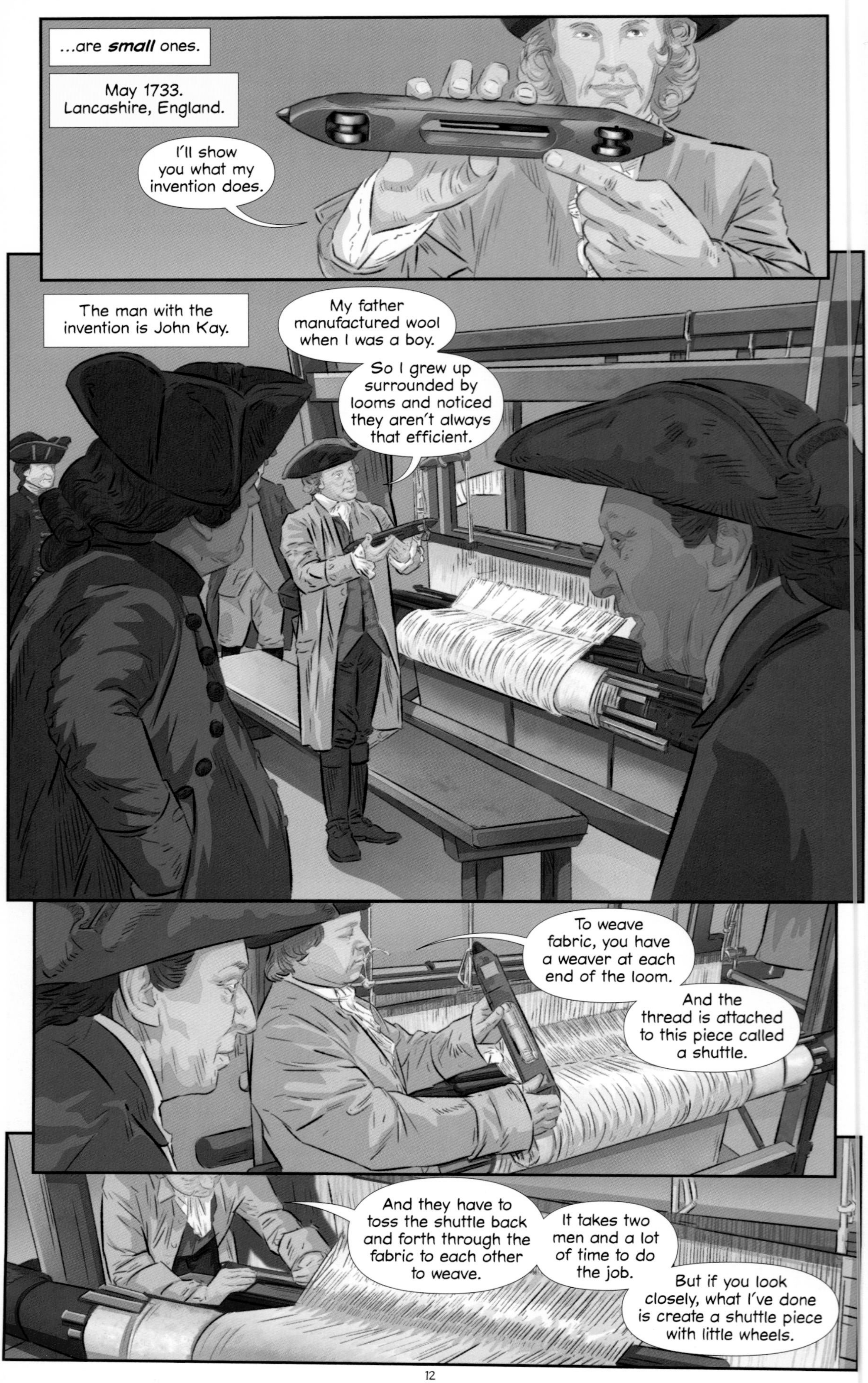
...are *small* ones.
May 1733. Lancashire, England.
I'll show you what my invention does.
The man with the invention is John Kay.
My father manufactured wool when I was a boy.
So I grew up surrounded by looms and noticed they aren't always that efficient.
To weave fabric, you have a weaver at each end of the loom.
And the thread is attached to this piece called a shuttle.
And they have to toss the shuttle back and forth through the fabric to each other to weave.
It takes two men and a lot of time to do the job.
But if you look closely, what I've done is create a shuttle piece with little wheels.

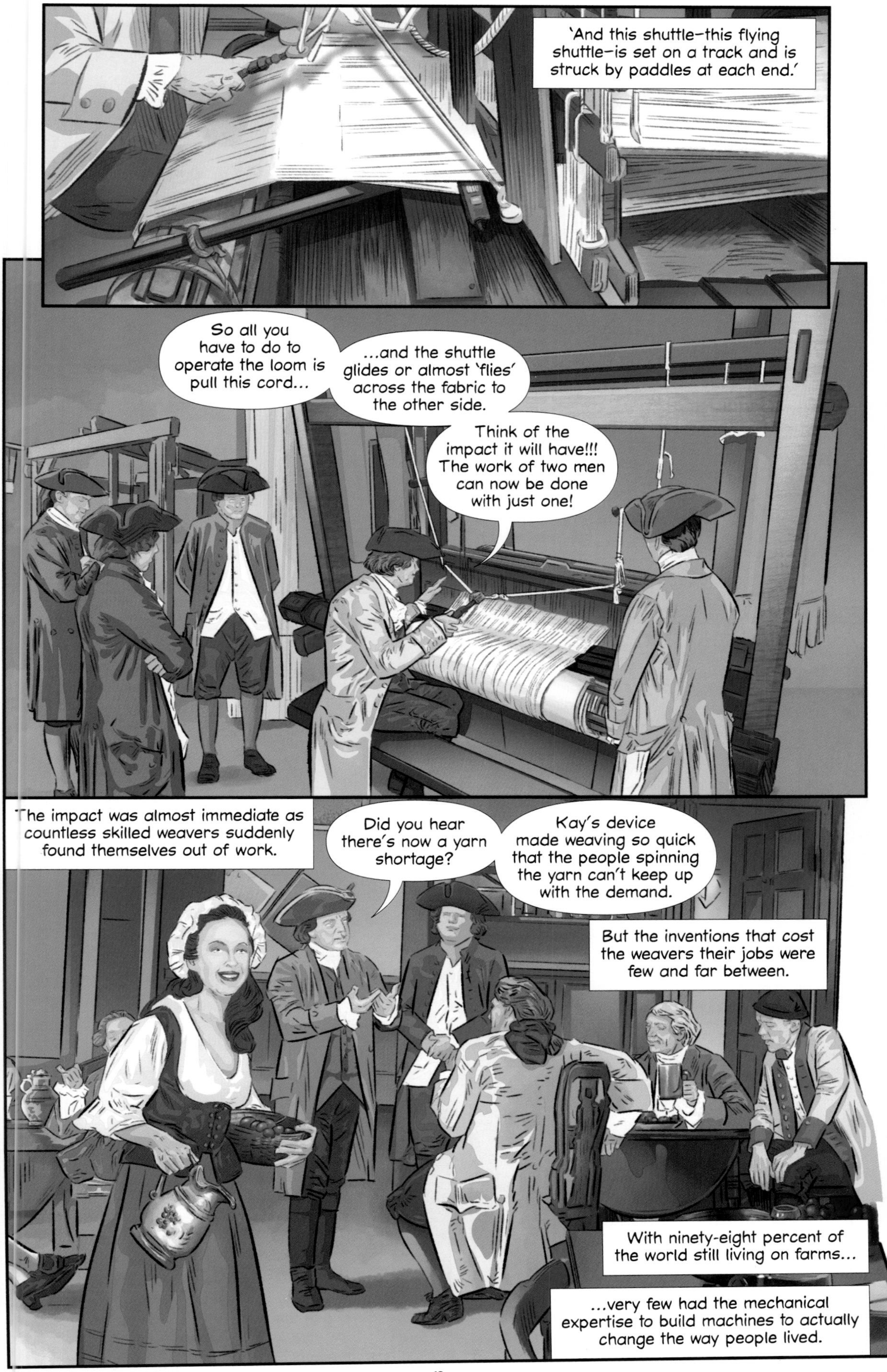

'And this shuttle–this flying shuttle–is set on a track and is struck by paddles at each end.'
So all you have to do to operate the loom is pull this cord...
...and the shuttle glides or almost 'flies' across the fabric to the other side.
Think of the impact it will have!!! The work of two men can now be done with just one!
The impact was almost immediate as countless skilled weavers suddenly found themselves out of work.
Did you hear there's now a yarn shortage?
Kay's device made weaving so quick that the people spinning the yarn can't keep up with the demand.
But the inventions that cost the weavers their jobs were few and far between.
With ninety-eight percent of the world still living on farms...
...very few had the mechanical expertise to build machines to actually change the way people lived.

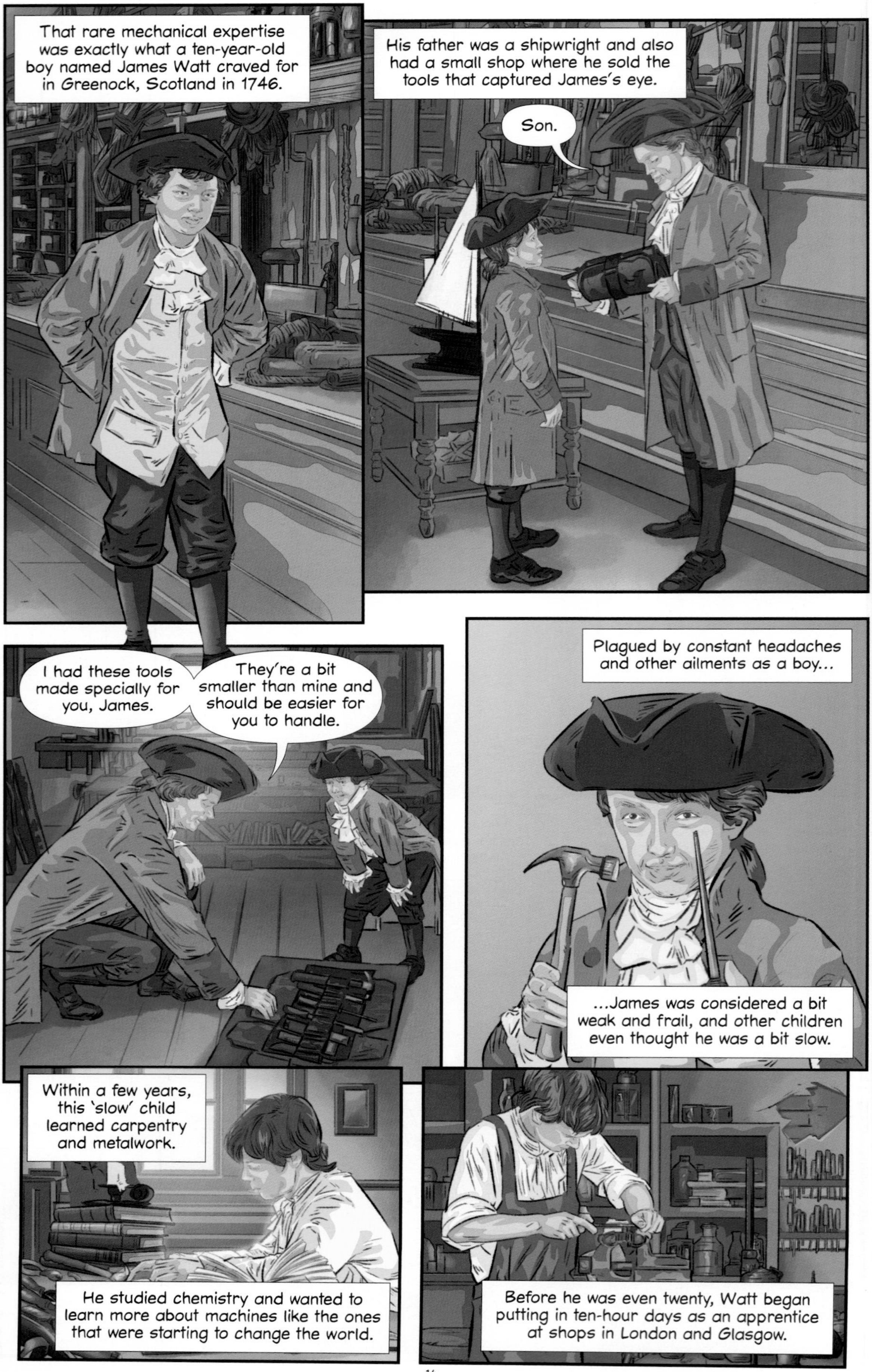
That rare mechanical expertise was exactly what a ten-year-old boy named James Watt craved for in Greenock, Scotland in 1746.
His father was a shipwright and also had a small shop where he sold the tools that captured James's eye.
Son.
I had these tools made specially for you, James.
They're a bit smaller than mine and should be easier for you to handle.
Plagued by constant headaches and other ailments as a boy...
...James was considered a bit weak and frail, and other children even thought he was a bit slow.
Within a few years, this 'slow' child learned carpentry and metalwork.
He studied chemistry and wanted to learn more about machines like the ones that were starting to change the world.
Before he was even twenty, Watt began putting in ten-hour days as an apprentice at shops in London and Glasgow.

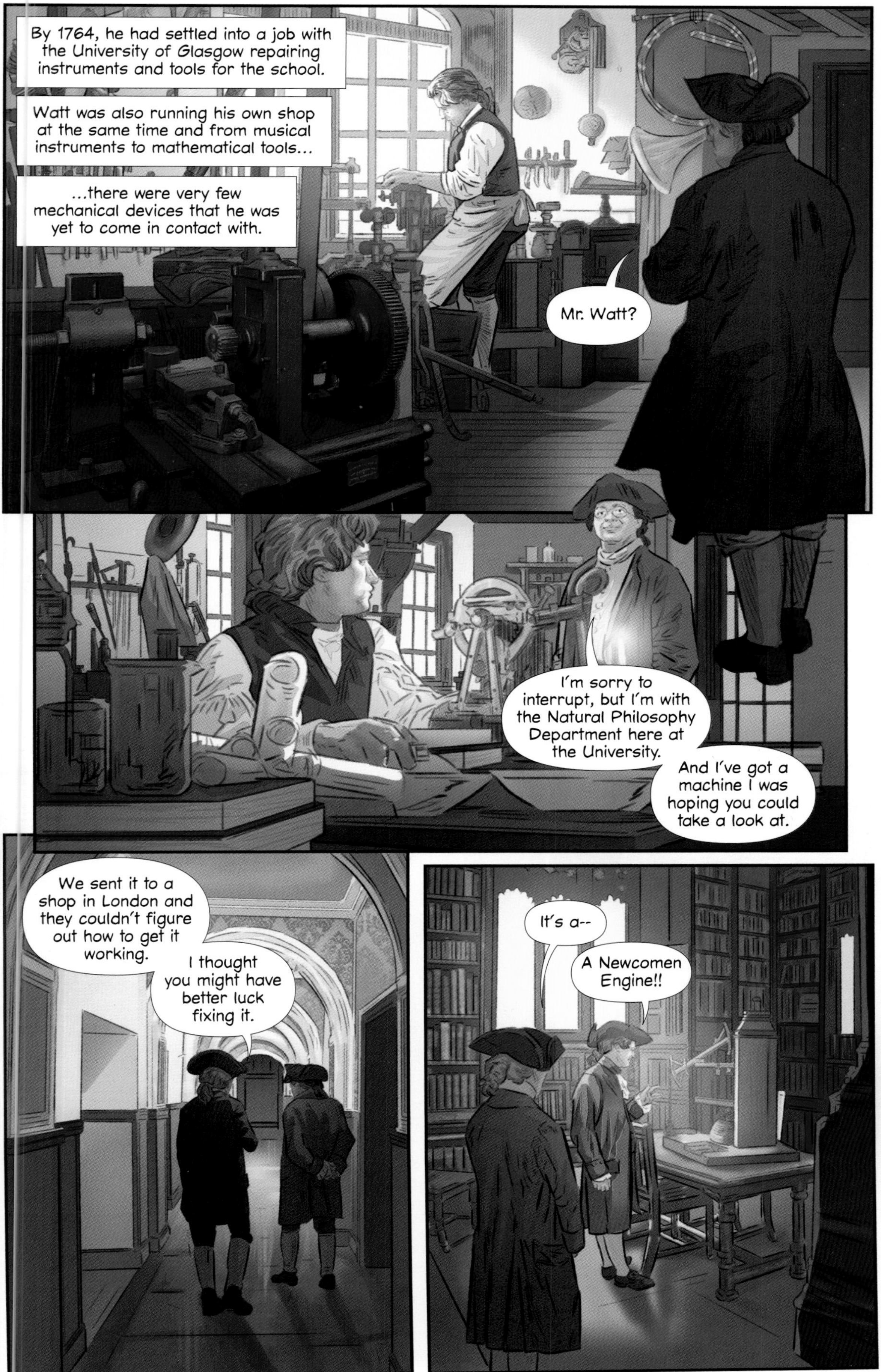

By 1764, he had settled into a job with the University of Glasgow repairing instruments and tools for the school.
Watt was also running his own shop at the same time and from musical instruments to mathematical tools...
...there were very few mechanical devices that he was yet to come in contact with.
Mr. Watt?
I'm sorry to interrupt, but I'm with the Natural Philosophy Department here at the University.
And I've got a machine I was hoping you could take a look at.
We sent it to a shop in London and they couldn't figure out how to get it working.
I thought you might have better luck fixing it.
It's a--
A Newcomen Engine!!

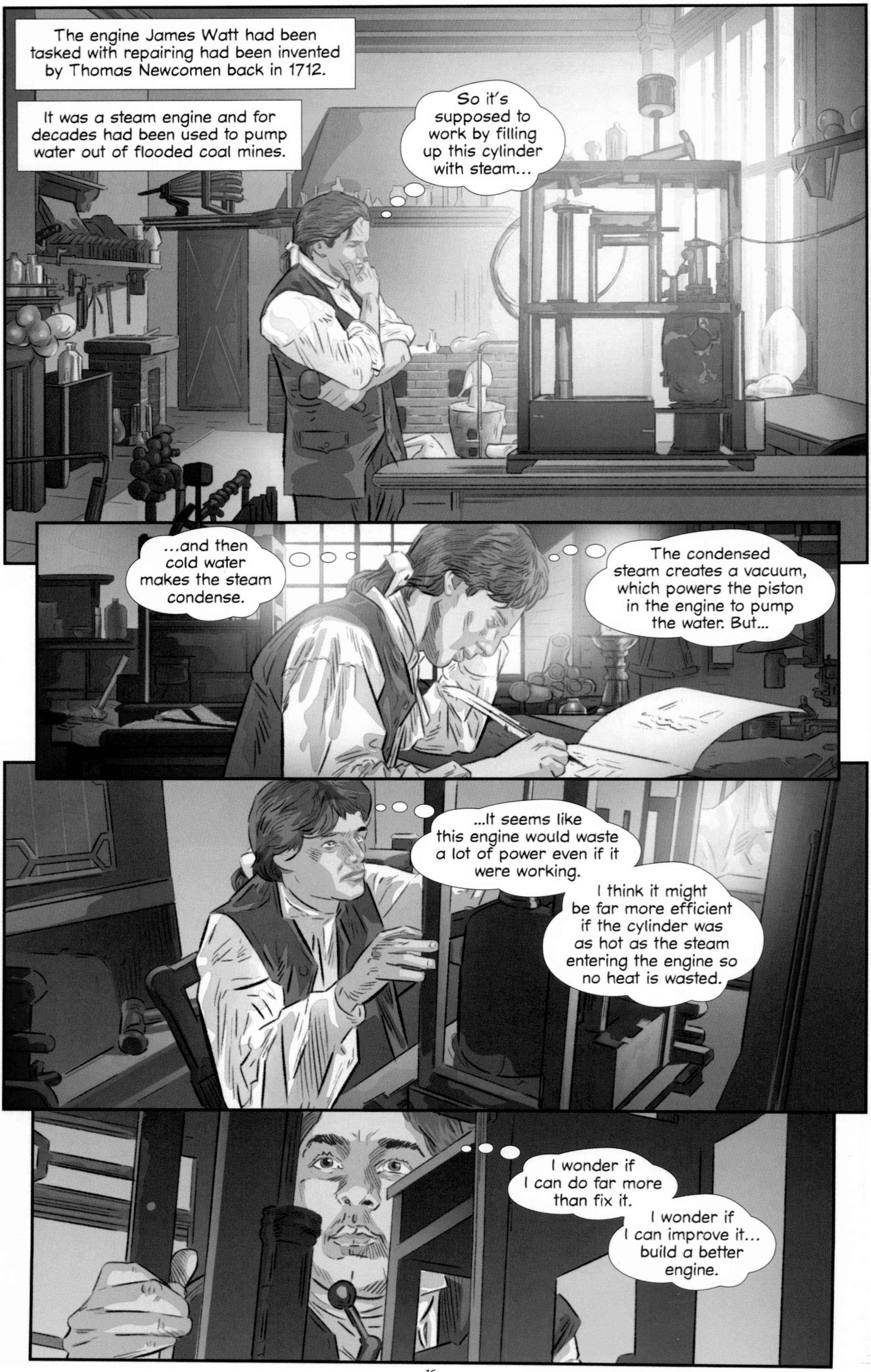
The engine James Watt had been tasked with repairing had been invented by Thomas Newcomen back in 1712.
It was a steam engine and for decades had been used to pump water out of flooded coal mines.
So it's supposed to work by filling up this cylinder with steam...
...and then cold water makes the steam condense.
The condensed steam creates a vacuum, which powers the piston in the engine to pump the water. But...
...It seems like this engine would waste a lot of power even if it were working.
I think it might be far more efficient if the cylinder was as hot as the steam entering the engine so no heat is wasted.
I wonder if I can do far more than fix it.
I wonder if I can improve it... build a better engine.

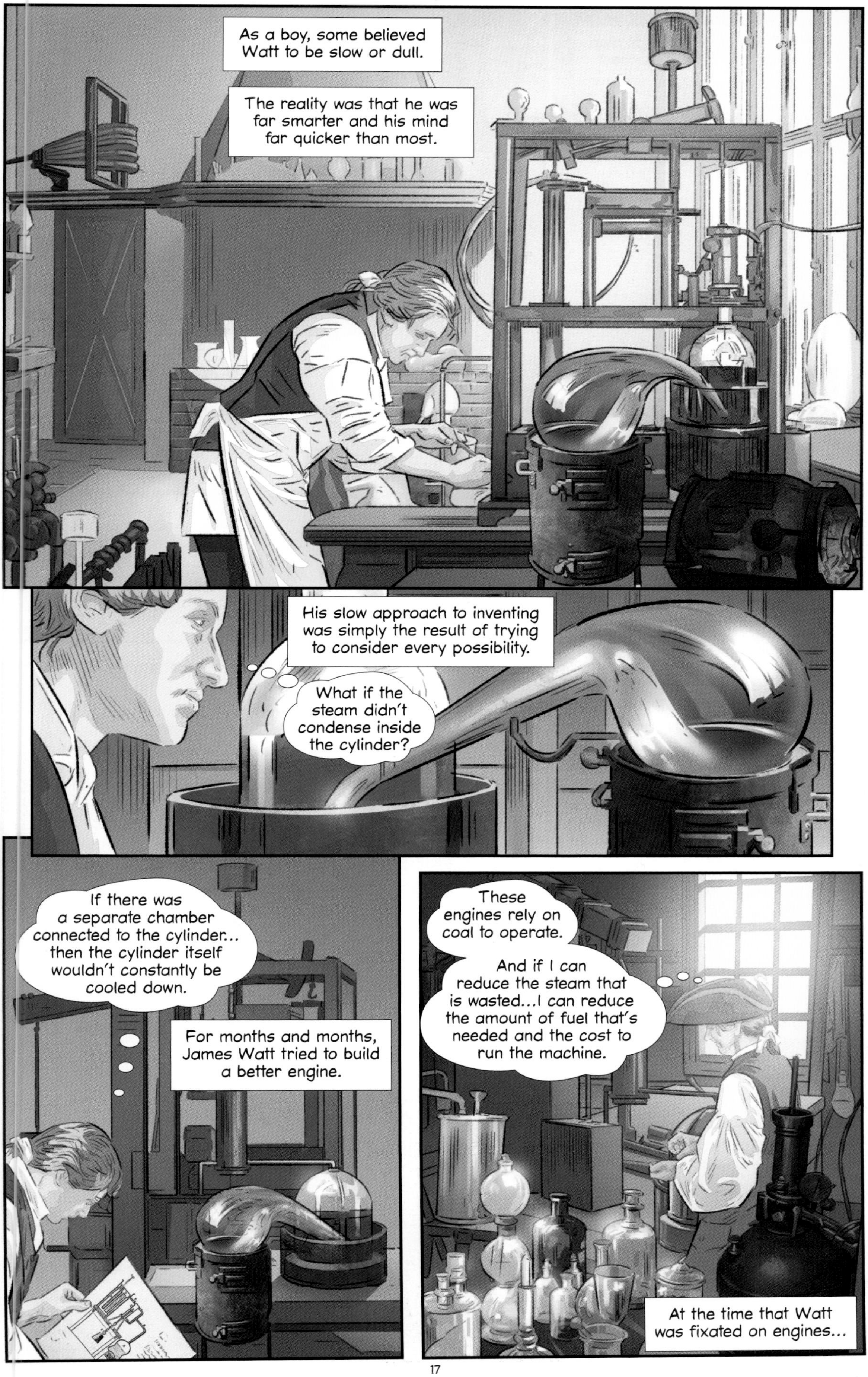
As a boy, some believed Watt to be slow or dull.
The reality was that he was far smarter and his mind far quicker than most.
His slow approach to inventing was simply the result of trying to consider every possibility.
What if the steam didn't condense inside the cylinder?
If there was a separate chamber connected to the cylinder... then the cylinder itself wouldn't constantly be cooled down.
For months and months, James Watt tried to build a better engine.
These engines rely on coal to operate.
And if I can reduce the steam that is wasted...I can reduce the amount of fuel that's needed and the cost to run the machine.
At the time that Watt was fixated on engines...

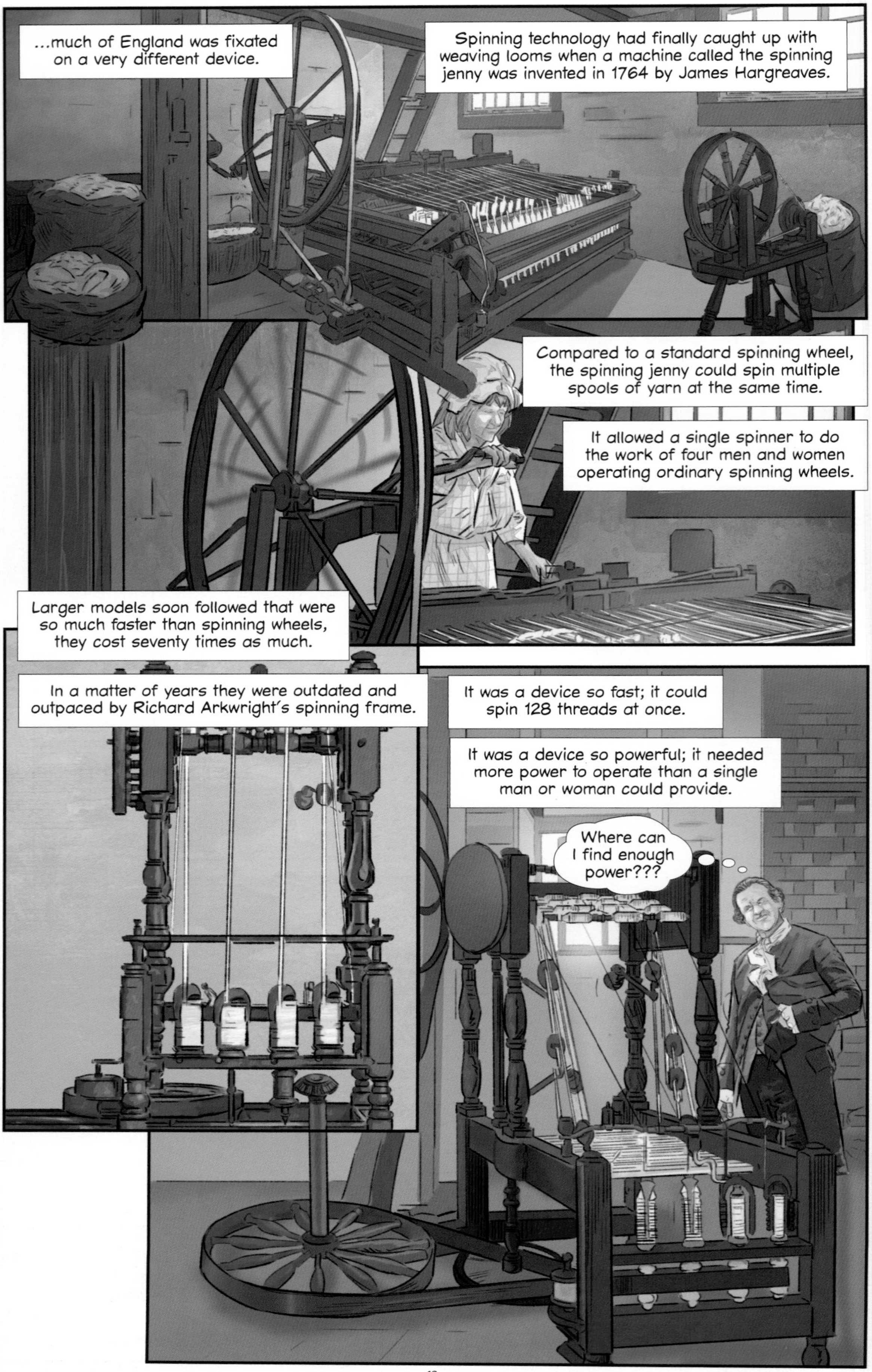
...much of England was fixated on a very different device.
Spinning technology had finally caught up with weaving looms when a machine called the spinning jenny was invented in 1764 by James Hargreaves.
Compared to a standard spinning wheel, the spinning jenny could spin multiple spools of yarn at the same time.
It allowed a single spinner to do the work of four men and women operating ordinary spinning wheels.
Larger models soon followed that were so much faster than spinning wheels, they cost seventy times as much.
In a matter of years they were outdated and outpaced by Richard Arkwright's spinning frame.
It was a device so fast; it could spin 128 threads at once.
It was a device so powerful; it needed more power to operate than a single man or woman could provide.
Where can I find enough power???

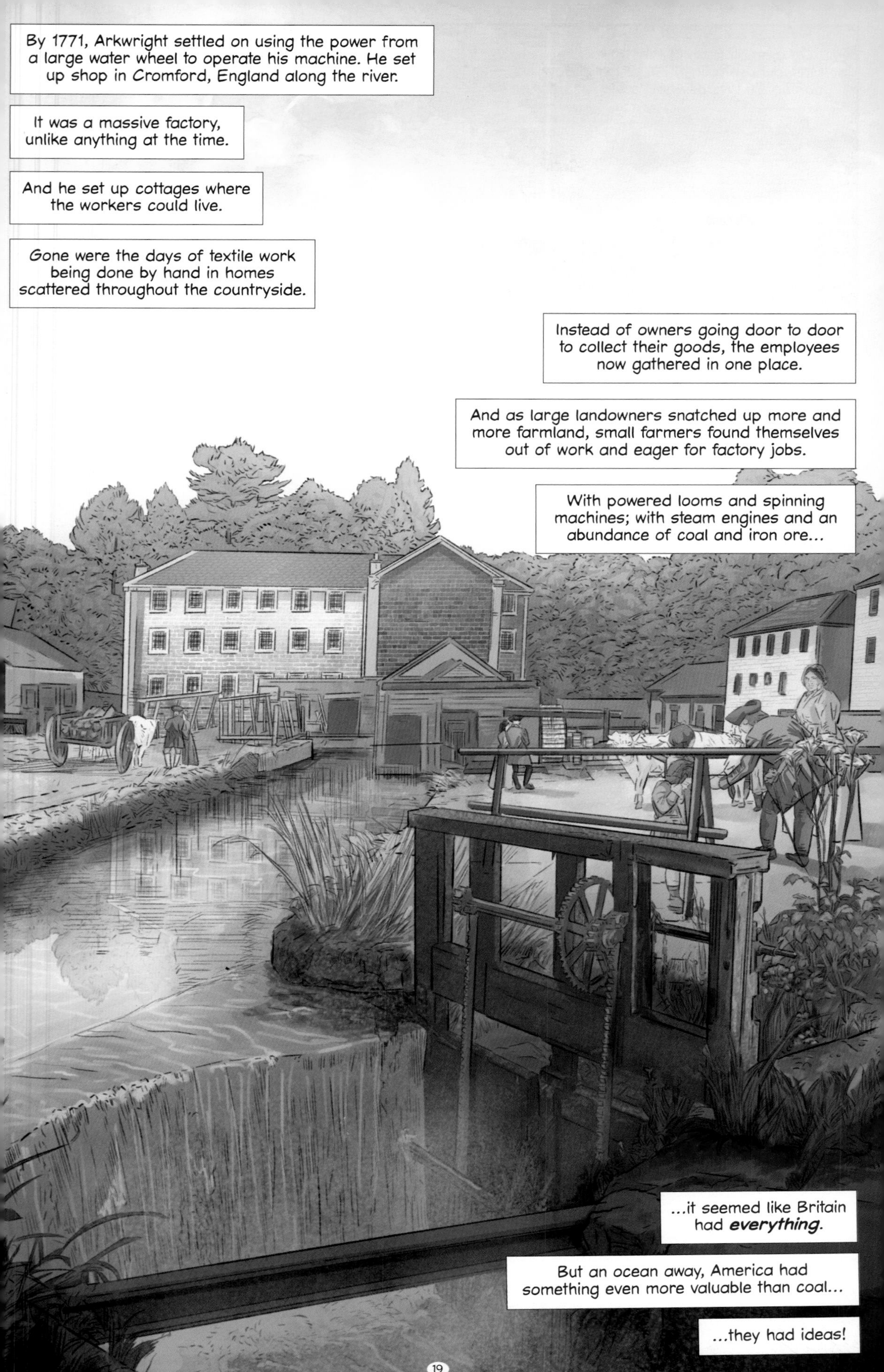

By 1771, Arkwright settled on using the power from a large water wheel to operate his machine. He set up shop in Cromford, England along the river.
It was a massive factory, unlike anything at the time.
And he set up cottages where the workers could live.
Gone were the days of textile work being done by hand in homes scattered throughout the countryside.
Instead of owners going door to door to collect their goods, the employees now gathered in one place.
And as large landowners snatched up more and more farmland, small farmers found themselves out of work and eager for factory jobs.
With powered looms and spinning machines; with steam engines and an abundance of coal and iron ore...
...it seemed like Britain had ***everything***.
But an ocean away, America had something even more valuable than coal...
...they had ideas!

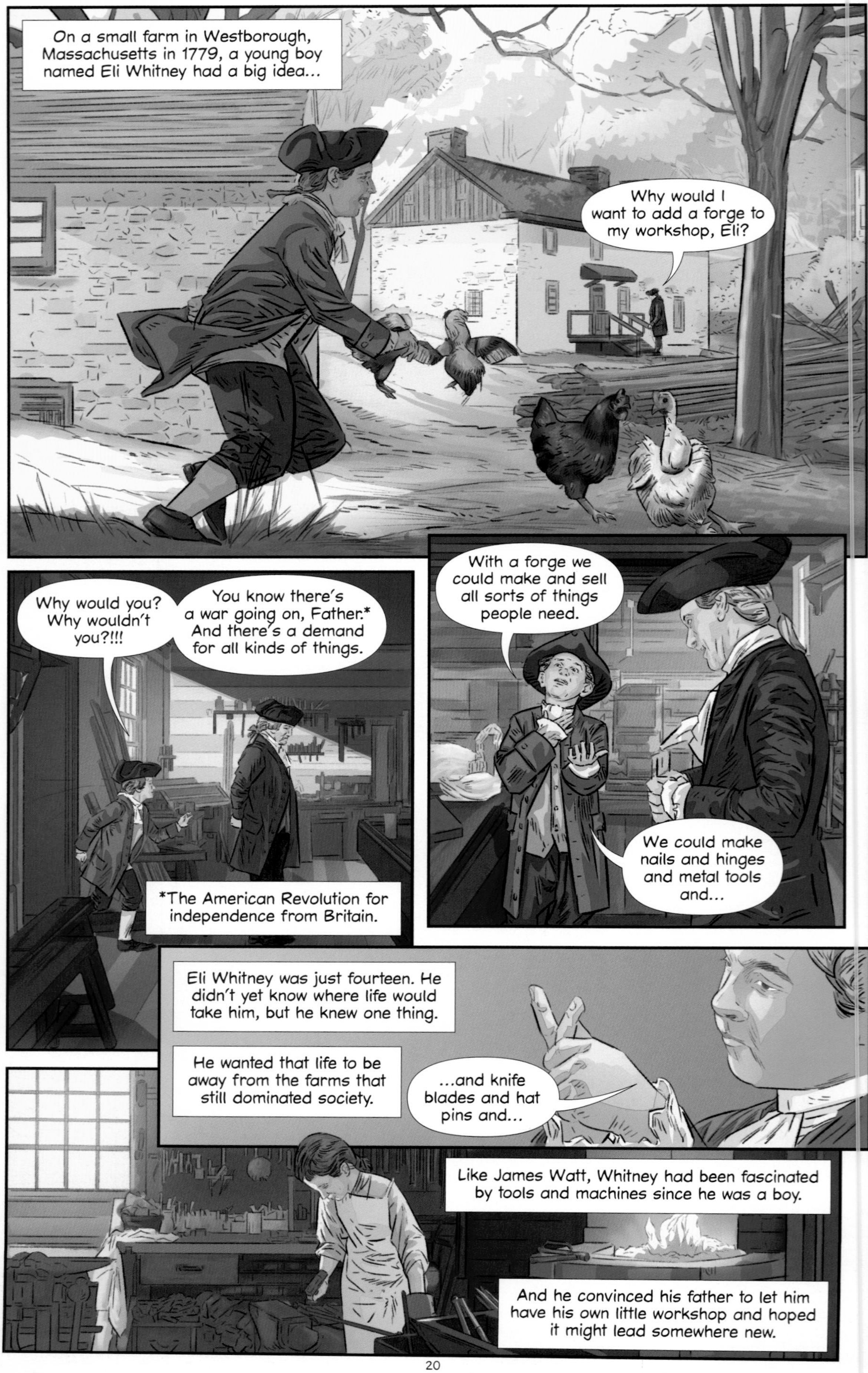

On a small farm in Westborough, Massachusetts in 1779, a young boy named Eli Whitney had a big idea...
Why would I want to add a forge to my workshop, Eli?
Why would you? Why wouldn't you?!!!
You know there's a war going on, Father.* And there's a demand for all kinds of things.
*The American Revolution for independence from Britain.
With a forge we could make and sell all sorts of things people need.
We could make nails and hinges and metal tools and...
Eli Whitney was just fourteen. He didn't yet know where life would take him, but he knew one thing.
He wanted that life to be away from the farms that still dominated society.
...and knife blades and hat pins and...
Like James Watt, Whitney had been fascinated by tools and machines since he was a boy.
And he convinced his father to let him have his own little workshop and hoped it might lead somewhere new.

But that was also the hope of Robert Fulton, hundreds of kilometers away in Philadelphia, Pennsylvania in 1783.

Try not to move, okay?

Of course. Have you been painting portraits in Philadelphia for a while?

I actually just moved to Philadelphia this year.

I was born outside the city on a farm.

And spent a bit of time working as a gunsmith in Lancaster, Pennsylvania.

Very nice work, Mr. Fulton.

Do you get your artistic talent from your father?

No, ma'am. He was a tailor and he passed away when I was a boy.

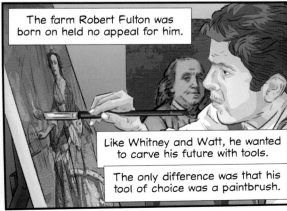

The farm Robert Fulton was born on held no appeal for him.

Like Whitney and Watt, he wanted to carve his future with tools.

The only difference was that his tool of choice was a paintbrush.

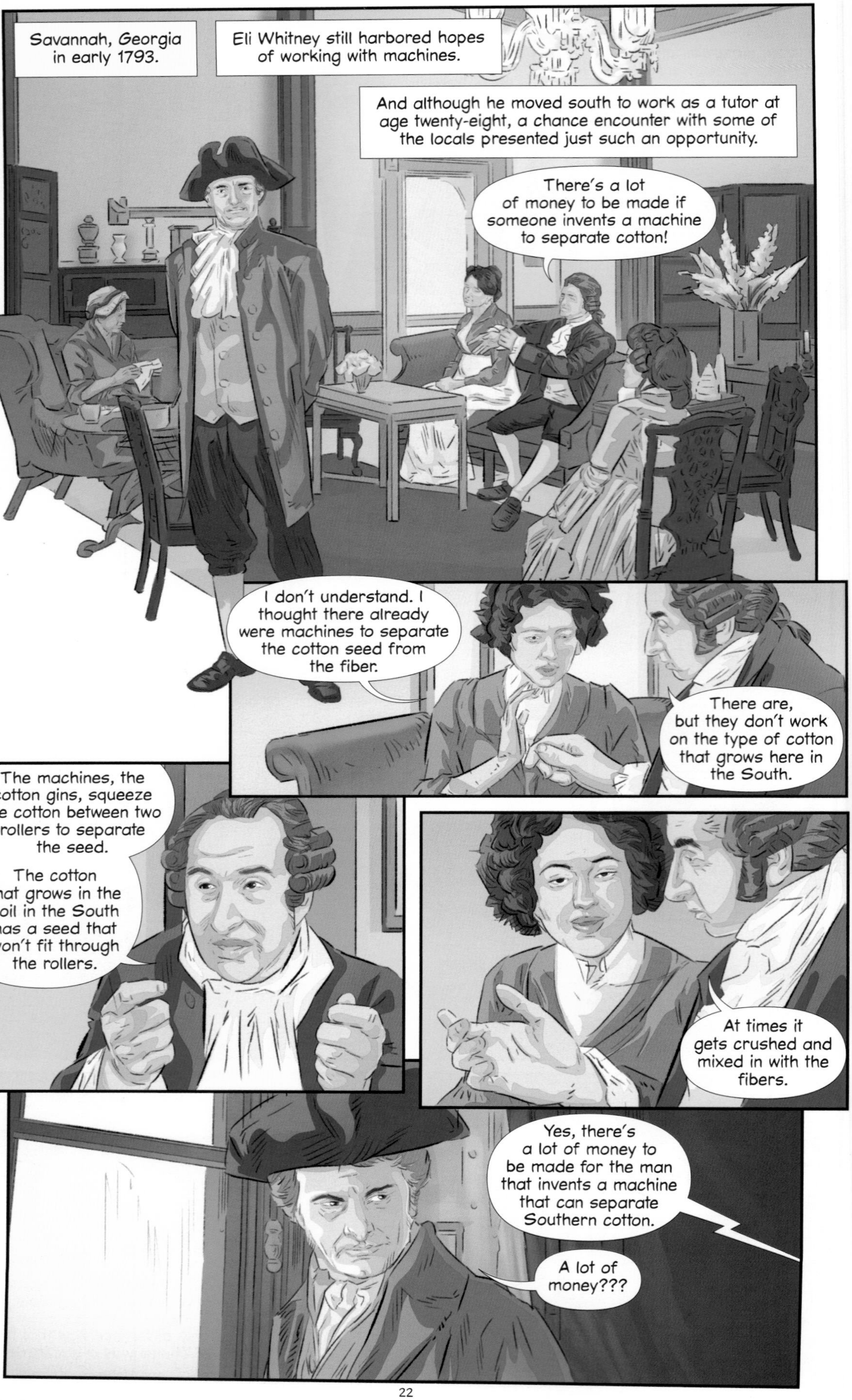
Savannah, Georgia in early 1793.
Eli Whitney still harbored hopes of working with machines.
And although he moved south to work as a tutor at age twenty-eight, a chance encounter with some of the locals presented just such an opportunity.
There's a lot of money to be made if someone invents a machine to separate cotton!
I don't understand. I thought there already were machines to separate the cotton seed from the fiber.
There are, but they don't work on the type of cotton that grows here in the South.
The machines, the cotton gins, squeeze the cotton between two rollers to separate the seed.
The cotton that grows in the soil in the South has a seed that won't fit through the rollers.
At times it gets crushed and mixed in with the fibers.
Yes, there's a lot of money to be made for the man that invents a machine that can separate Southern cotton.
A lot of money???

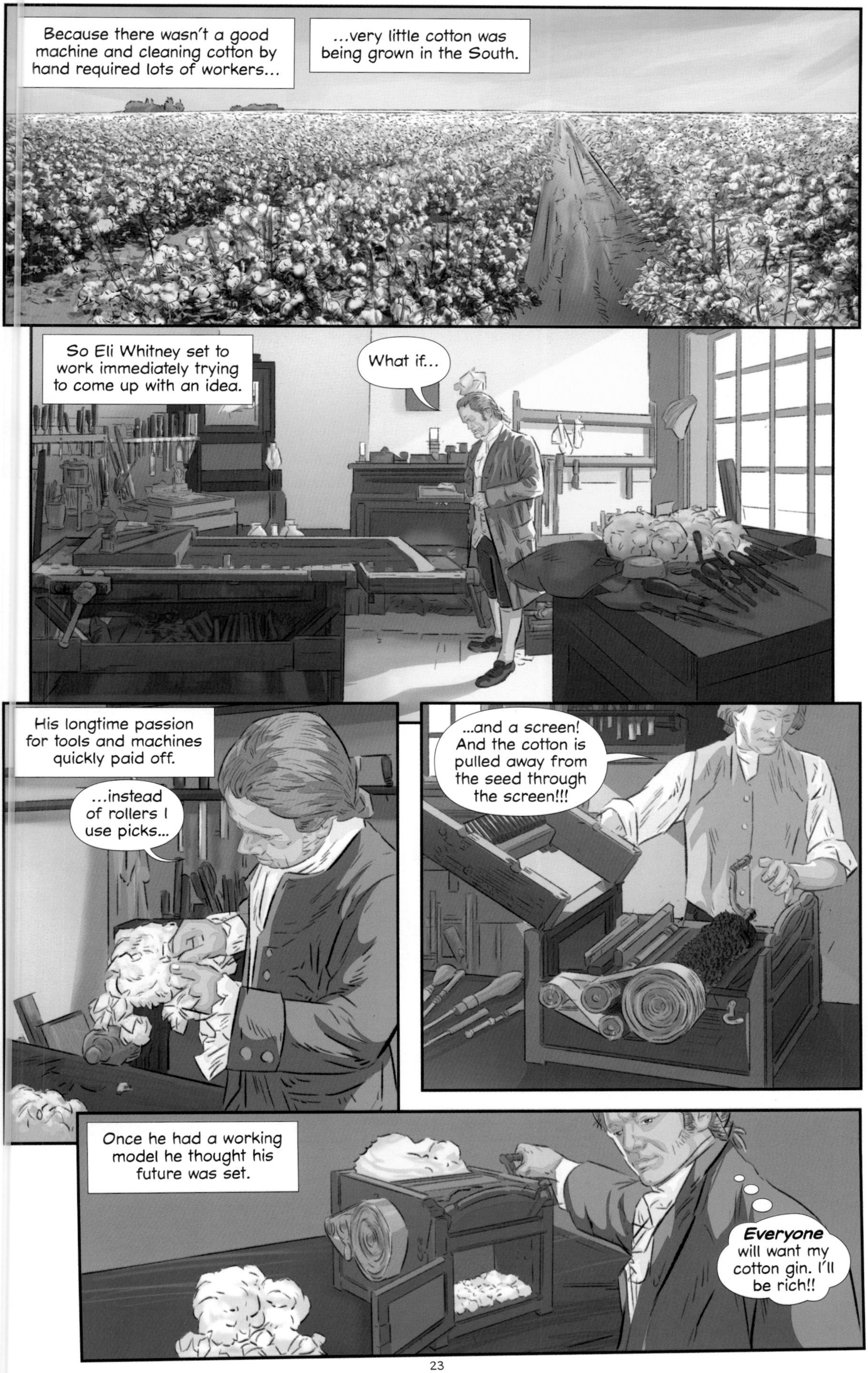
Because there wasn't a good machine and cleaning cotton by hand required lots of workers...
...very little cotton was being grown in the South.
So Eli Whitney set to work immediately trying to come up with an idea.
What if...
His longtime passion for tools and machines quickly paid off.
...instead of rollers I use picks...
...and a screen! And the cotton is pulled away from the seed through the screen!!!
Once he had a working model he thought his future was set.
Everyone will want my cotton gin. I'll be rich!!

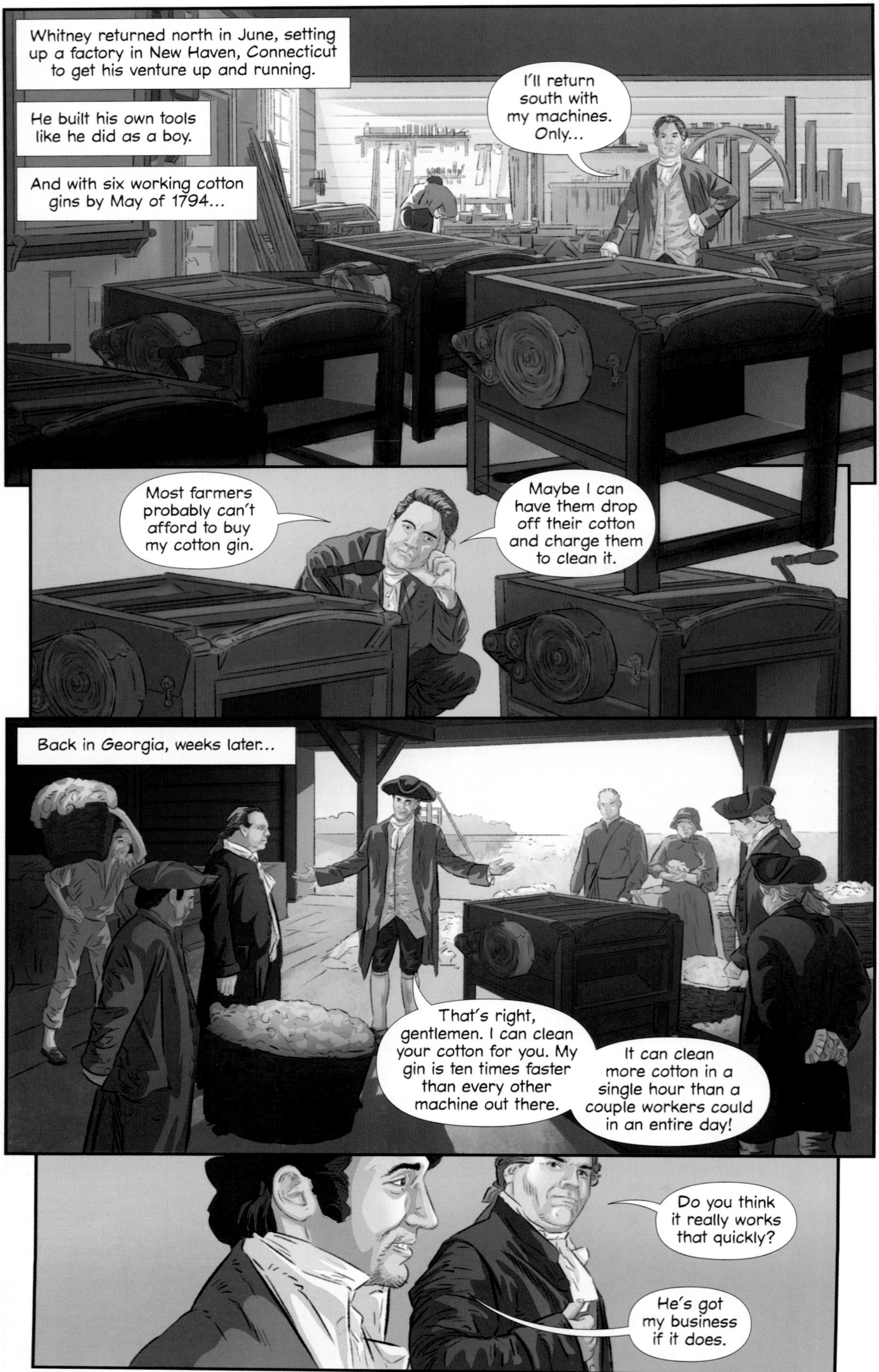

Whitney returned north in June, setting up a factory in New Haven, Connecticut to get his venture up and running.
He built his own tools like he did as a boy.
And with six working cotton gins by May of 1794...
I'll return south with my machines. Only...
Most farmers probably can't afford to buy my cotton gin.
Maybe I can have them drop off their cotton and charge them to clean it.
Back in Georgia, weeks later...
That's right, gentlemen. I can clean your cotton for you. My gin is ten times faster than every other machine out there.
It can clean more cotton in a single hour than a couple workers could in an entire day!
Do you think it really works that quickly?
He's got my business if it does.

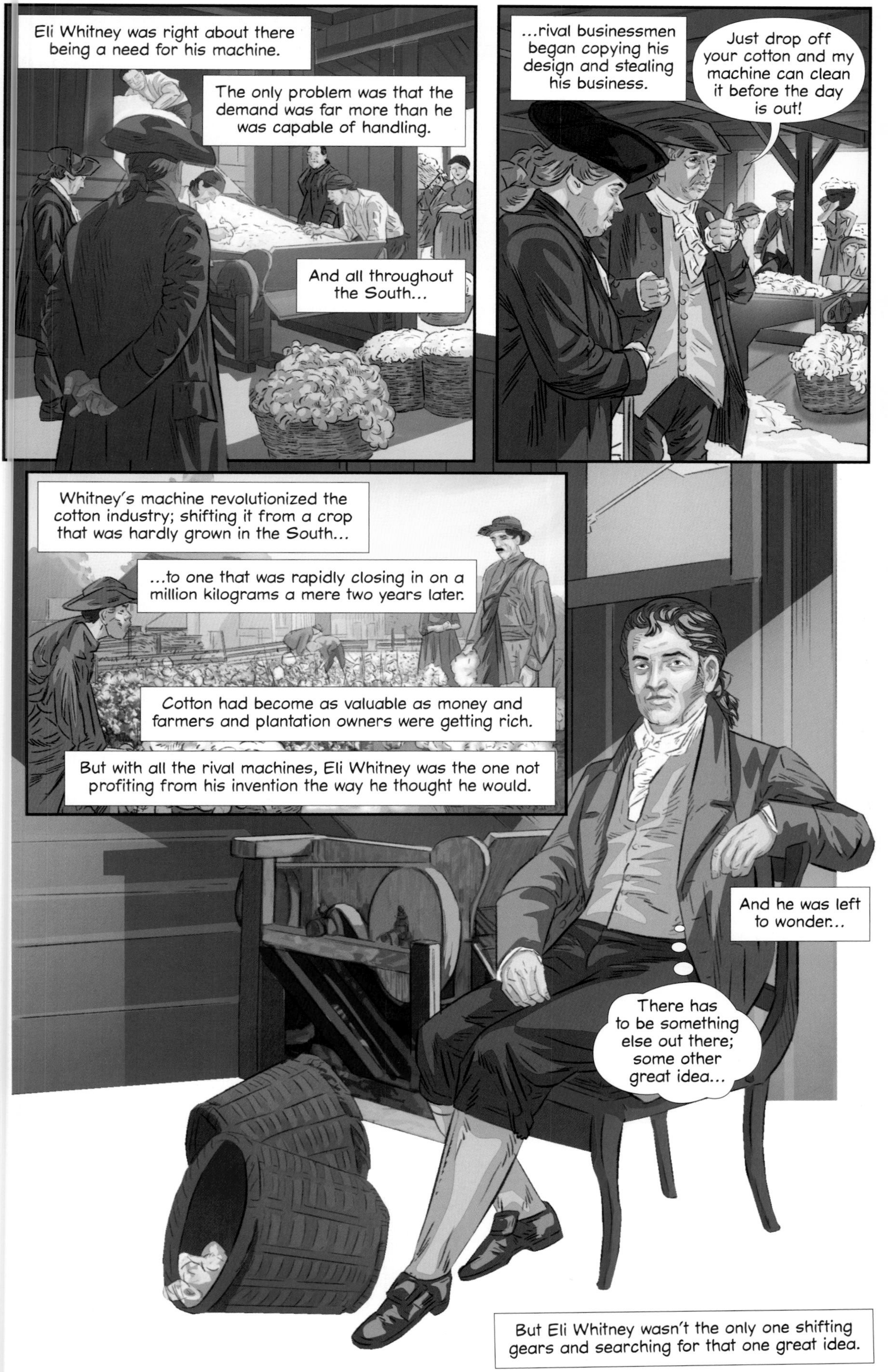
Eli Whitney was right about there being a need for his machine.
The only problem was that the demand was far more than he was capable of handling.
And all throughout the South...
...rival businessmen began copying his design and stealing his business.
Just drop off your cotton and my machine can clean it before the day is out!
Whitney's machine revolutionized the cotton industry; shifting it from a crop that was hardly grown in the South...
...to one that was rapidly closing in on a million kilograms a mere two years later.
Cotton had become as valuable as money and farmers and plantation owners were getting rich.
But with all the rival machines, Eli Whitney was the one not profiting from his invention the way he thought he would.
And he was left to wonder...
There has to be something else out there; some other great idea...
But Eli Whitney wasn't the only one shifting gears and searching for that one great idea.

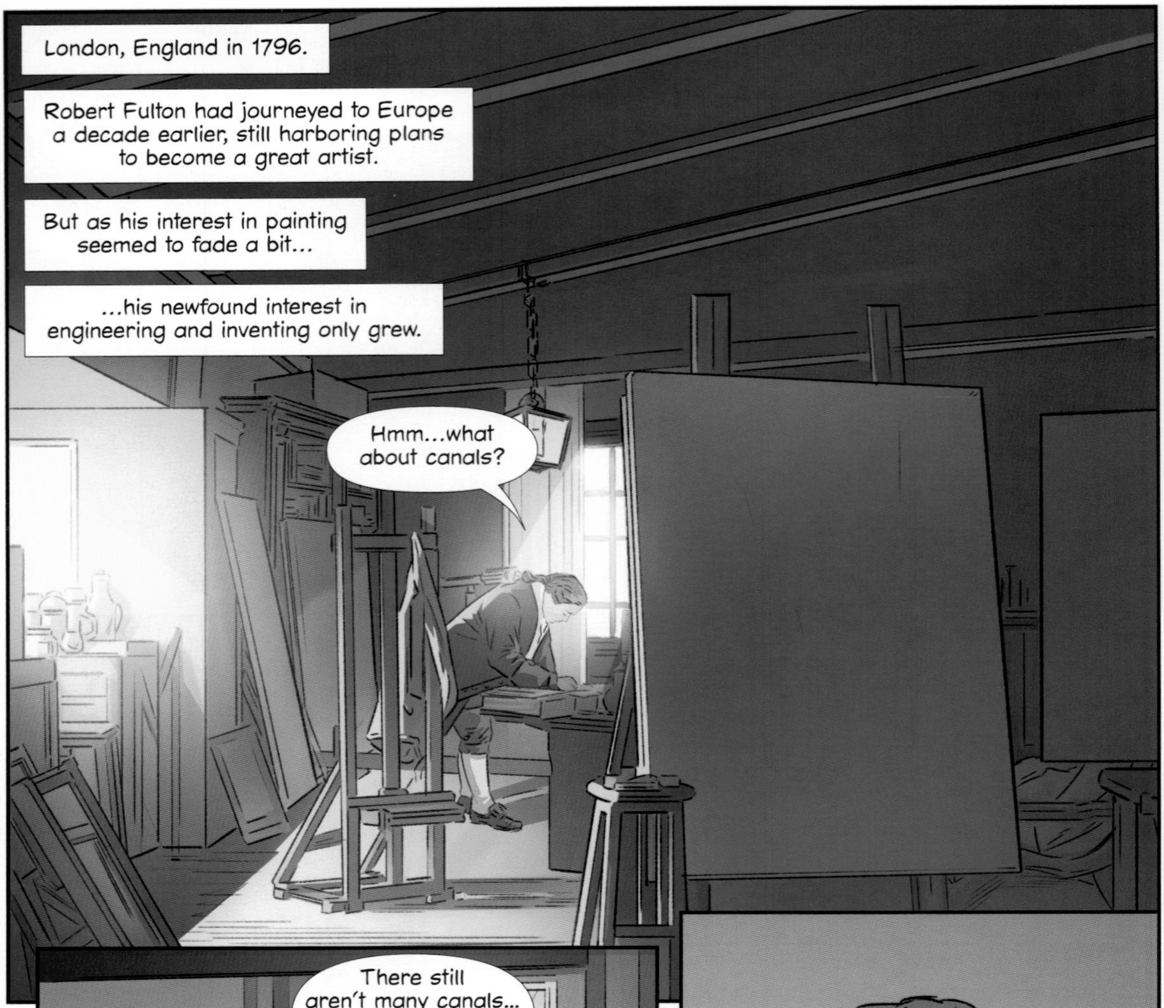
London, England in 1796.
Robert Fulton had journeyed to Europe a decade earlier, still harboring plans to become a great artist.
But as his interest in painting seemed to fade a bit...
...his newfound interest in engineering and inventing only grew.
Hmm...what about canals?

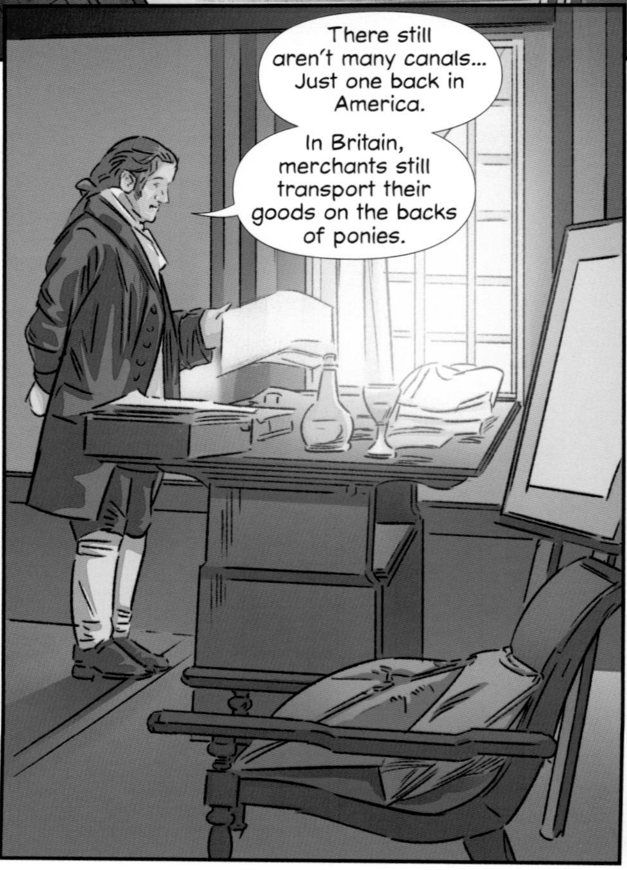
There still aren't many canals... Just one back in America.
In Britain, merchants still transport their goods on the backs of ponies.

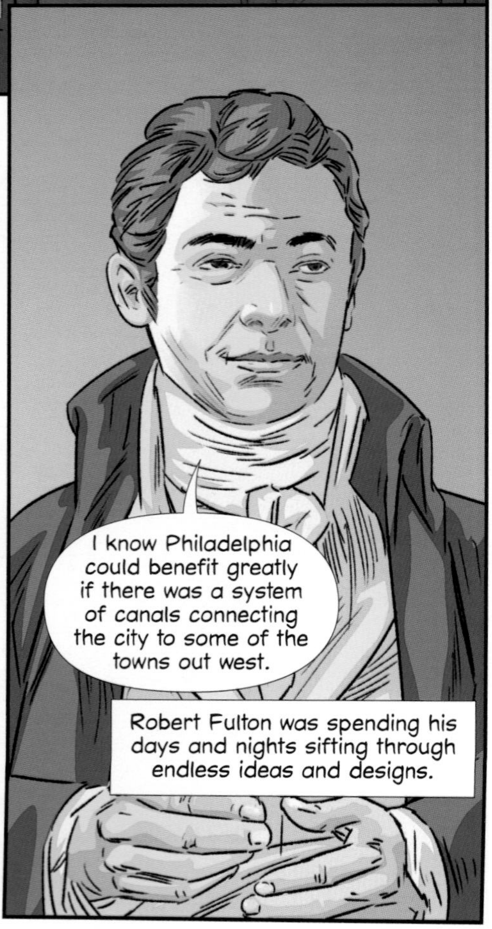
I know Philadelphia could benefit greatly if there was a system of canals connecting the city to some of the towns out west.
Robert Fulton was spending his days and nights sifting through endless ideas and designs.

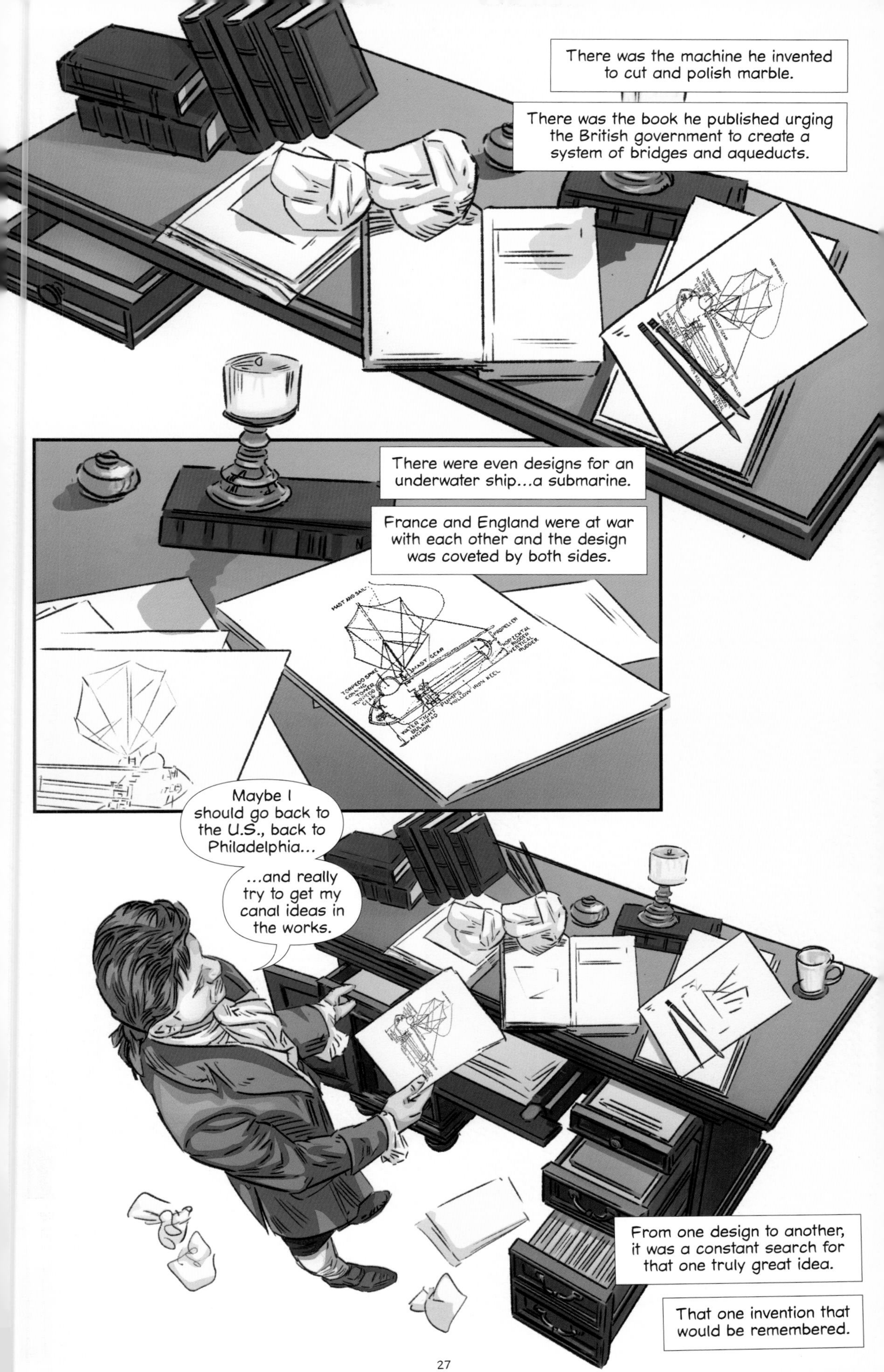

There was the machine he invented to cut and polish marble.
There was the book he published urging the British government to create a system of bridges and aqueducts.
There were even designs for an underwater ship...a submarine.
France and England were at war with each other and the design was coveted by both sides.
Maybe I should go back to the U.S., back to Philadelphia...
...and really try to get my canal ideas in the works.
From one design to another, it was a constant search for that one truly great idea.
That one invention that would be remembered.

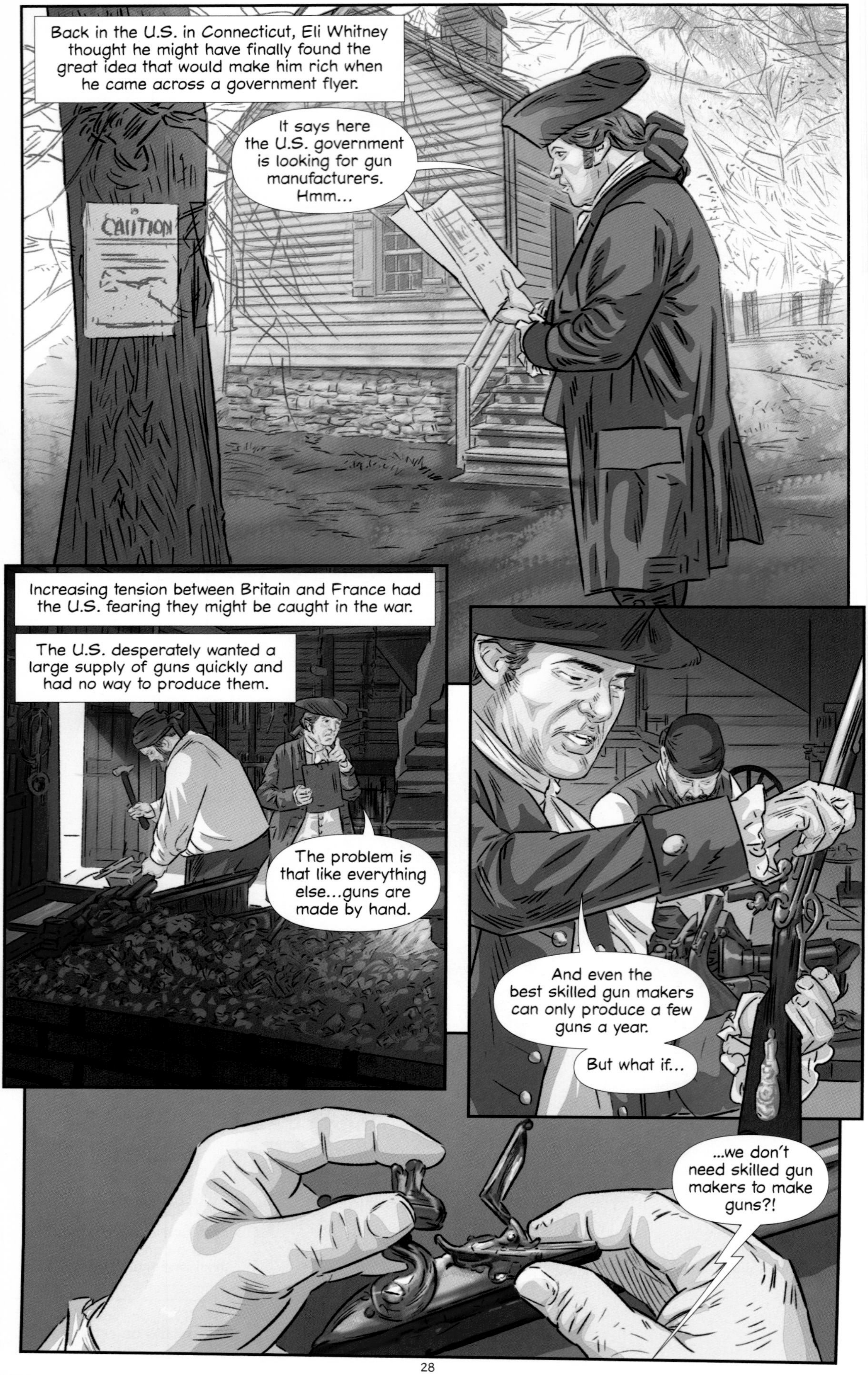
Back in the U.S. in Connecticut, Eli Whitney thought he might have finally found the great idea that would make him rich when he came across a government flyer.
It says here the U.S. government is looking for gun manufacturers. Hmm...
CAUTION
Increasing tension between Britain and France had the U.S. fearing they might be caught in the war.
The U.S. desperately wanted a large supply of guns quickly and had no way to produce them.
The problem is that like everything else...guns are made by hand.
And even the best skilled gun makers can only produce a few guns a year.
But what if...
...we don't need skilled gun makers to make guns?!

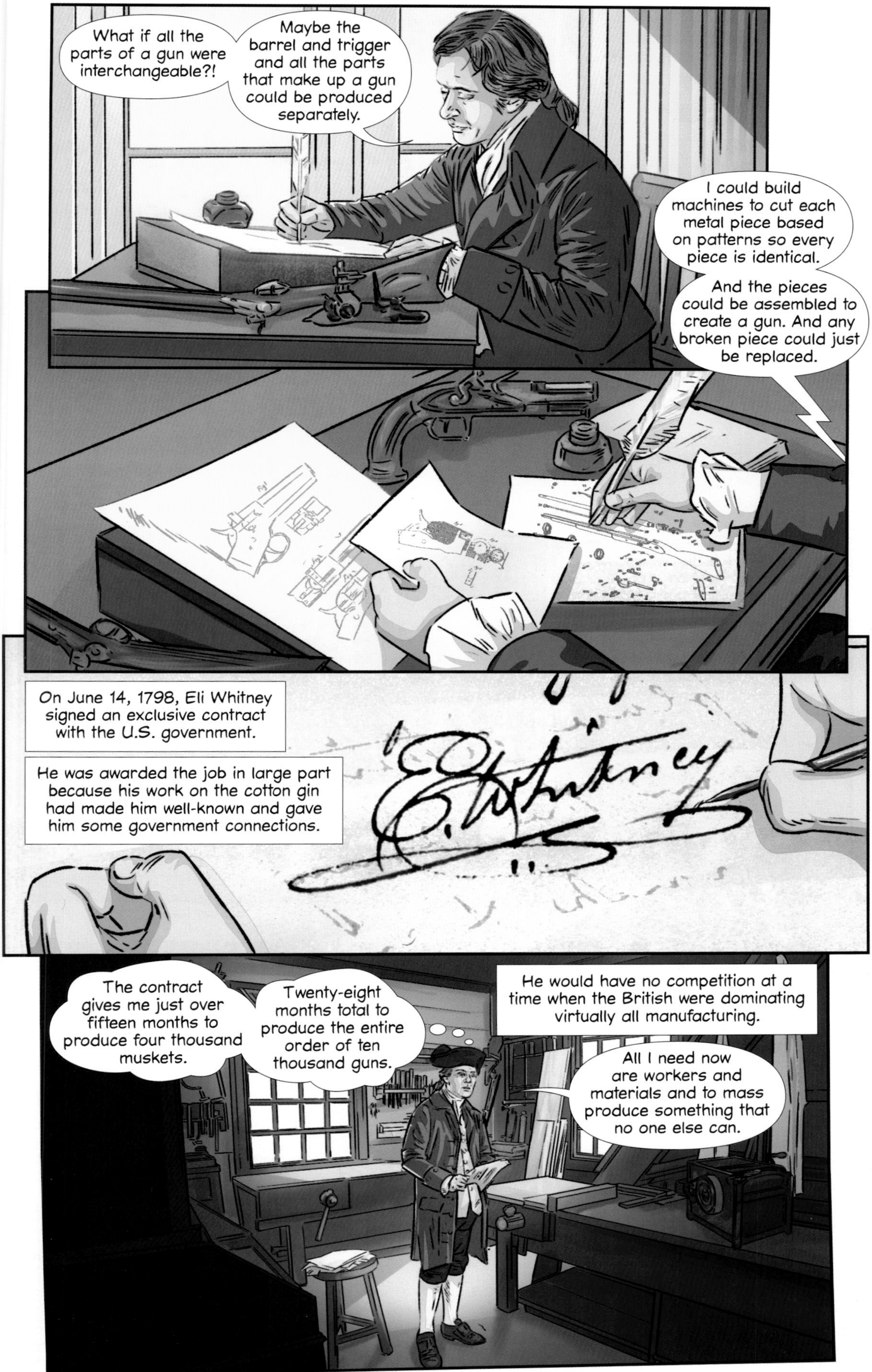
What if all the parts of a gun were interchangeable?!
Maybe the barrel and trigger and all the parts that make up a gun could be produced separately.
I could build machines to cut each metal piece based on patterns so every piece is identical.
And the pieces could be assembled to create a gun. And any broken piece could just be replaced.
On June 14, 1798, Eli Whitney signed an exclusive contract with the U.S. government.
He was awarded the job in large part because his work on the cotton gin had made him well-known and gave him some government connections.
The contract gives me just over fifteen months to produce four thousand muskets.
Twenty-eight months total to produce the entire order of ten thousand guns.
He would have no competition at a time when the British were dominating virtually all manufacturing.
All I need now are workers and materials and to mass produce something that no one else can.

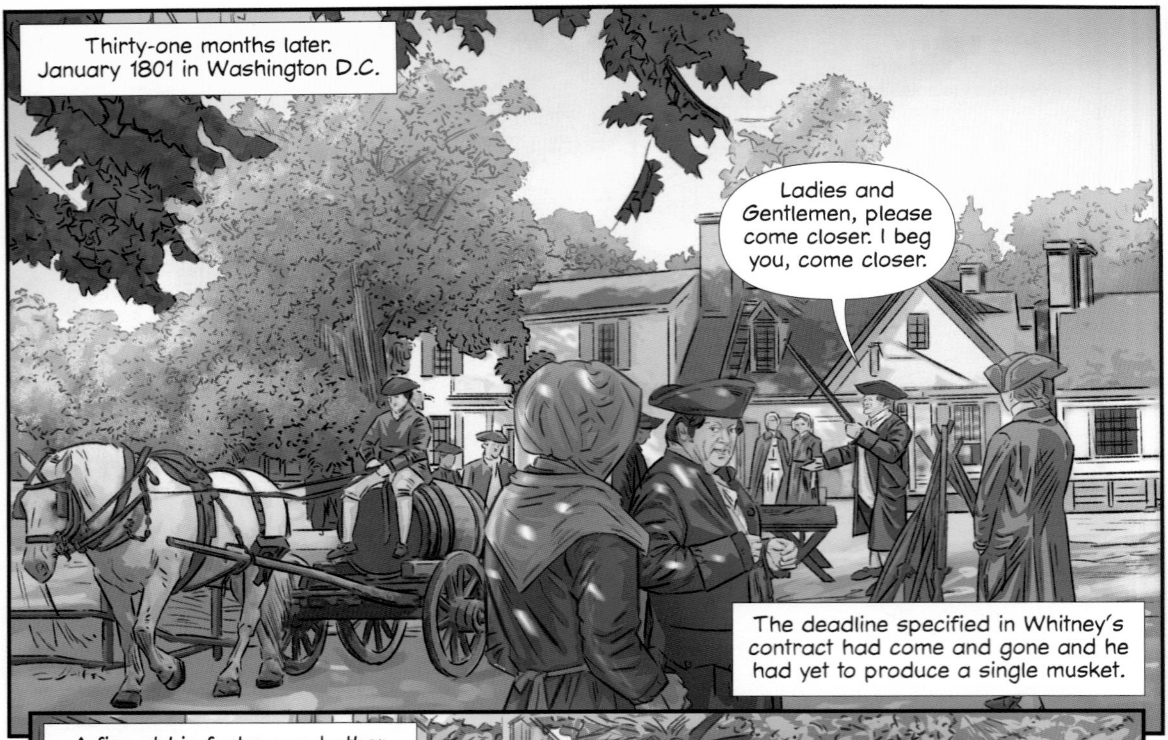
Thirty-one months later. January 1801 in Washington D.C.
Ladies and Gentlemen, please come closer. I beg you, come closer.
The deadline specified in Whitney's contract had come and gone and he had yet to produce a single musket.

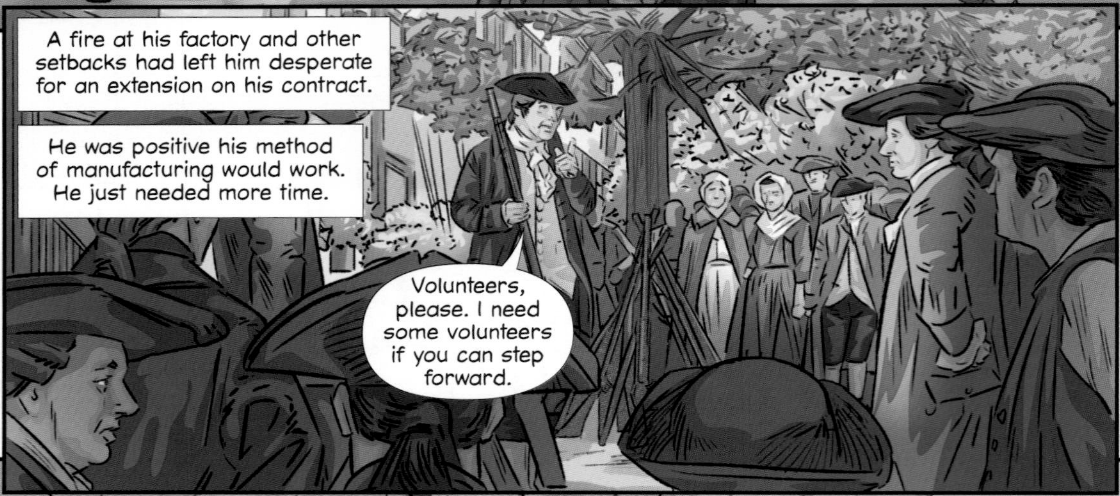
A fire at his factory and other setbacks had left him desperate for an extension on his contract.
He was positive his method of manufacturing would work. He just needed more time.
Volunteers, please. I need some volunteers if you can step forward.

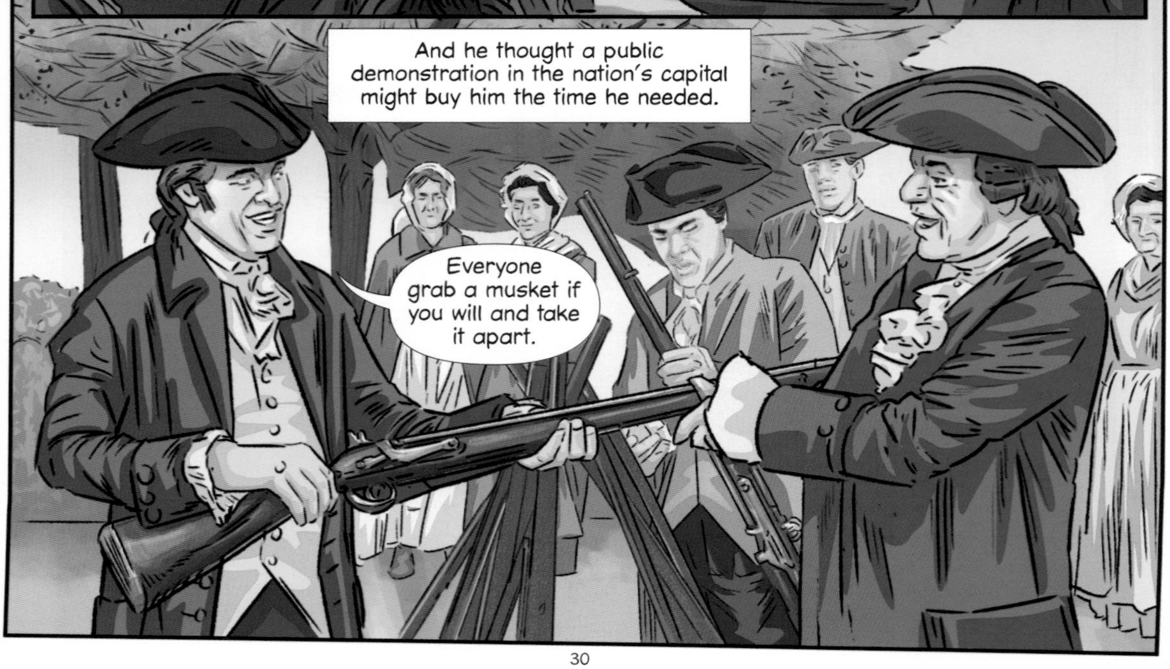
And he thought a public demonstration in the nation's capital might buy him the time he needed.
Everyone grab a musket if you will and take it apart.

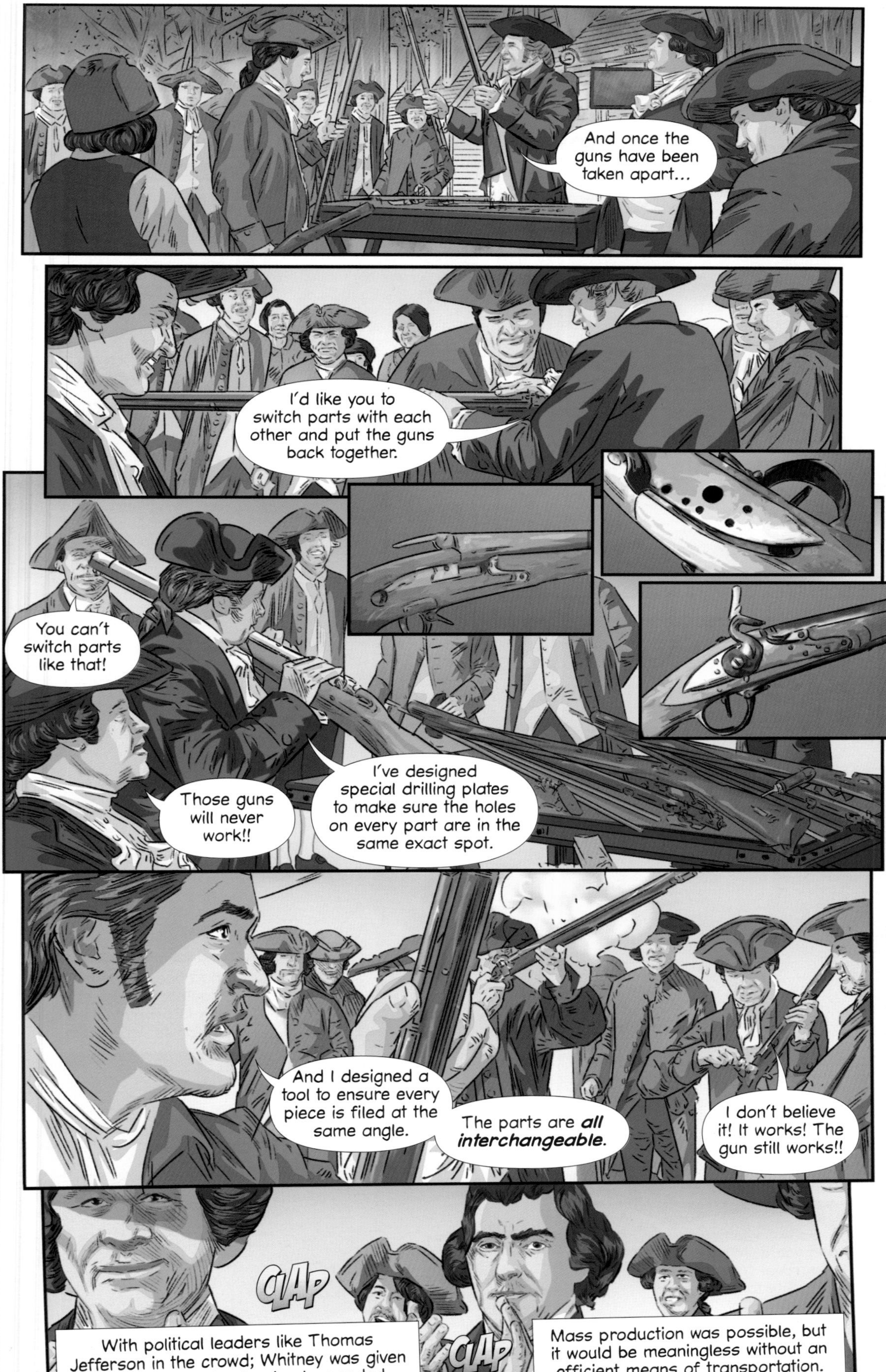

And once the guns have been taken apart...
I'd like you to switch parts with each other and put the guns back together.
You can't switch parts like that!
Those guns will never work!!
I've designed special drilling plates to make sure the holes on every part are in the same exact spot.
And I designed a tool to ensure every piece is filed at the same angle.
The parts are ***all interchangeable***.
I don't believe it! It works! The gun still works!!
CLAP
CLAP
With political leaders like Thomas Jefferson in the crowd; Whitney was given the support and extension he needed.
Mass production was possible, but it would be meaningless without an efficient means of transportation.

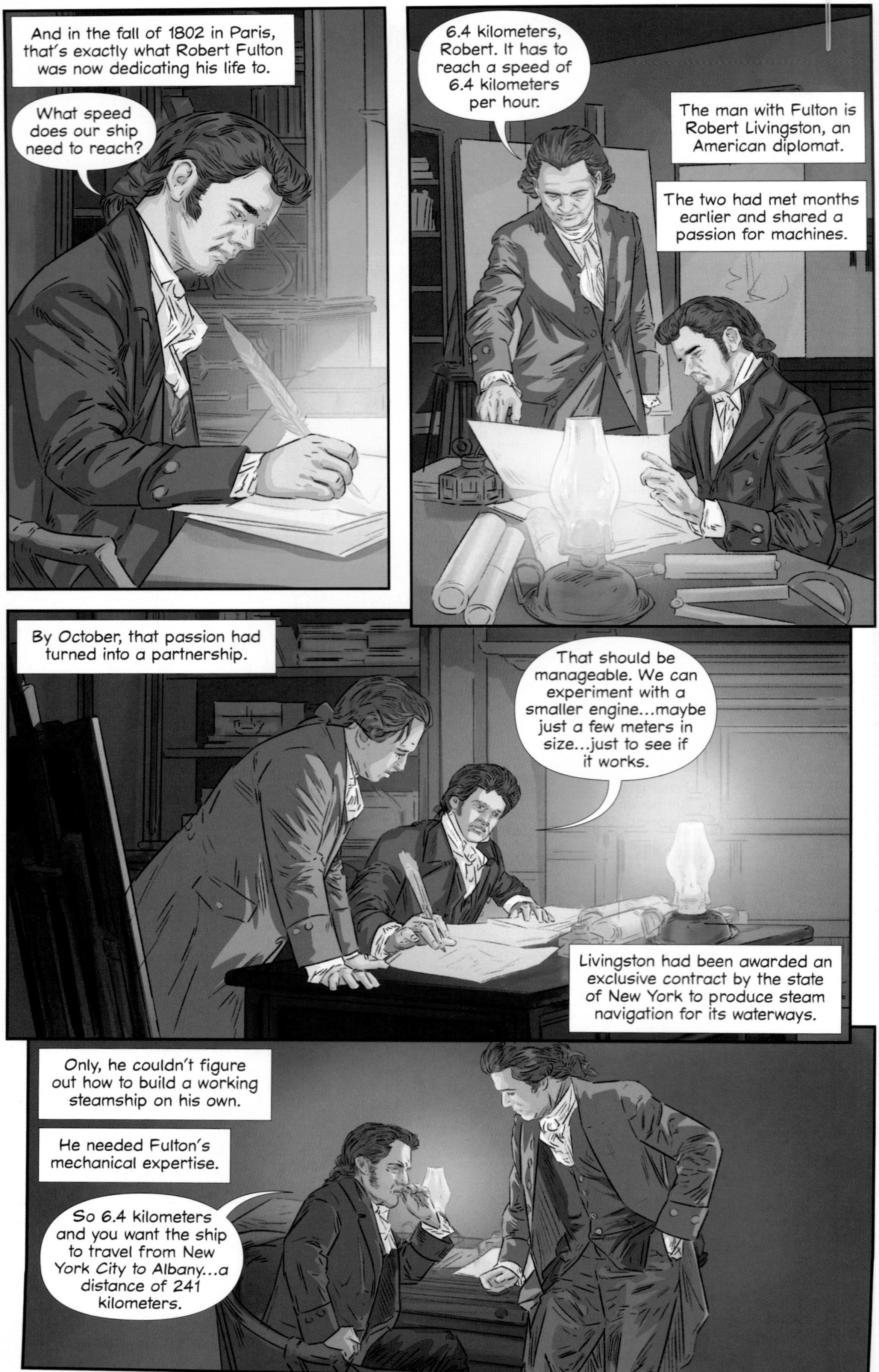
And in the fall of 1802 in Paris, that's exactly what Robert Fulton was now dedicating his life to.
What speed does our ship need to reach?
6.4 kilometers, Robert. It has to reach a speed of 6.4 kilometers per hour.
The man with Fulton is Robert Livingston, an American diplomat.
The two had met months earlier and shared a passion for machines.
By October, that passion had turned into a partnership.
That should be manageable. We can experiment with a smaller engine...maybe just a few meters in size...just to see if it works.
Livingston had been awarded an exclusive contract by the state of New York to produce steam navigation for its waterways.
Only, he couldn't figure out how to build a working steamship on his own.
He needed Fulton's mechanical expertise.
So 6.4 kilometers and you want the ship to travel from New York City to Albany...a distance of 241 kilometers.

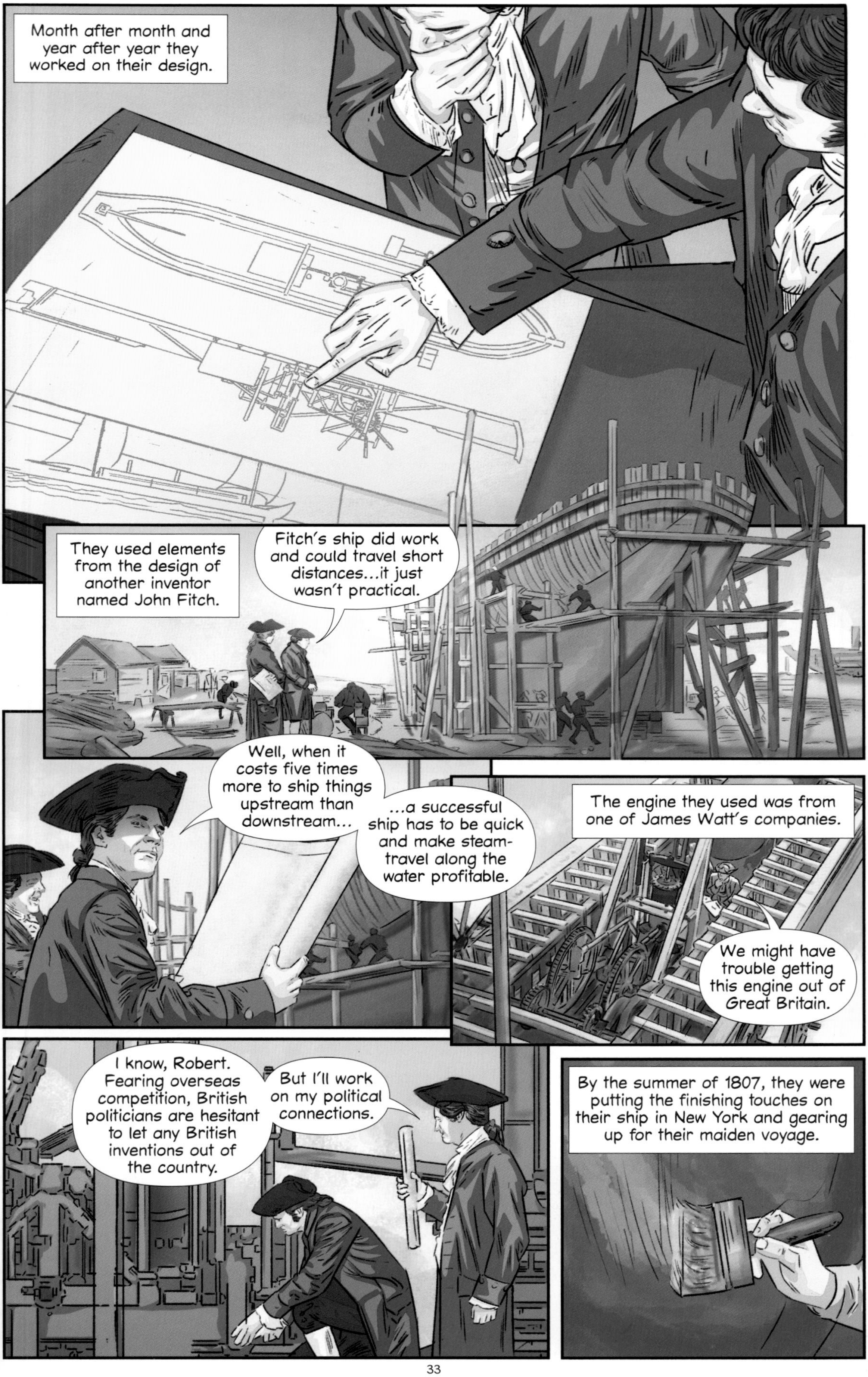

Month after month and year after year they worked on their design.
They used elements from the design of another inventor named John Fitch.
Fitch's ship did work and could travel short distances...it just wasn't practical.
Well, when it costs five times more to ship things upstream than downstream...
...a successful ship has to be quick and make steam-travel along the water profitable.
The engine they used was from one of James Watt's companies.
We might have trouble getting this engine out of Great Britain.
I know, Robert. Fearing overseas competition, British politicians are hesitant to let any British inventions out of the country.
But I'll work on my political connections.
By the summer of 1807, they were putting the finishing touches on their ship in New York and gearing up for their maiden voyage.

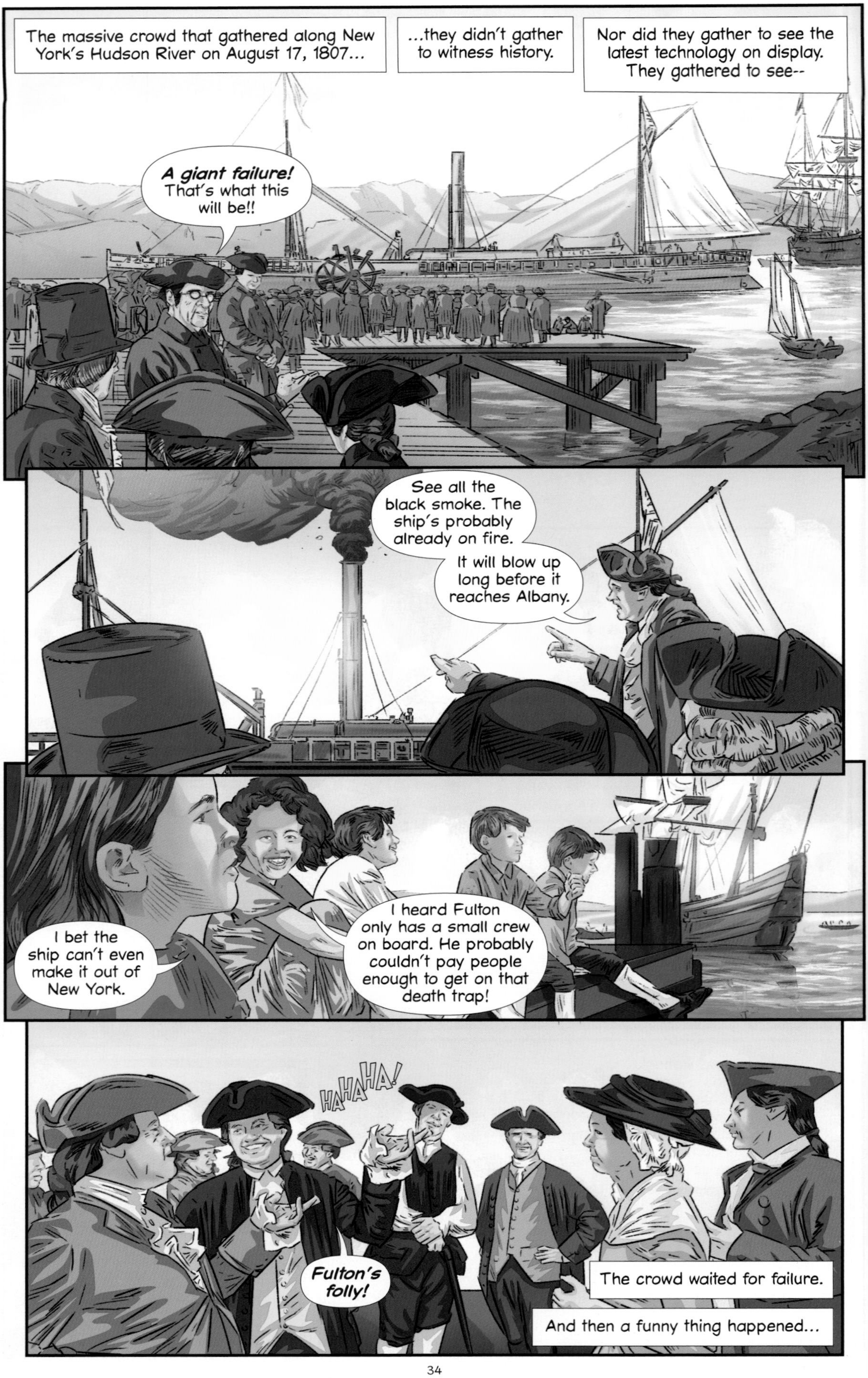

The massive crowd that gathered along New York's Hudson River on August 17, 1807...
...they didn't gather to witness history.
Nor did they gather to see the latest technology on display. They gathered to see--
A giant failure! That's what this will be!!
See all the black smoke. The ship's probably already on fire.
It will blow up long before it reaches Albany.
I bet the ship can't even make it out of New York.
I heard Fulton only has a small crew on board. He probably couldn't pay people enough to get on that death trap!
HAHAHA!
Fulton's folly!
The crowd waited for failure.
And then a funny thing happened...

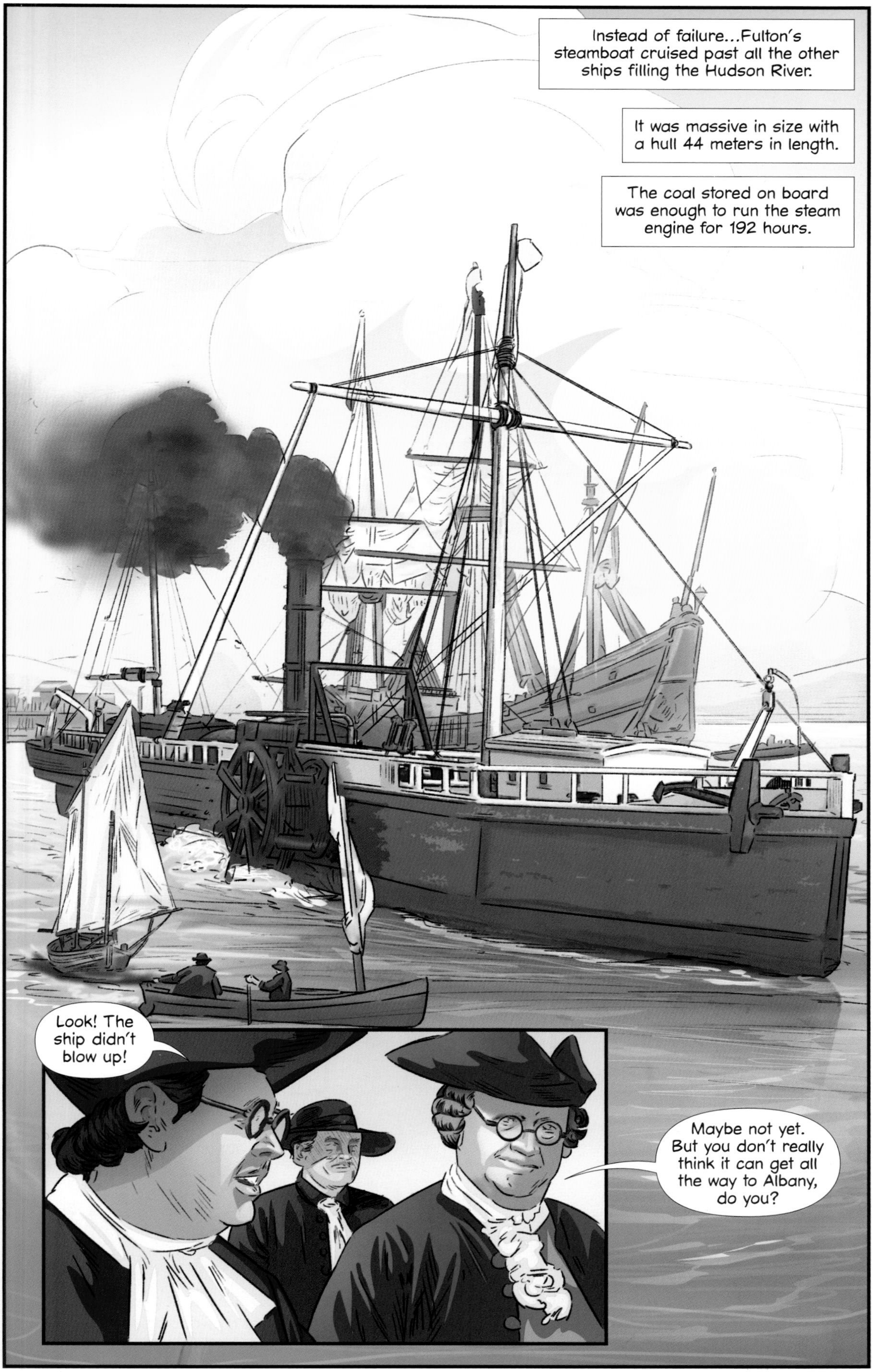
Instead of failure...Fulton's steamboat cruised past all the other ships filling the Hudson River.
It was massive in size with a hull 44 meters in length.
The coal stored on board was enough to run the steam engine for 192 hours.
Look! The ship didn't blow up!
Maybe not yet. But you don't really think it can get all the way to Albany, do you?

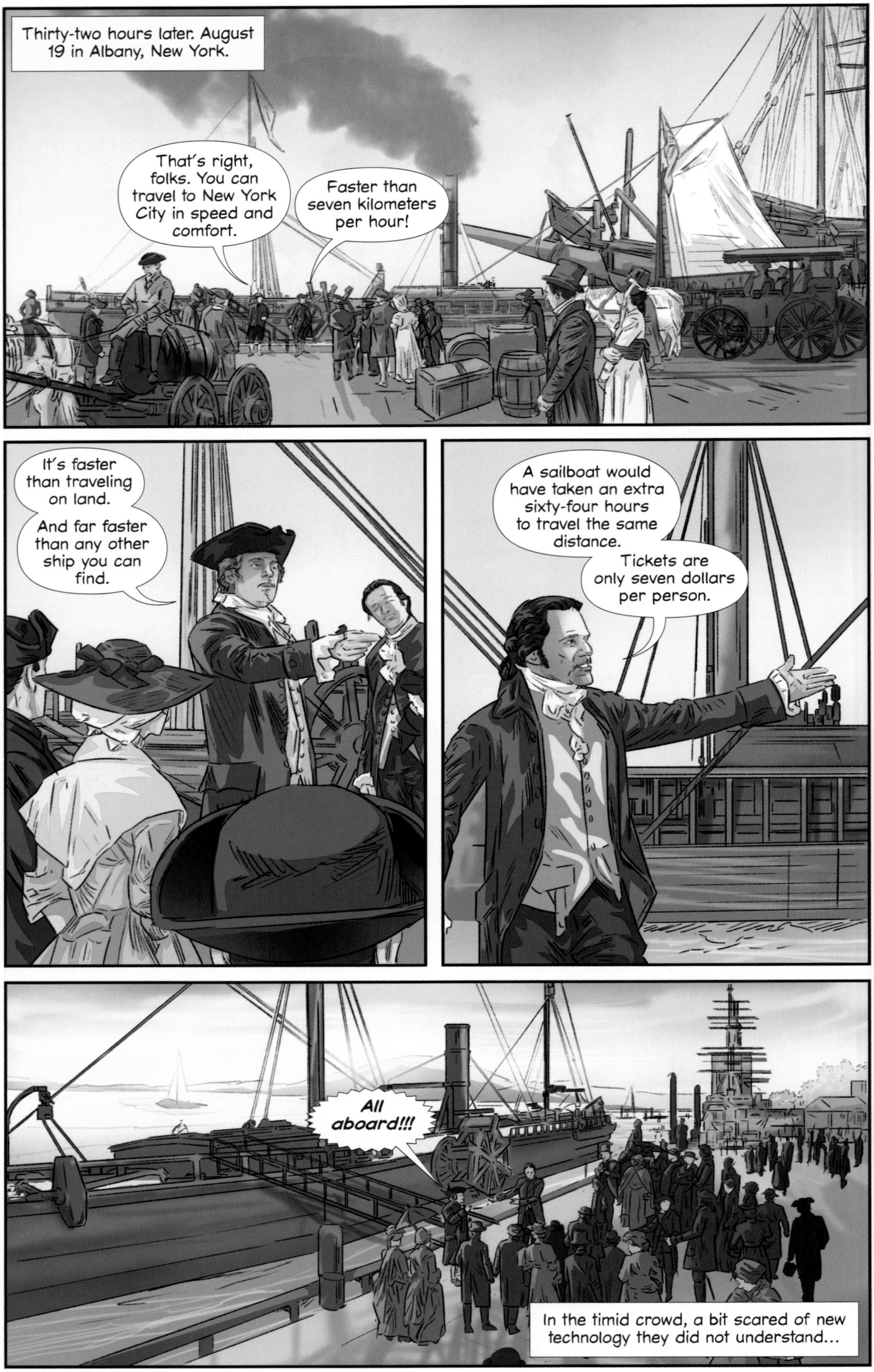
Thirty-two hours later. August 19 in Albany, New York.
That's right, folks. You can travel to New York City in speed and comfort.
Faster than seven kilometers per hour!
It's faster than traveling on land.
And far faster than any other ship you can find.
A sailboat would have taken an extra sixty-four hours to travel the same distance.
Tickets are only seven dollars per person.
All aboard!!!
In the timid crowd, a bit scared of new technology they did not understand...

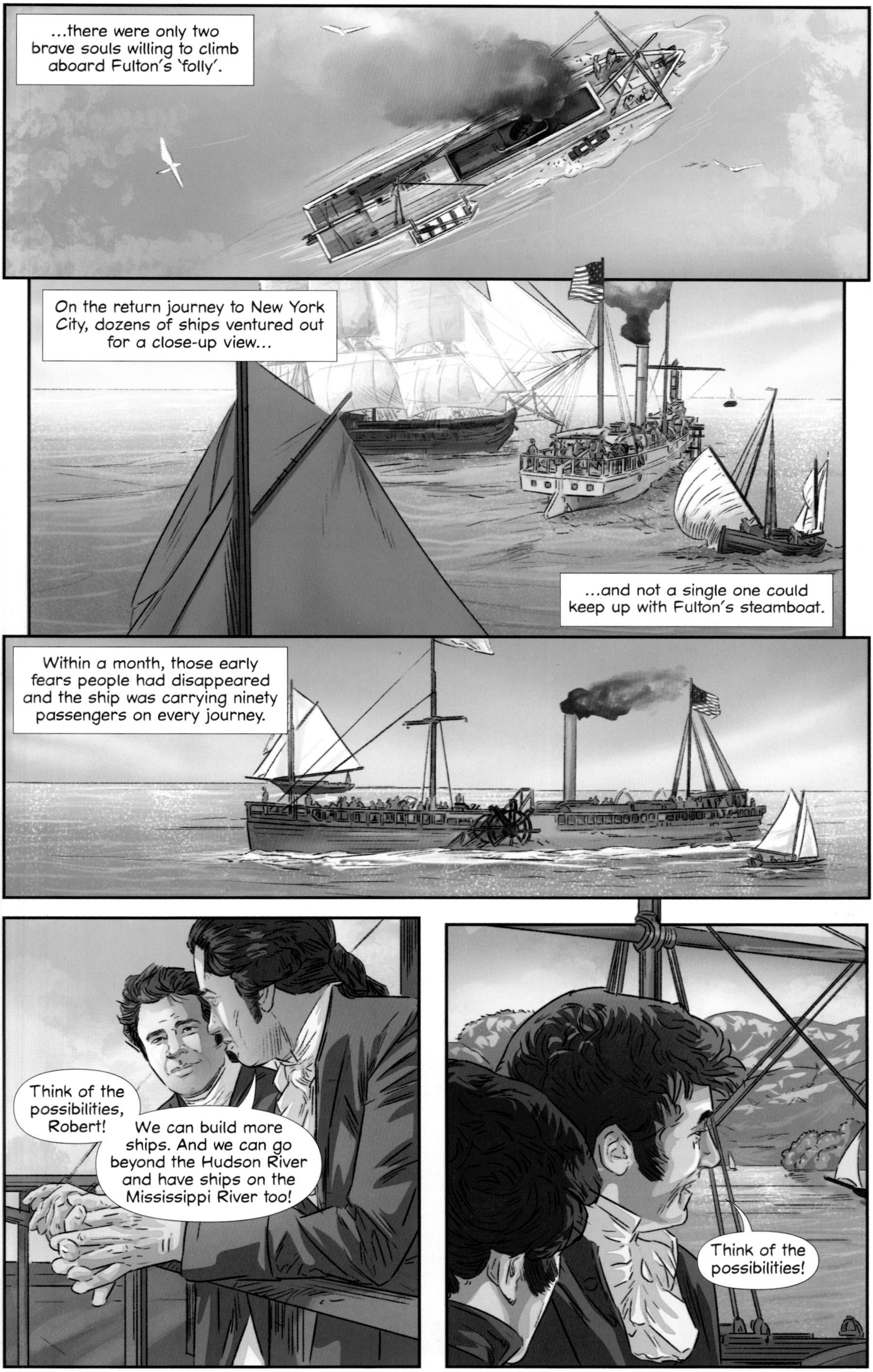
...there were only two brave souls willing to climb aboard Fulton's 'folly'.
On the return journey to New York City, dozens of ships ventured out for a close-up view...
...and not a single one could keep up with Fulton's steamboat.
Within a month, those early fears people had disappeared and the ship was carrying ninety passengers on every journey.
Think of the possibilities, Robert!
We can build more ships. And we can go beyond the Hudson River and have ships on the Mississippi River too!
Think of the possibilities!

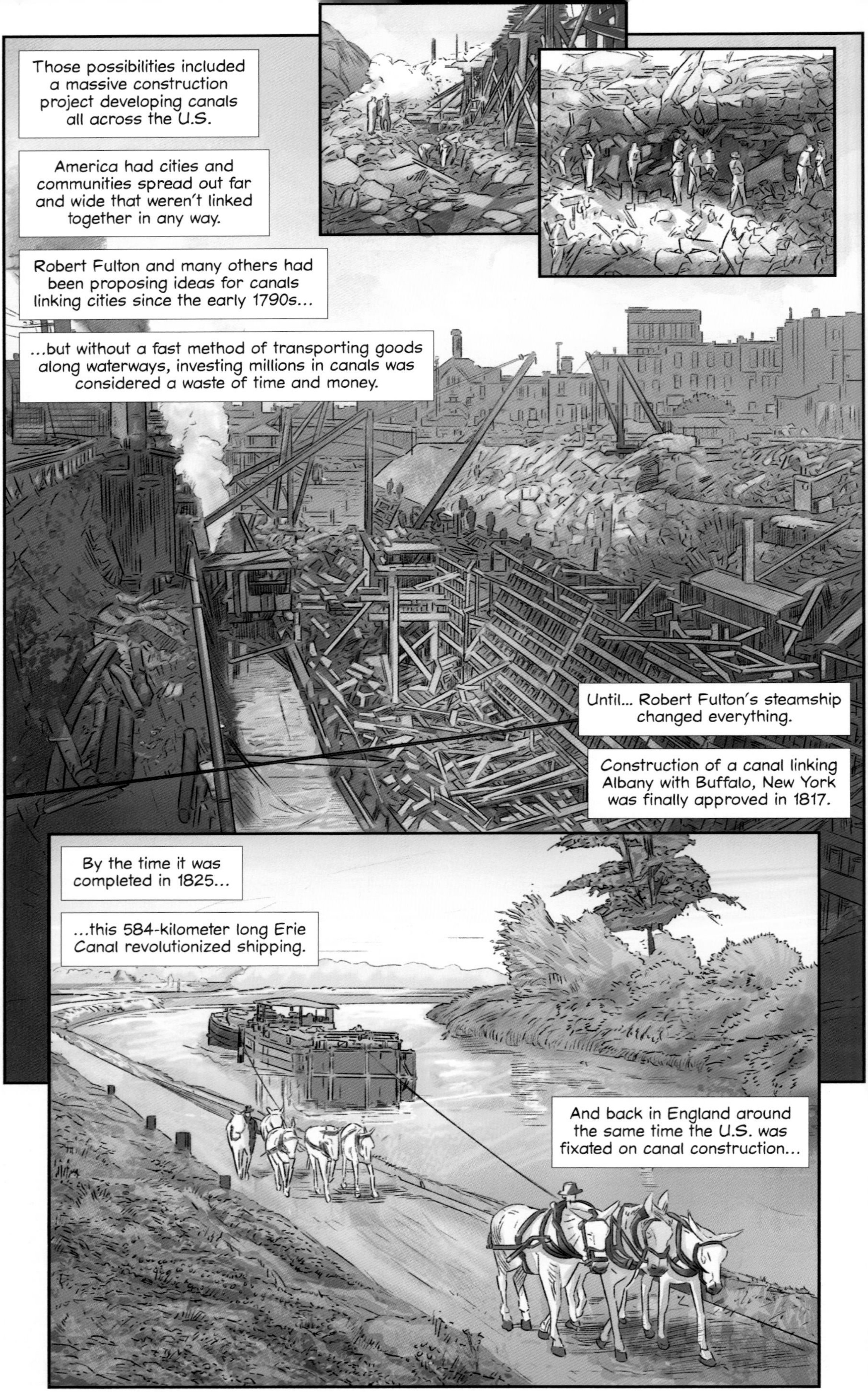
Those possibilities included a massive construction project developing canals all across the U.S.
America had cities and communities spread out far and wide that weren't linked together in any way.
Robert Fulton and many others had been proposing ideas for canals linking cities since the early 1790s...
...but without a fast method of transporting goods along waterways, investing millions in canals was considered a waste of time and money.
Until... Robert Fulton's steamship changed everything.
Construction of a canal linking Albany with Buffalo, New York was finally approved in 1817.
By the time it was completed in 1825...
...this 584-kilometer long Erie Canal revolutionized shipping.
And back in England around the same time the U.S. was fixated on canal construction...

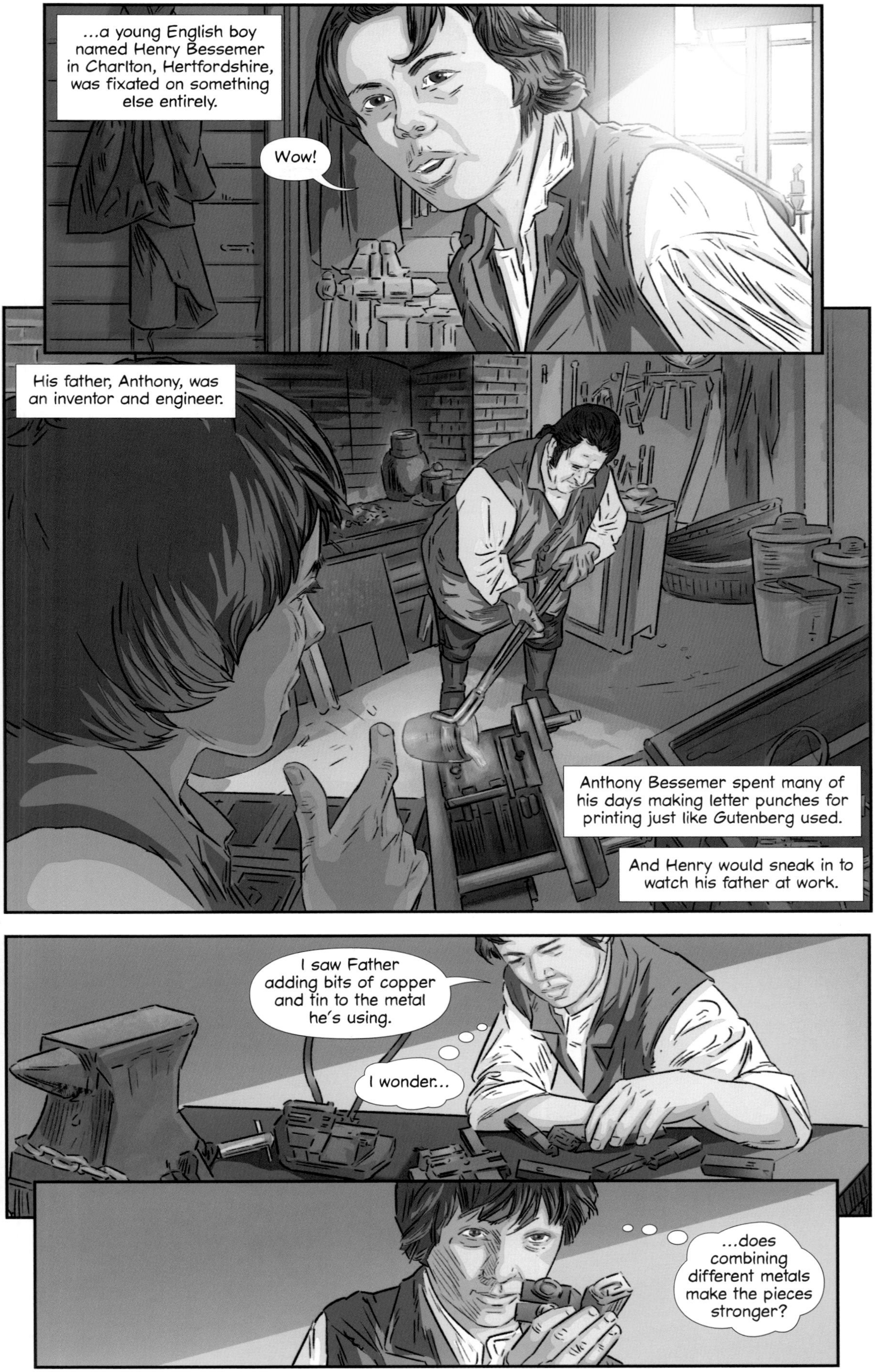

...a young English boy named Henry Bessemer in Charlton, Hertfordshire, was fixated on something else entirely.
Wow!
His father, Anthony, was an inventor and engineer.
Anthony Bessemer spent many of his days making letter punches for printing just like Gutenberg used.
And Henry would sneak in to watch his father at work.
I saw Father adding bits of copper and tin to the metal he's using.
I wonder...
...does combining different metals make the pieces stronger?

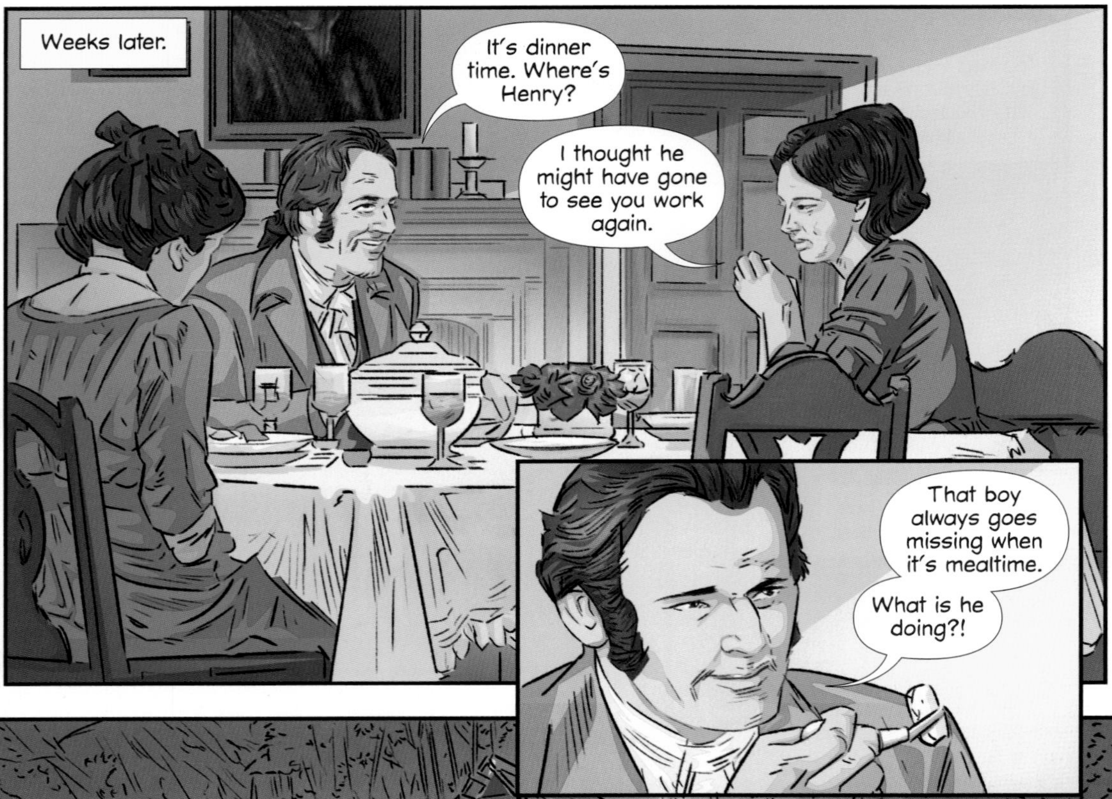
Weeks later.
It's dinner time. Where's Henry?
I thought he might have gone to see you work again.
That boy always goes missing when it's mealtime.
What is he doing?!

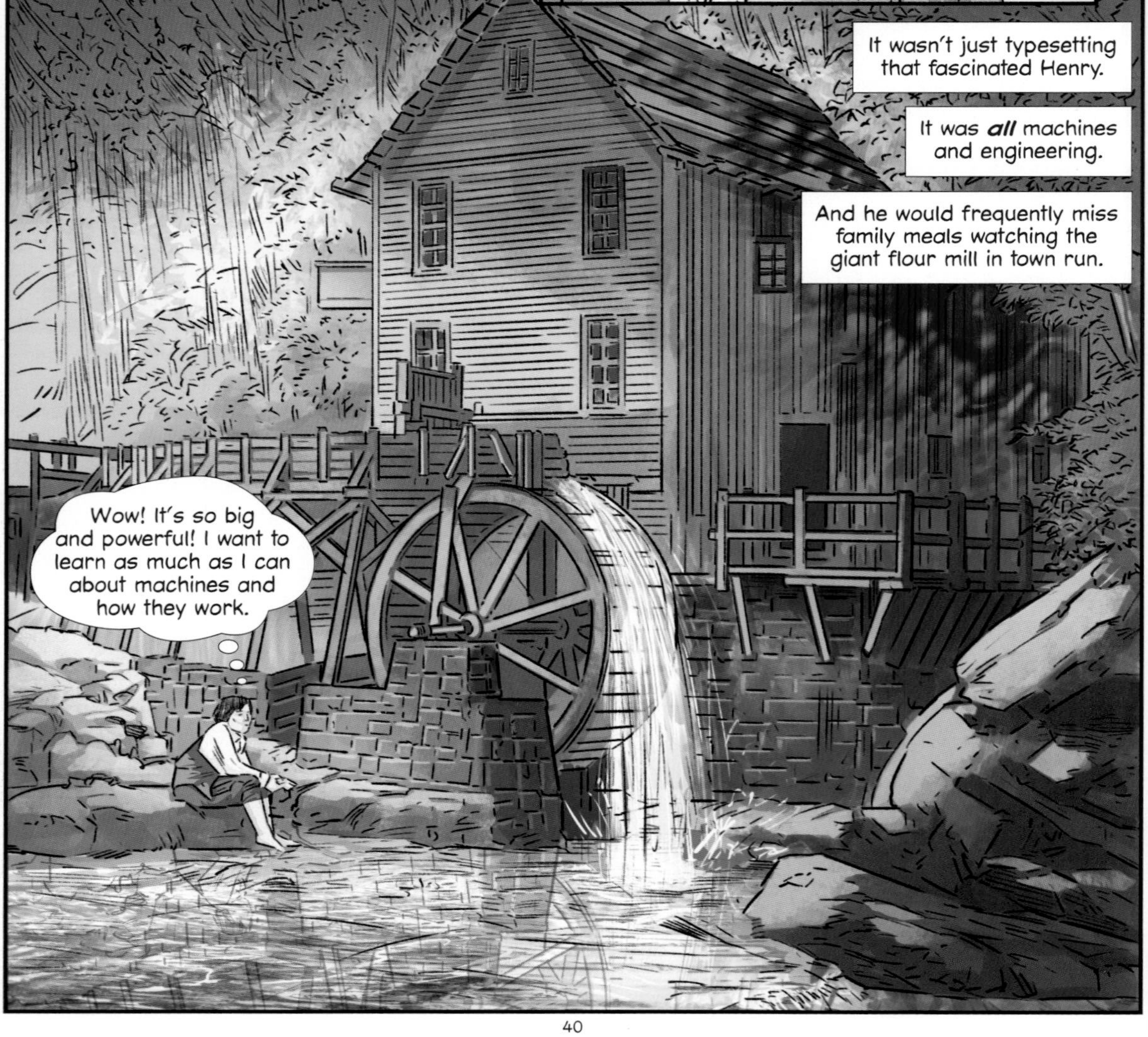
It wasn't just typesetting that fascinated Henry.
It was ***all*** machines and engineering.
And he would frequently miss family meals watching the giant flour mill in town run.
Wow! It's so big and powerful! I want to learn as much as I can about machines and how they work.

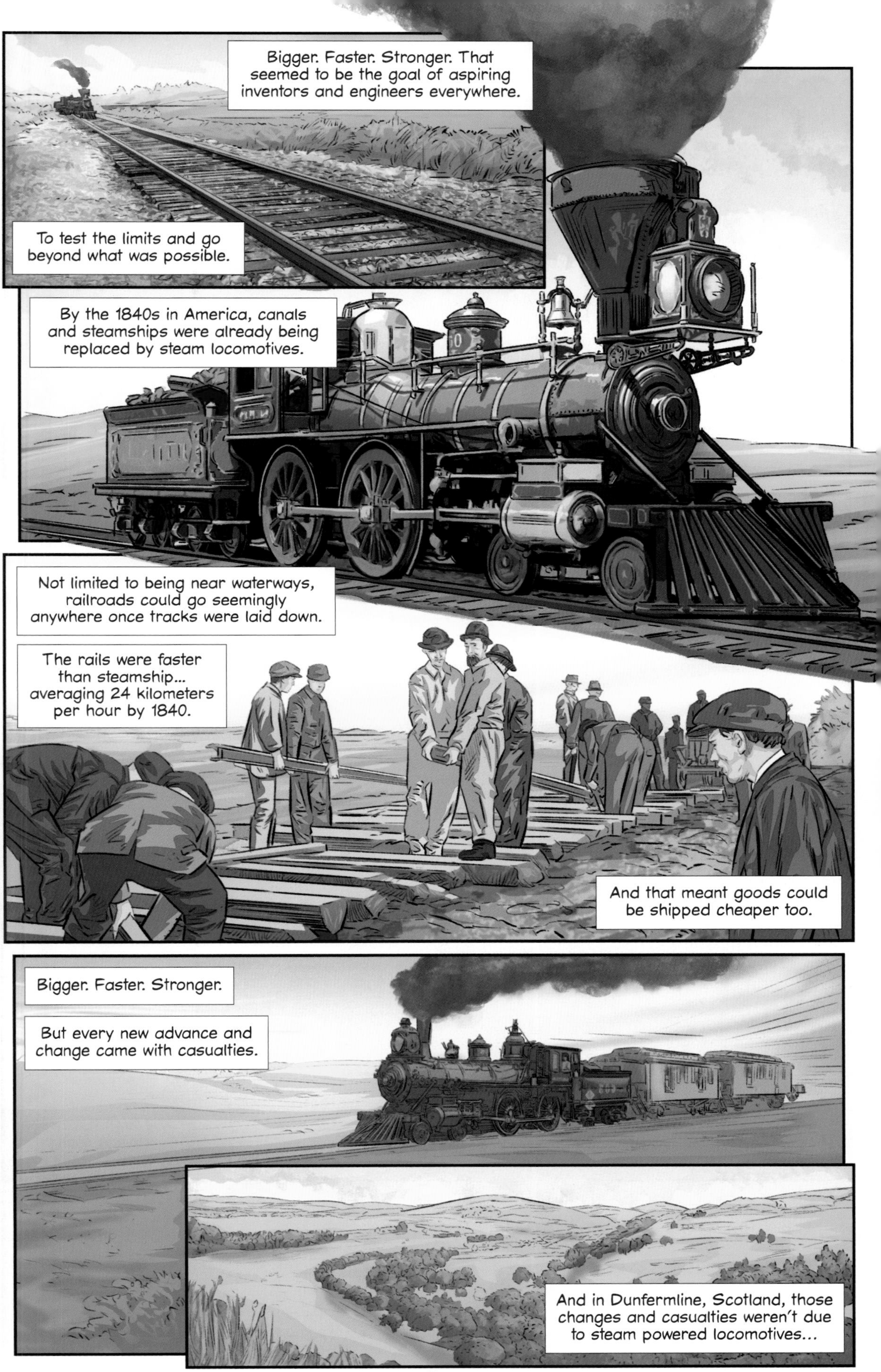
Bigger. Faster. Stronger. That seemed to be the goal of aspiring inventors and engineers everywhere.
To test the limits and go beyond what was possible.
By the 1840s in America, canals and steamships were already being replaced by steam locomotives.
Not limited to being near waterways, railroads could go seemingly anywhere once tracks were laid down.
The rails were faster than steamship... averaging 24 kilometers per hour by 1840.
And that meant goods could be shipped cheaper too.
Bigger. Faster. Stronger.
But every new advance and change came with casualties.
And in Dunfermline, Scotland, those changes and casualties weren't due to steam powered locomotives...

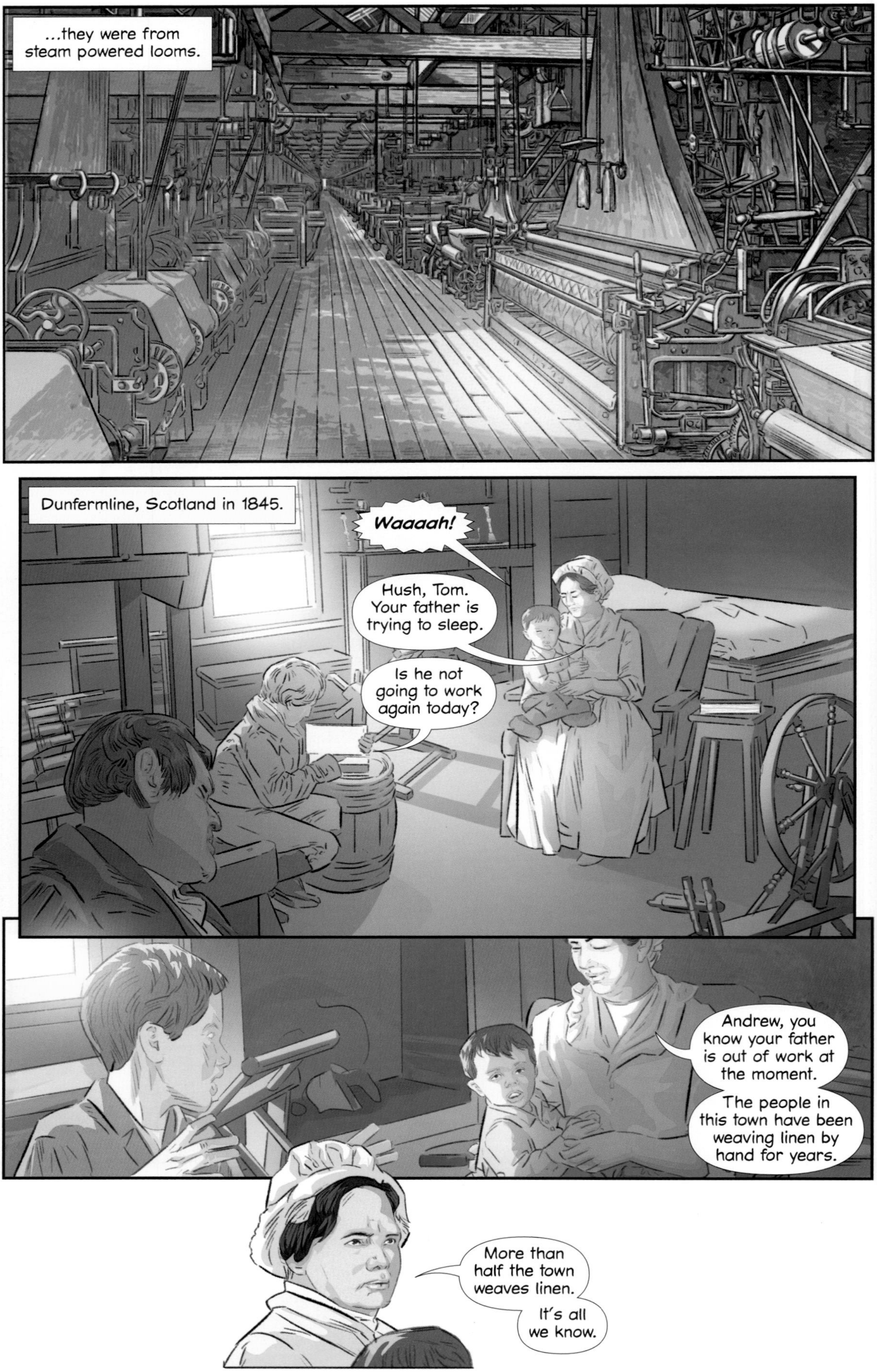
...they were from steam powered looms.
Dunfermline, Scotland in 1845.
Waaaah!
Hush, Tom. Your father is trying to sleep.
Is he not going to work again today?
Andrew, you know your father is out of work at the moment.
The people in this town have been weaving linen by hand for years.
More than half the town weaves linen.
It's all we know.

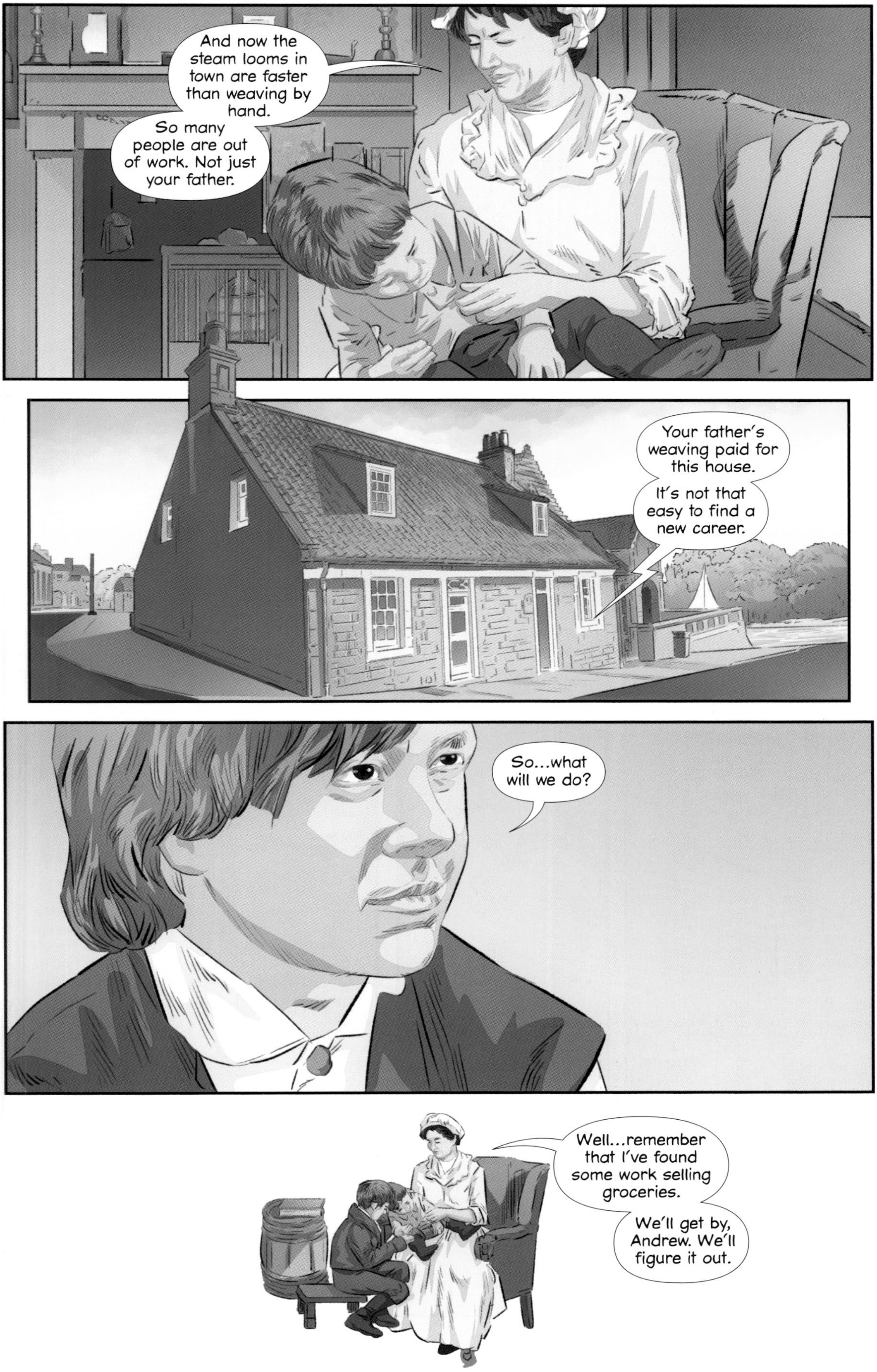
And now the steam looms in town are faster than weaving by hand.
So many people are out of work. Not just your father.
Your father's weaving paid for this house.
It's not that easy to find a new career.
So...what will we do?
Well...remember that I've found some work selling groceries.
We'll get by, Andrew. We'll figure it out.

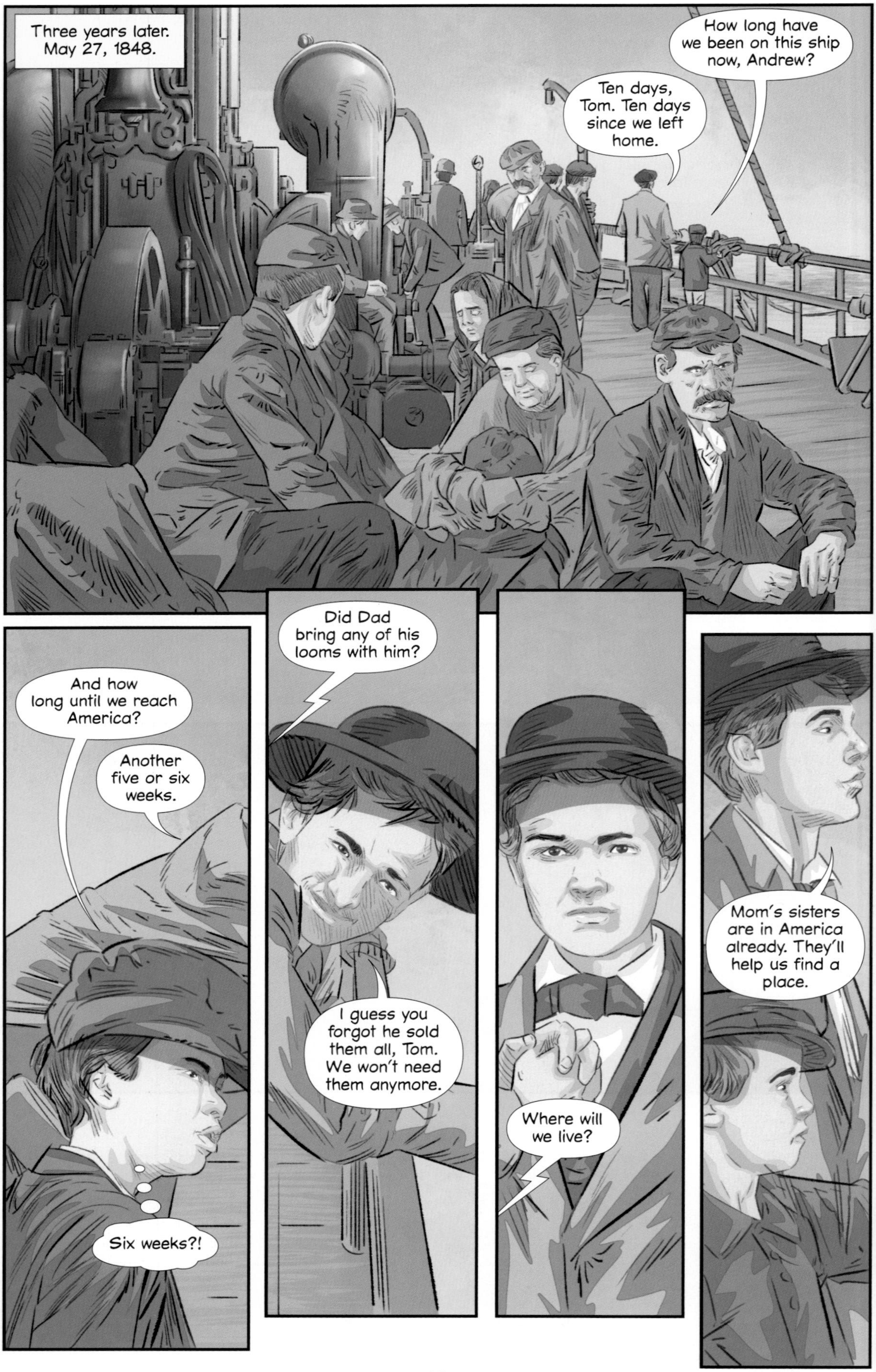
Three years later. May 27, 1848.
How long have we been on this ship now, Andrew?
Ten days, Tom. Ten days since we left home.
And how long until we reach America?
Another five or six weeks.
Six weeks?!
Did Dad bring any of his looms with him?
I guess you forgot he sold them all, Tom. We won't need them anymore.
Where will we live?
Mom's sisters are in America already. They'll help us find a place.

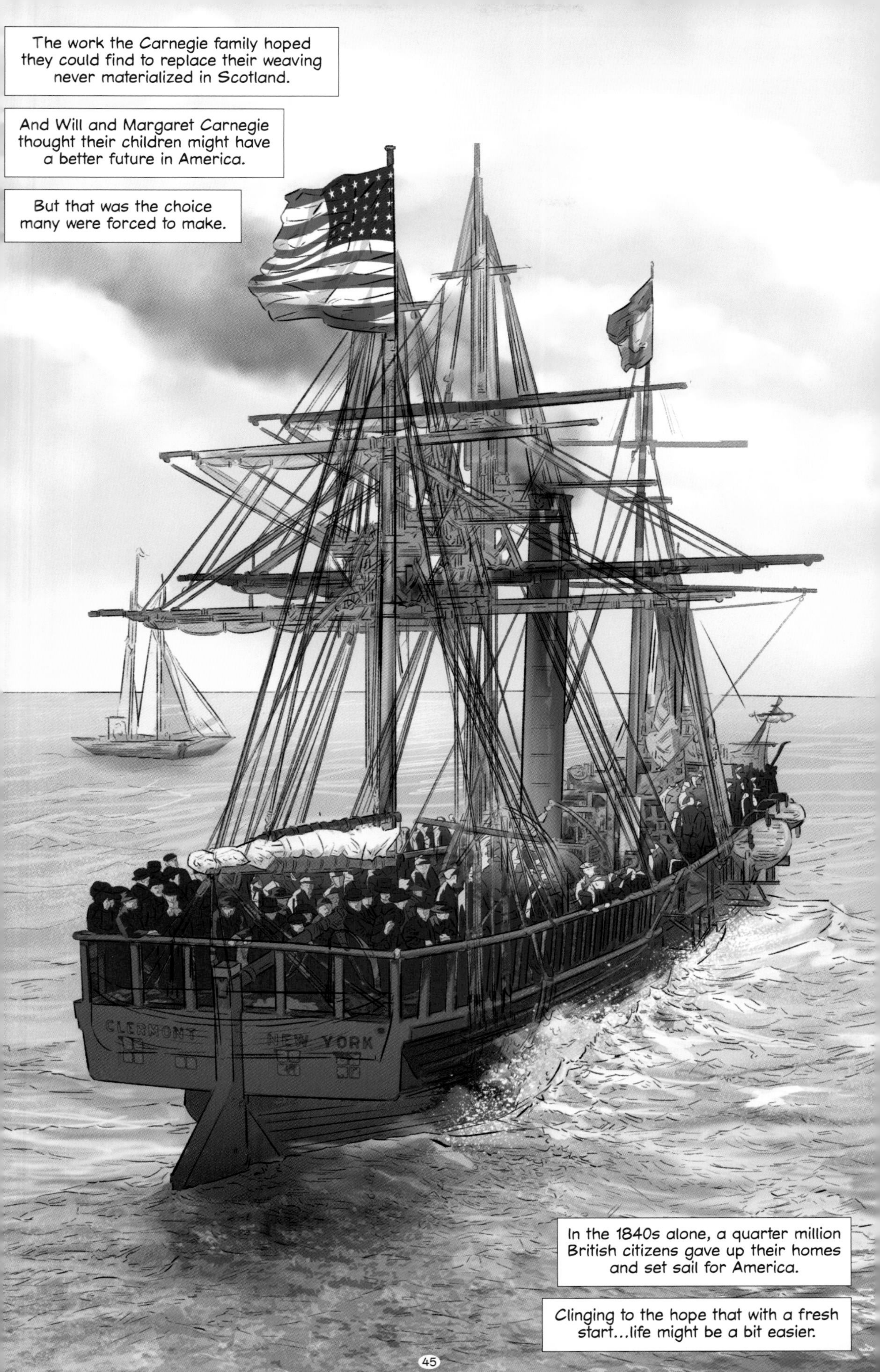
The work the Carnegie family hoped they could find to replace their weaving never materialized in Scotland.
And Will and Margaret Carnegie thought their children might have a better future in America.
But that was the choice many were forced to make.
CLERMONT
NEW YORK
In the 1840s alone, a quarter million British citizens gave up their homes and set sail for America.
Clinging to the hope that with a fresh start...life might be a bit easier.

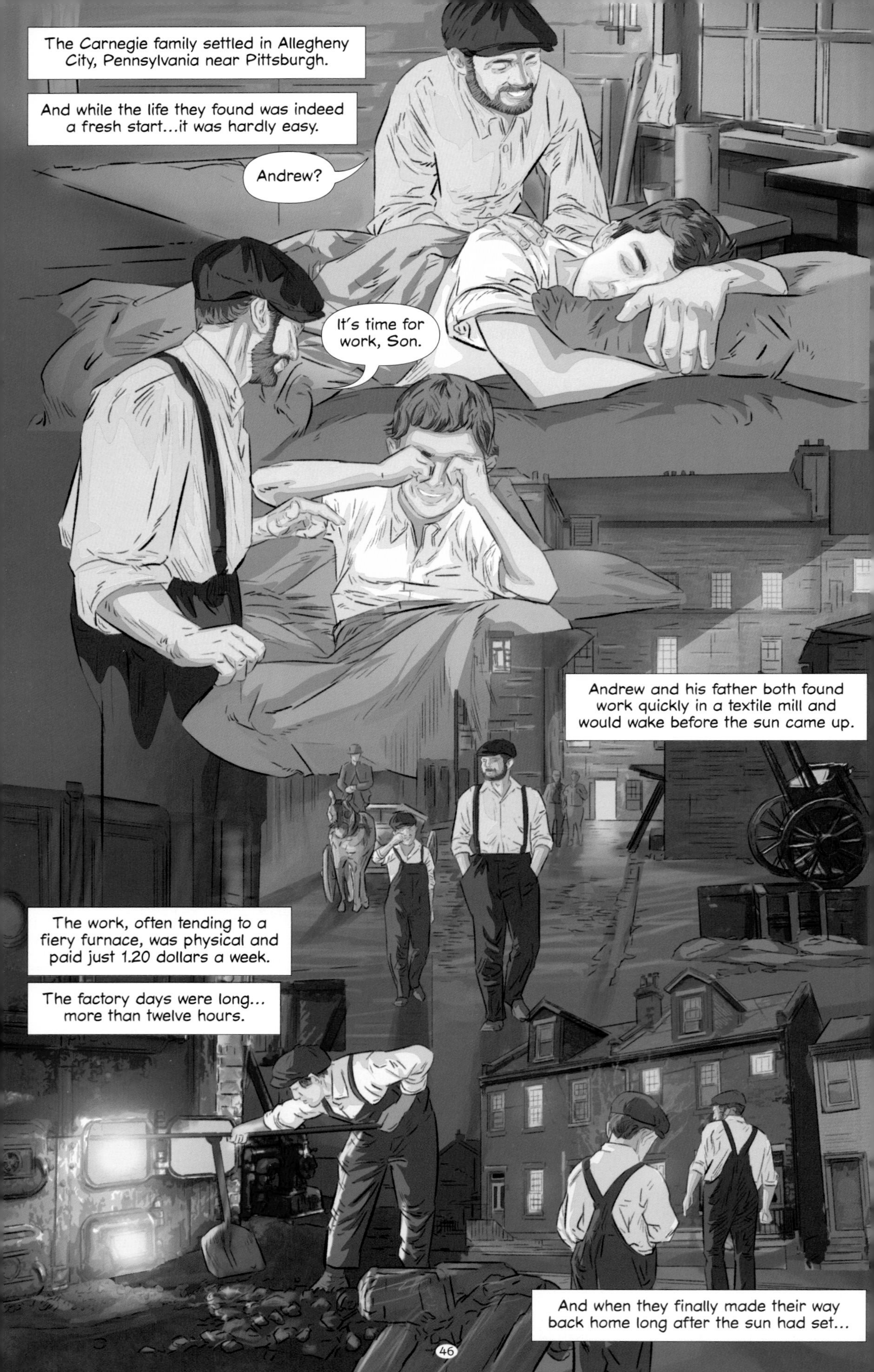
The Carnegie family settled in Allegheny City, Pennsylvania near Pittsburgh.
And while the life they found was indeed a fresh start…it was hardly easy.
Andrew?
It's time for work, Son.
Andrew and his father both found work quickly in a textile mill and would wake before the sun came up.
The work, often tending to a fiery furnace, was physical and paid just 1.20 dollars a week.
The factory days were long… more than twelve hours.
And when they finally made their way back home long after the sun had set…

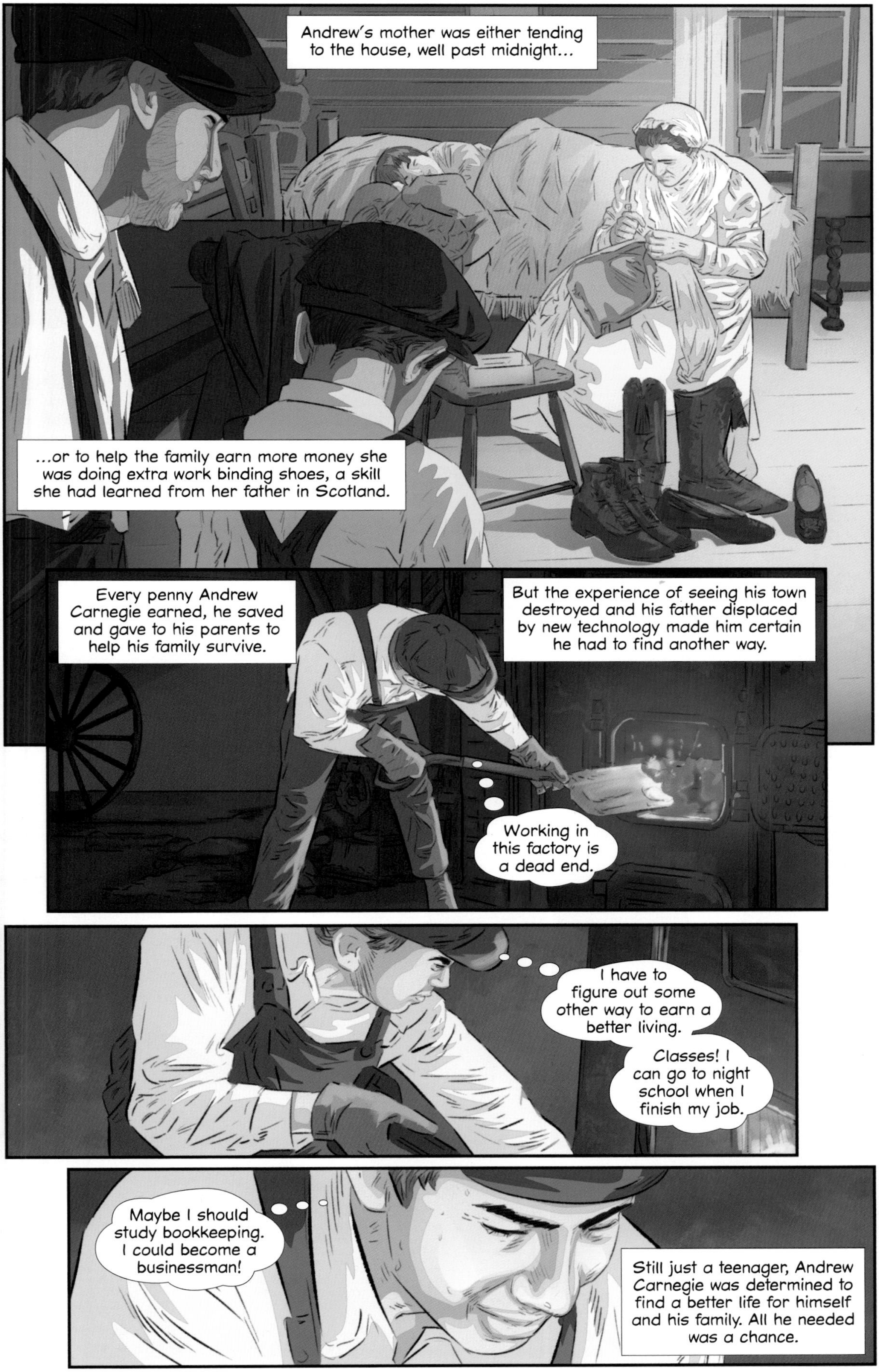
Andrew's mother was either tending to the house, well past midnight...
...or to help the family earn more money she was doing extra work binding shoes, a skill she had learned from her father in Scotland.
Every penny Andrew Carnegie earned, he saved and gave to his parents to help his family survive.
But the experience of seeing his town destroyed and his father displaced by new technology made him certain he had to find another way.
Working in this factory is a dead end.
I have to figure out some other way to earn a better living.
Classes! I can go to night school when I finish my job.
Maybe I should study bookkeeping. I could become a businessman!
Still just a teenager, Andrew Carnegie was determined to find a better life for himself and his family. All he needed was a chance.

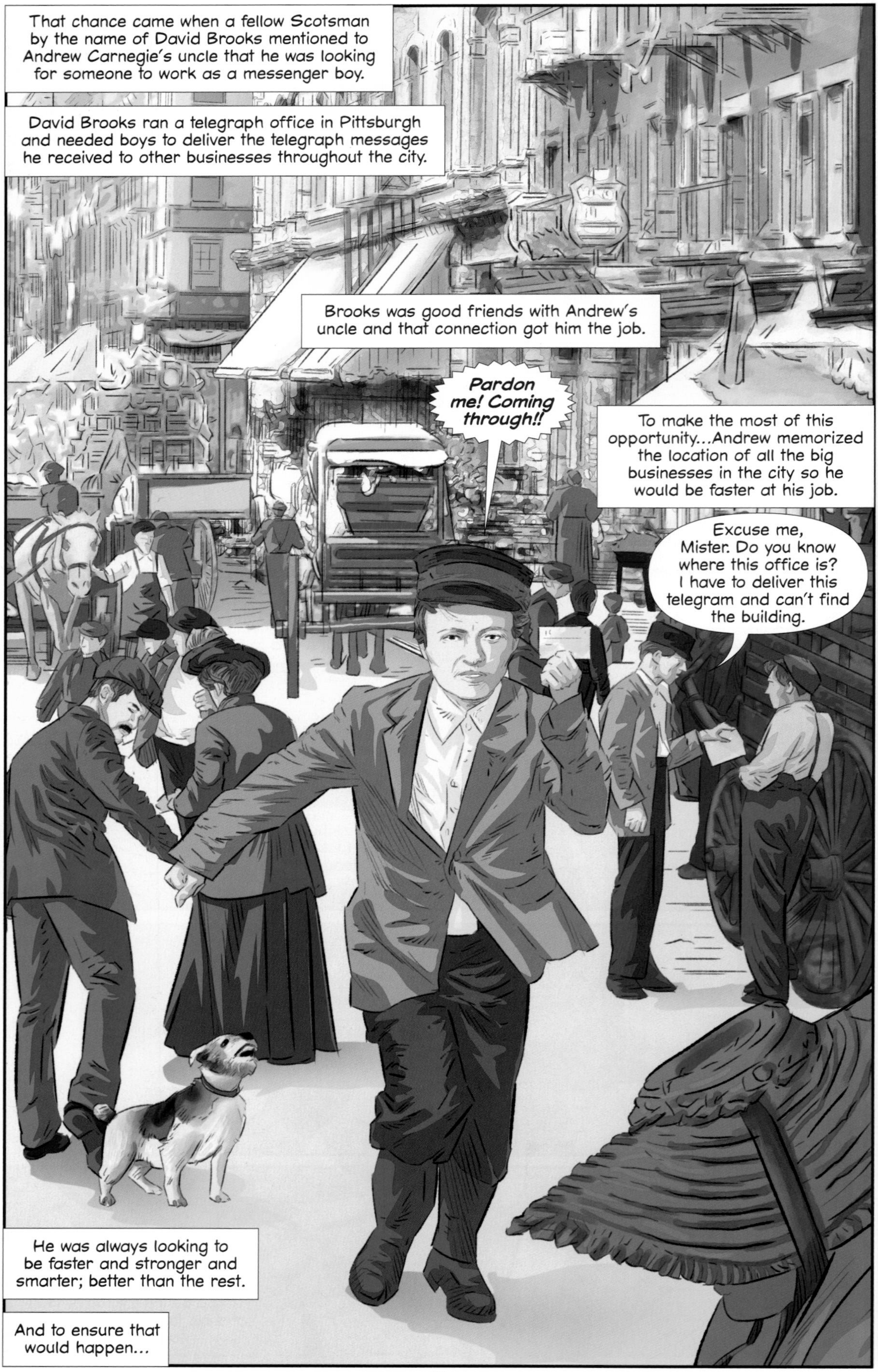

That chance came when a fellow Scotsman by the name of David Brooks mentioned to Andrew Carnegie's uncle that he was looking for someone to work as a messenger boy.
David Brooks ran a telegraph office in Pittsburgh and needed boys to deliver the telegraph messages he received to other businesses throughout the city.
Brooks was good friends with Andrew's uncle and that connection got him the job.
Pardon me! Coming through!!
To make the most of this opportunity...Andrew memorized the location of all the big businesses in the city so he would be faster at his job.
Excuse me, Mister. Do you know where this office is? I have to deliver this telegram and can't find the building.
He was always looking to be faster and stronger and smarter; better than the rest.
And to ensure that would happen...

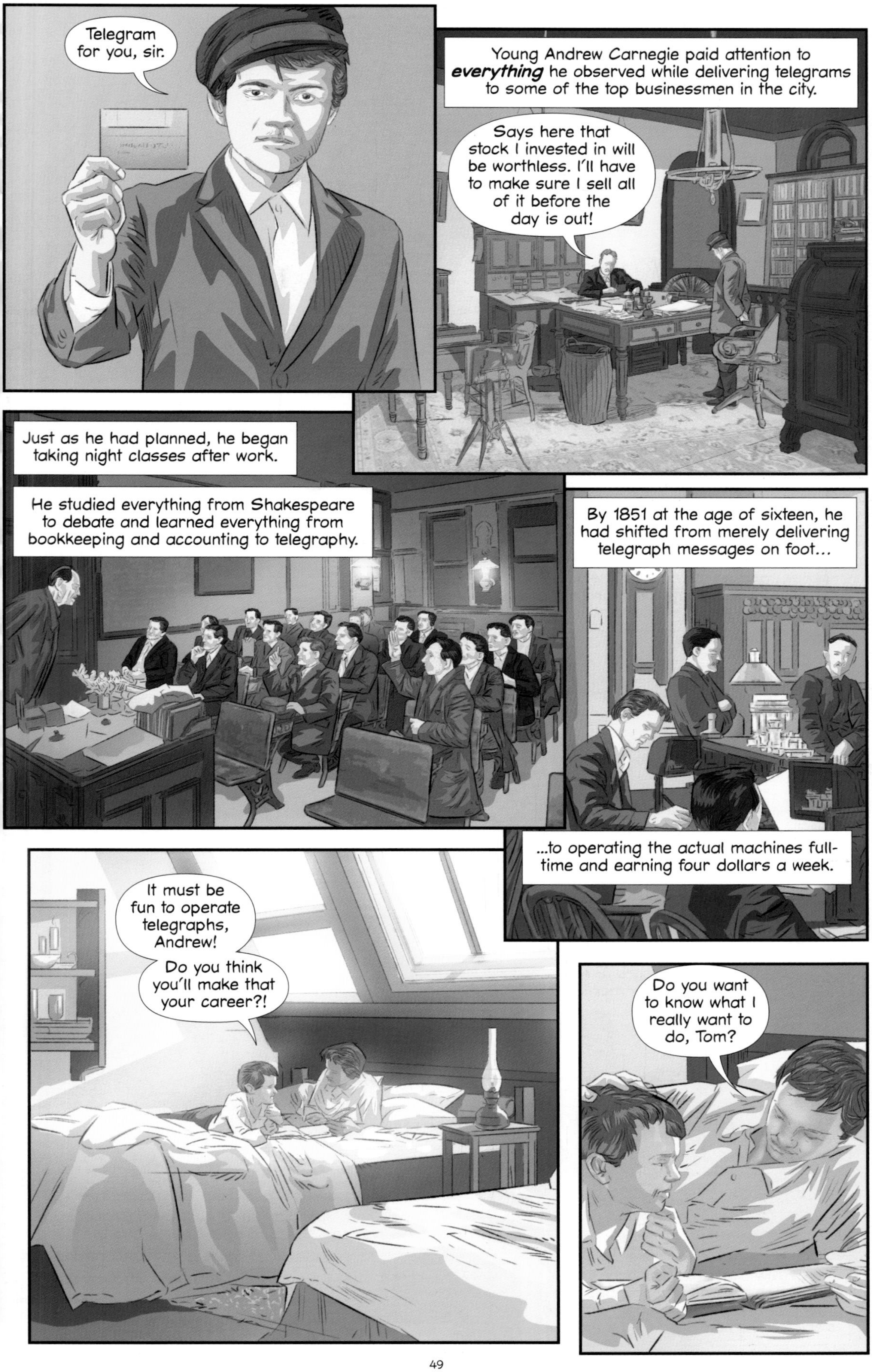
Telegram for you, sir.
Young Andrew Carnegie paid attention to **everything** he observed while delivering telegrams to some of the top businessmen in the city.
Says here that stock I invested in will be worthless. I'll have to make sure I sell all of it before the day is out!
Just as he had planned, he began taking night classes after work.
He studied everything from Shakespeare to debate and learned everything from bookkeeping and accounting to telegraphy.
By 1851 at the age of sixteen, he had shifted from merely delivering telegraph messages on foot...
...to operating the actual machines full-time and earning four dollars a week.
It must be fun to operate telegraphs, Andrew!
Do you think you'll make that your career?!
Do you want to know what I really want to do, Tom?

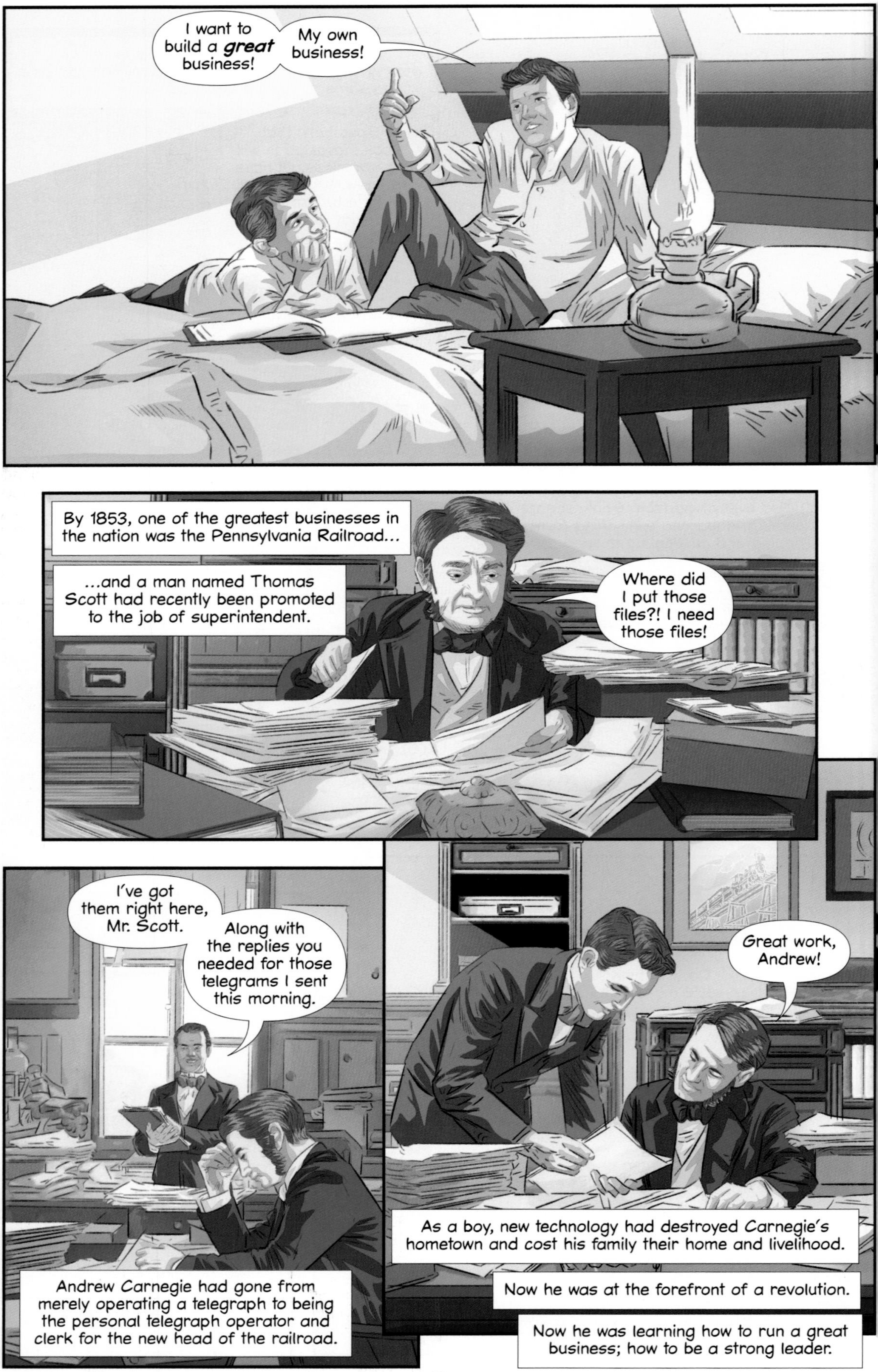
I want to build a *great* business!
My own business!
By 1853, one of the greatest businesses in the nation was the Pennsylvania Railroad...
...and a man named Thomas Scott had recently been promoted to the job of superintendent.
Where did I put those files?! I need those files!
I've got them right here, Mr. Scott.
Along with the replies you needed for those telegrams I sent this morning.
Andrew Carnegie had gone from merely operating a telegraph to being the personal telegraph operator and clerk for the new head of the railroad.
Great work, Andrew!
As a boy, new technology had destroyed Carnegie's hometown and cost his family their home and livelihood.
Now he was at the forefront of a revolution.
Now he was learning how to run a great business; how to be a strong leader.

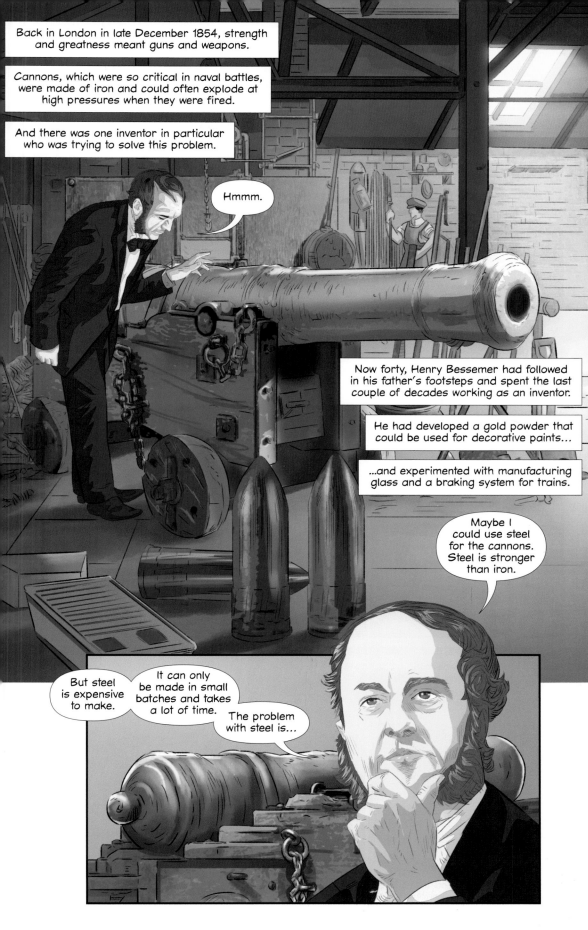

Back in London in late December 1854, strength and greatness meant guns and weapons.

Cannons, which were so critical in naval battles, were made of iron and could often explode at high pressures when they were fired.

And there was one inventor in particular who was trying to solve this problem.

Hmmm.

Now forty, Henry Bessemer had followed in his father's footsteps and spent the last couple of decades working as an inventor.

He had developed a gold powder that could be used for decorative paints...

...and experimented with manufacturing glass and a braking system for trains.

Maybe I could use steel for the cannons. Steel is stronger than iron.

But steel is expensive to make.

It can only be made in small batches and takes a lot of time.

The problem with steel is...

There were **many** problems with steel.

Steel was basically made by melting down iron. To convert iron into the much stronger steel...

...it had to be melted at extremely high temperatures to burn off the impurities in the iron.

And it had to be melted down in small batches of about twenty-seven kilograms at a time, with each batch taking about six weeks.

And to heat the iron, a massive amount of coke was needed, which was obtained by heating expensive coal.

And on top of the time and cost to produce steel in such small batches...

...there was also the labor.

Each batch of molten iron had to be stirred by hand...

...for hours!

This was done by teams of men called puddlers.

Hiring and training teams of men strong enough to handle the hard labor only added to the expense of producing steel.

All these factors were why steel was only being used for small tools and cutlery.

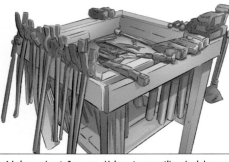

Using steel for anything large like bridges or buildings or ships or trains or even cannons would have been unthinkable.

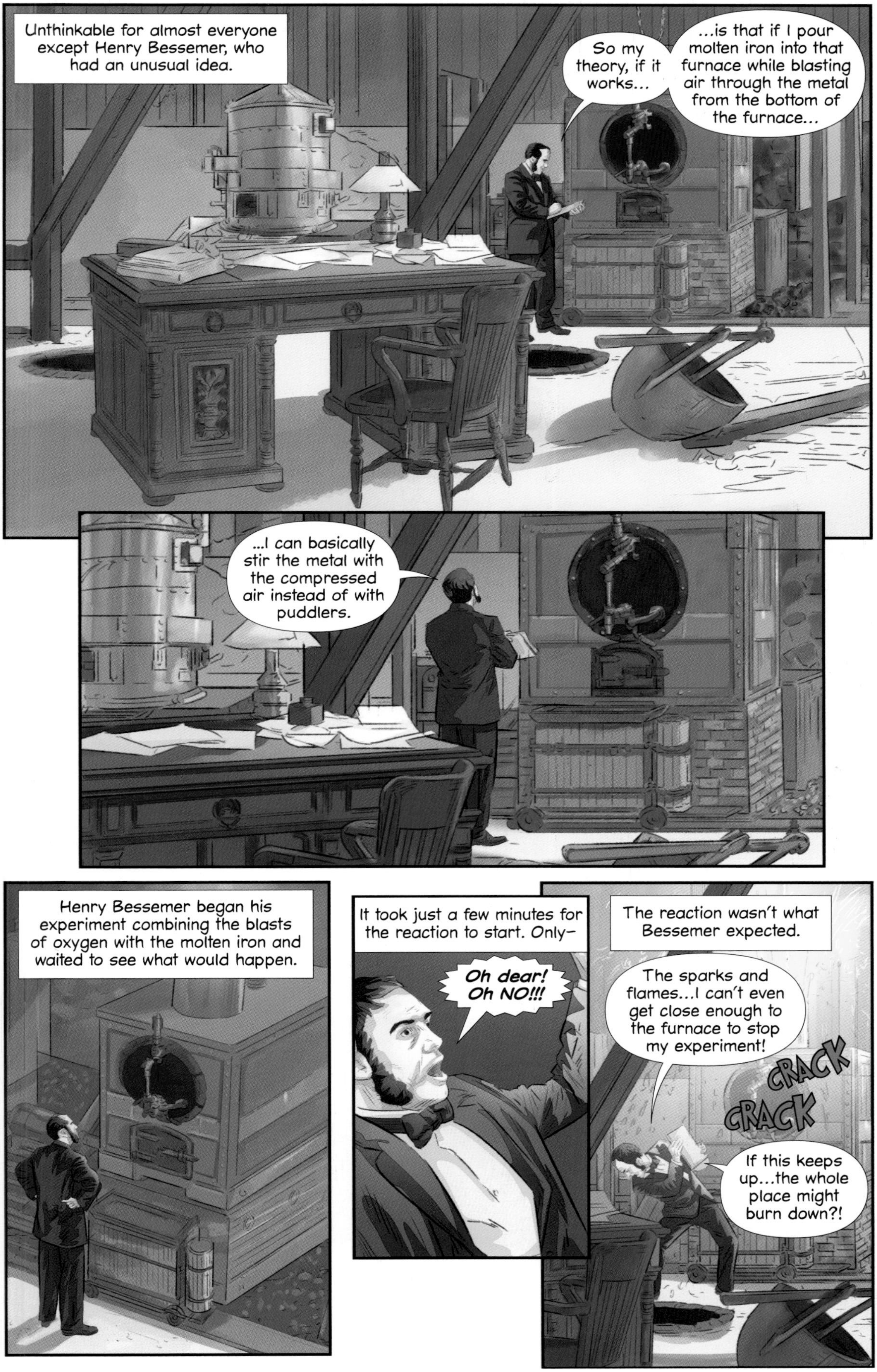
Unthinkable for almost everyone except Henry Bessemer, who had an unusual idea.
So my theory, if it works...
...is that if I pour molten iron into that furnace while blasting air through the metal from the bottom of the furnace...
...I can basically stir the metal with the compressed air instead of with puddlers.
Henry Bessemer began his experiment combining the blasts of oxygen with the molten iron and waited to see what would happen.
It took just a few minutes for the reaction to start. Only–
Oh dear! Oh NO!!!
The reaction wasn't what Bessemer expected.
The sparks and flames...I can't even get close enough to the furnace to stop my experiment!
CRACK
CRACK
If this keeps up...the whole place might burn down?!

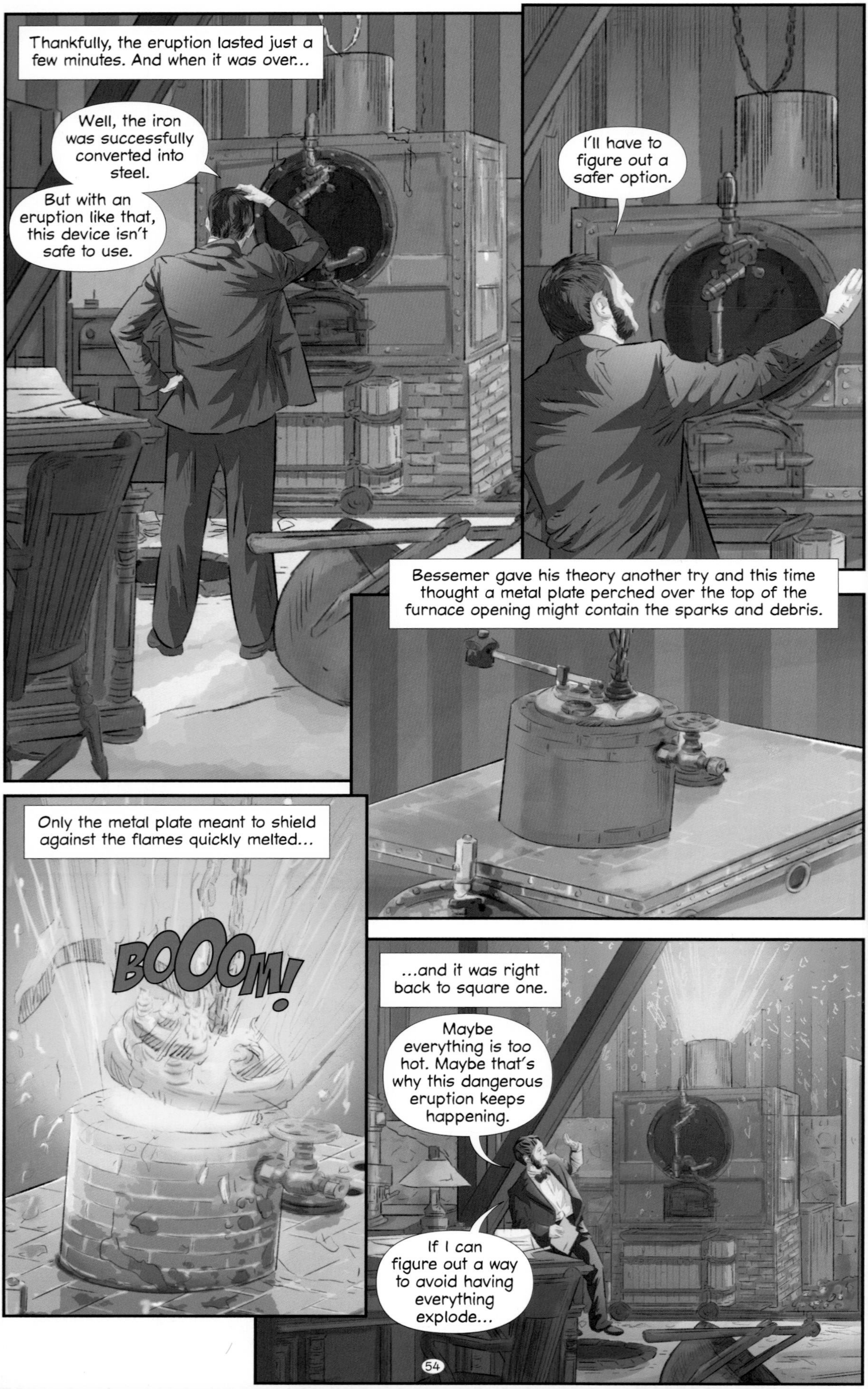

Thankfully, the eruption lasted just a few minutes. And when it was over...
Well, the iron was successfully converted into steel.
But with an eruption like that, this device isn't safe to use.
I'll have to figure out a safer option.
Bessemer gave his theory another try and this time thought a metal plate perched over the top of the furnace opening might contain the sparks and debris.
Only the metal plate meant to shield against the flames quickly melted...
BOOOM!
...and it was right back to square one.
Maybe everything is too hot. Maybe that's why this dangerous eruption keeps happening.
If I can figure out a way to avoid having everything explode...

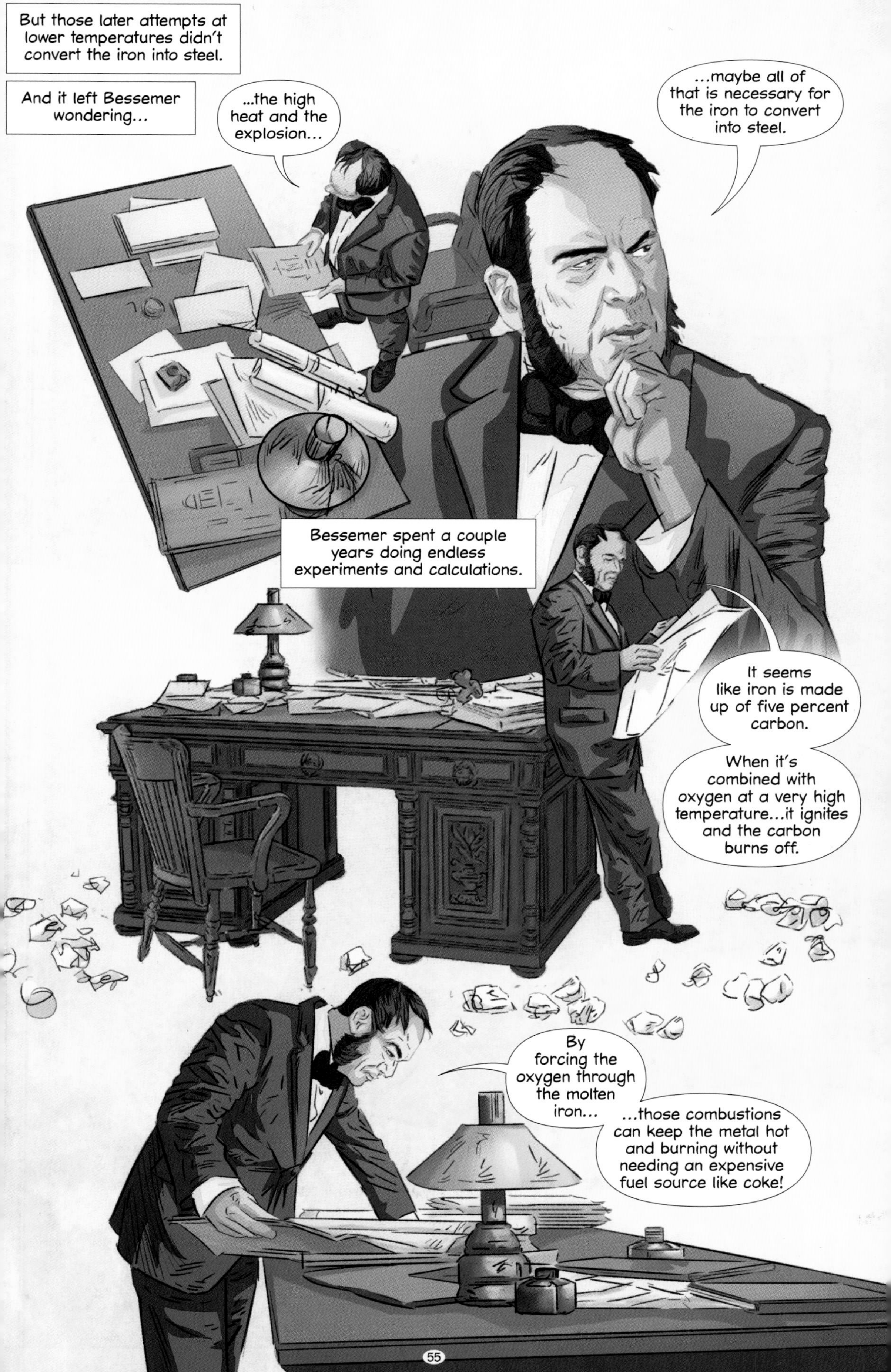

But those later attempts at lower temperatures didn't convert the iron into steel.
And it left Bessemer wondering...
...the high heat and the explosion...
...maybe all of that is necessary for the iron to convert into steel.
Bessemer spent a couple years doing endless experiments and calculations.
It seems like iron is made up of five percent carbon.
When it's combined with oxygen at a very high temperature...it ignites and the carbon burns off.
By forcing the oxygen through the molten iron...
...those combustions can keep the metal hot and burning without needing an expensive fuel source like coke!

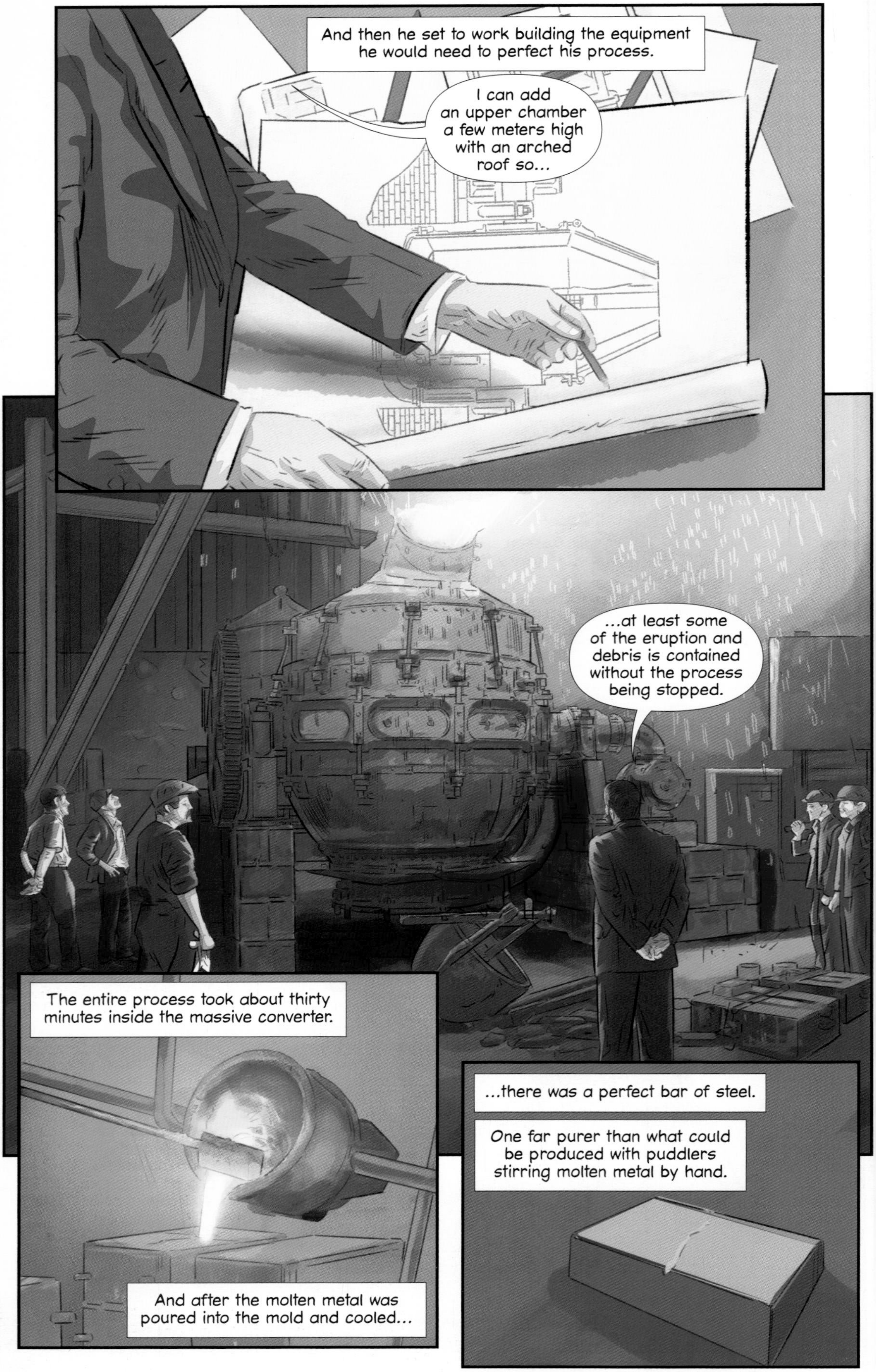
And then he set to work building the equipment he would need to perfect his process.
I can add an upper chamber a few meters high with an arched roof so...
...at least some of the eruption and debris is contained without the process being stopped.
The entire process took about thirty minutes inside the massive converter.
And after the molten metal was poured into the mold and cooled...
...there was a perfect bar of steel.
One far purer than what could be produced with puddlers stirring molten metal by hand.

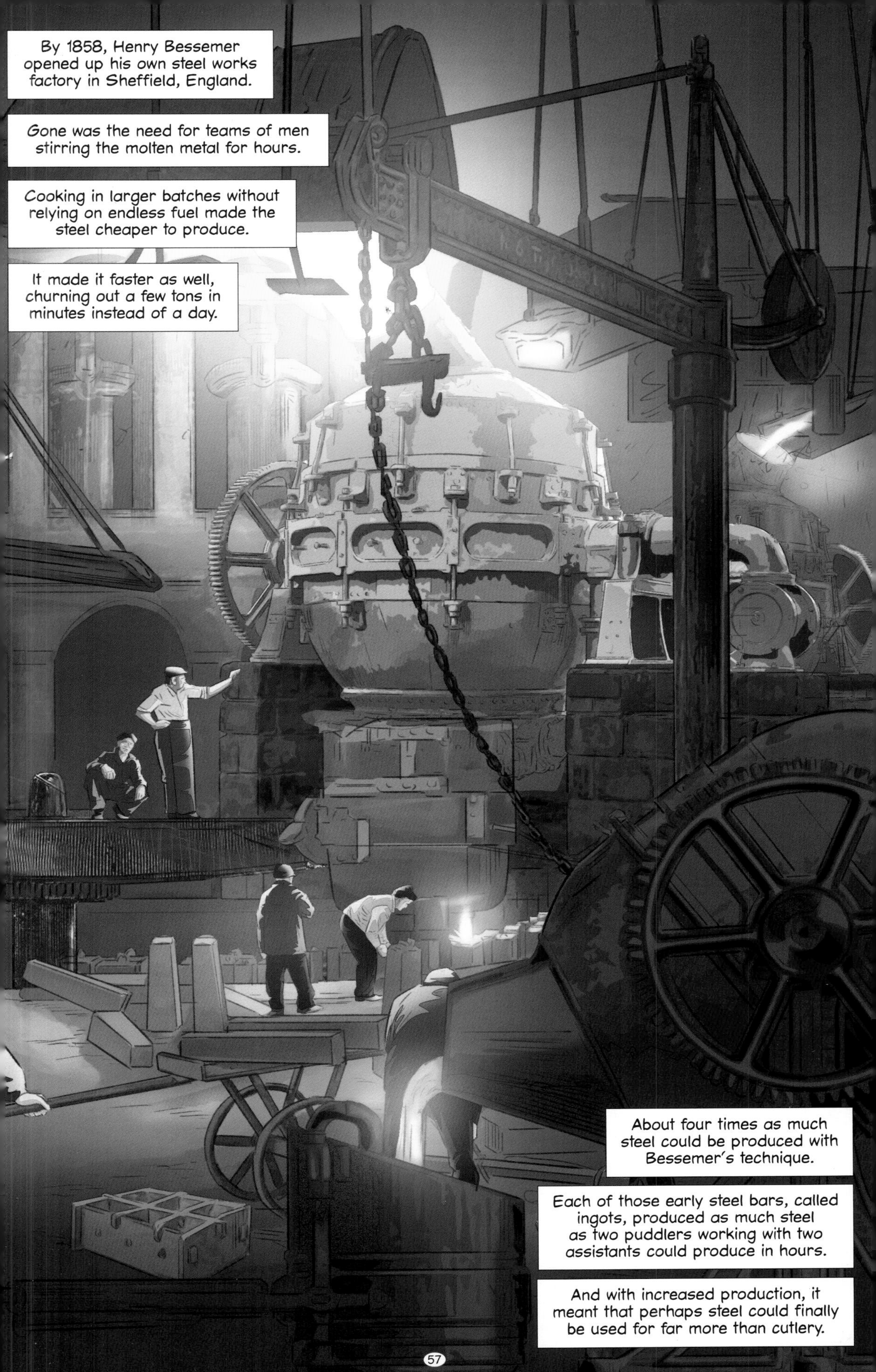
By 1858, Henry Bessemer opened up his own steel works factory in Sheffield, England.
Gone was the need for teams of men stirring the molten metal for hours.
Cooking in larger batches without relying on endless fuel made the steel cheaper to produce.
It made it faster as well, churning out a few tons in minutes instead of a day.
About four times as much steel could be produced with Bessemer's technique.
Each of those early steel bars, called ingots, produced as much steel as two puddlers working with two assistants could produce in hours.
And with increased production, it meant that perhaps steel could finally be used for far more than cutlery.

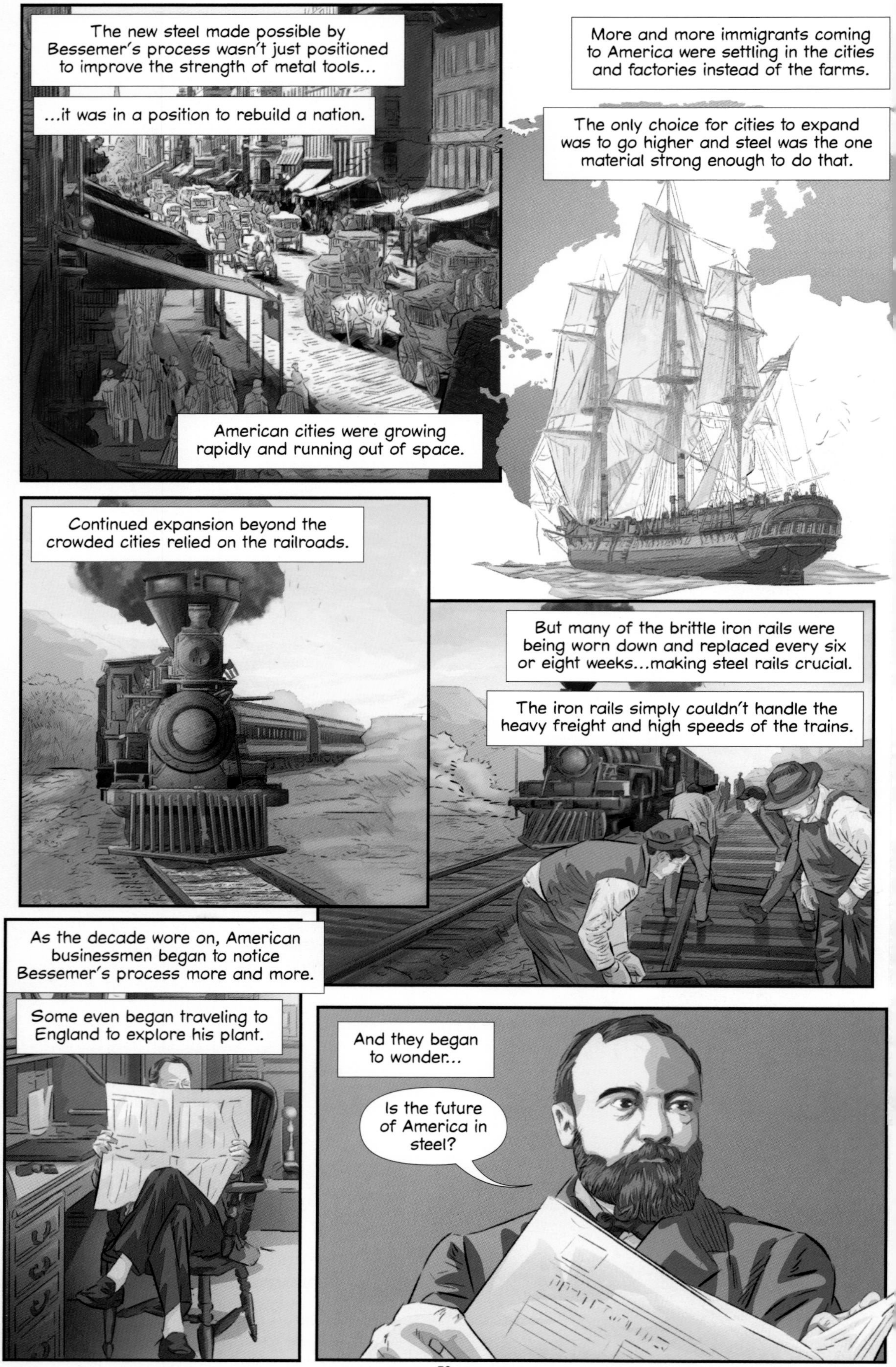
The new steel made possible by Bessemer's process wasn't just positioned to improve the strength of metal tools...
...it was in a position to rebuild a nation.
American cities were growing rapidly and running out of space.
More and more immigrants coming to America were settling in the cities and factories instead of the farms.
The only choice for cities to expand was to go higher and steel was the one material strong enough to do that.
Continued expansion beyond the crowded cities relied on the railroads.
But many of the brittle iron rails were being worn down and replaced every six or eight weeks...making steel rails crucial.
The iron rails simply couldn't handle the heavy freight and high speeds of the trains.
As the decade wore on, American businessmen began to notice Bessemer's process more and more.
Some even began traveling to England to explore his plant.
And they began to wonder...
Is the future of America in steel?

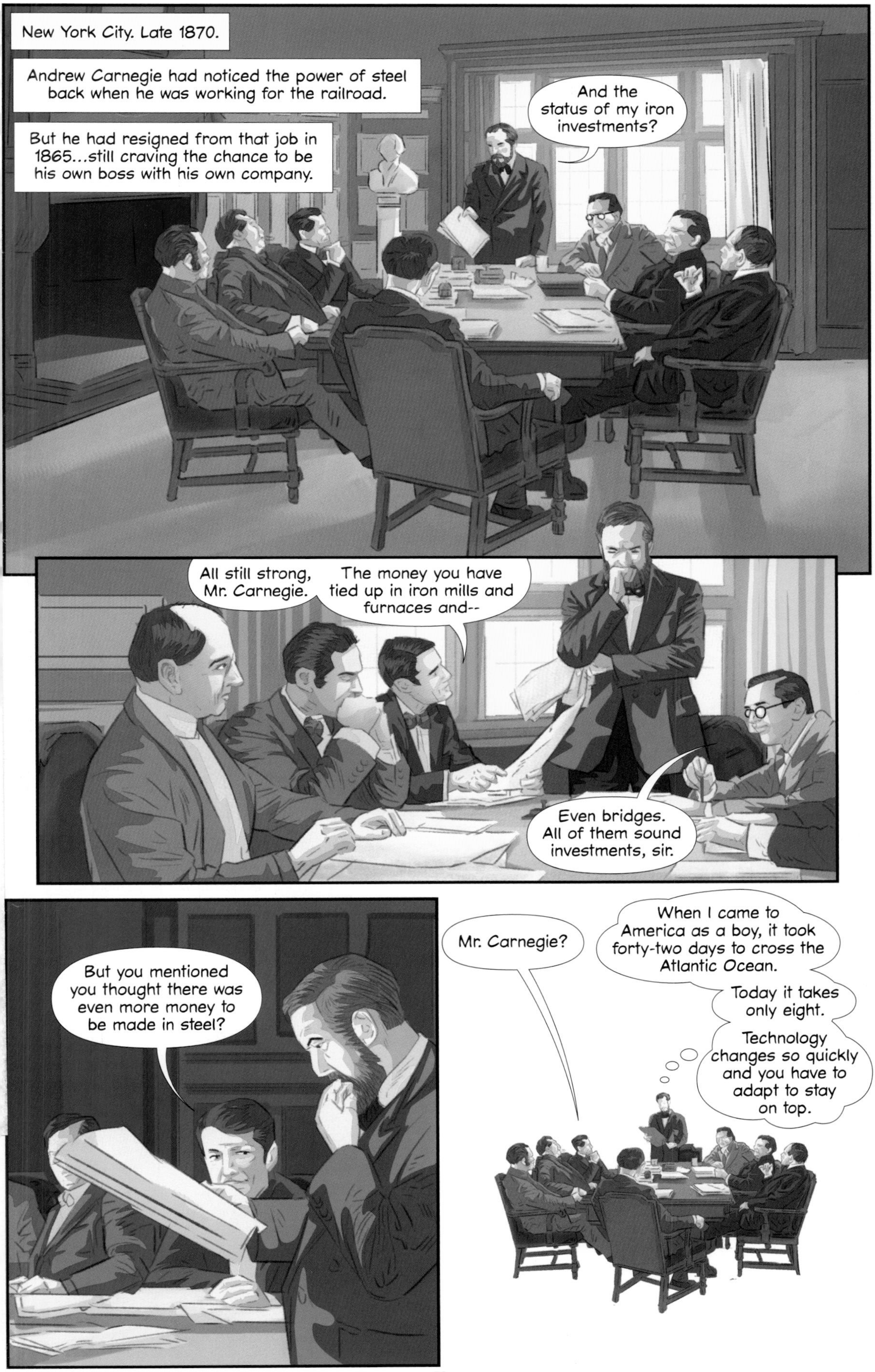

New York City. Late 1870.
Andrew Carnegie had noticed the power of steel back when he was working for the railroad.
But he had resigned from that job in 1865...still craving the chance to be his own boss with his own company.
And the status of my iron investments?
All still strong, Mr. Carnegie.
The money you have tied up in iron mills and furnaces and--
Even bridges. All of them sound investments, sir.
But you mentioned you thought there was even more money to be made in steel?
Mr. Carnegie?
When I came to America as a boy, it took forty-two days to cross the Atlantic Ocean.
Today it takes only eight.
Technology changes so quickly and you have to adapt to stay on top.

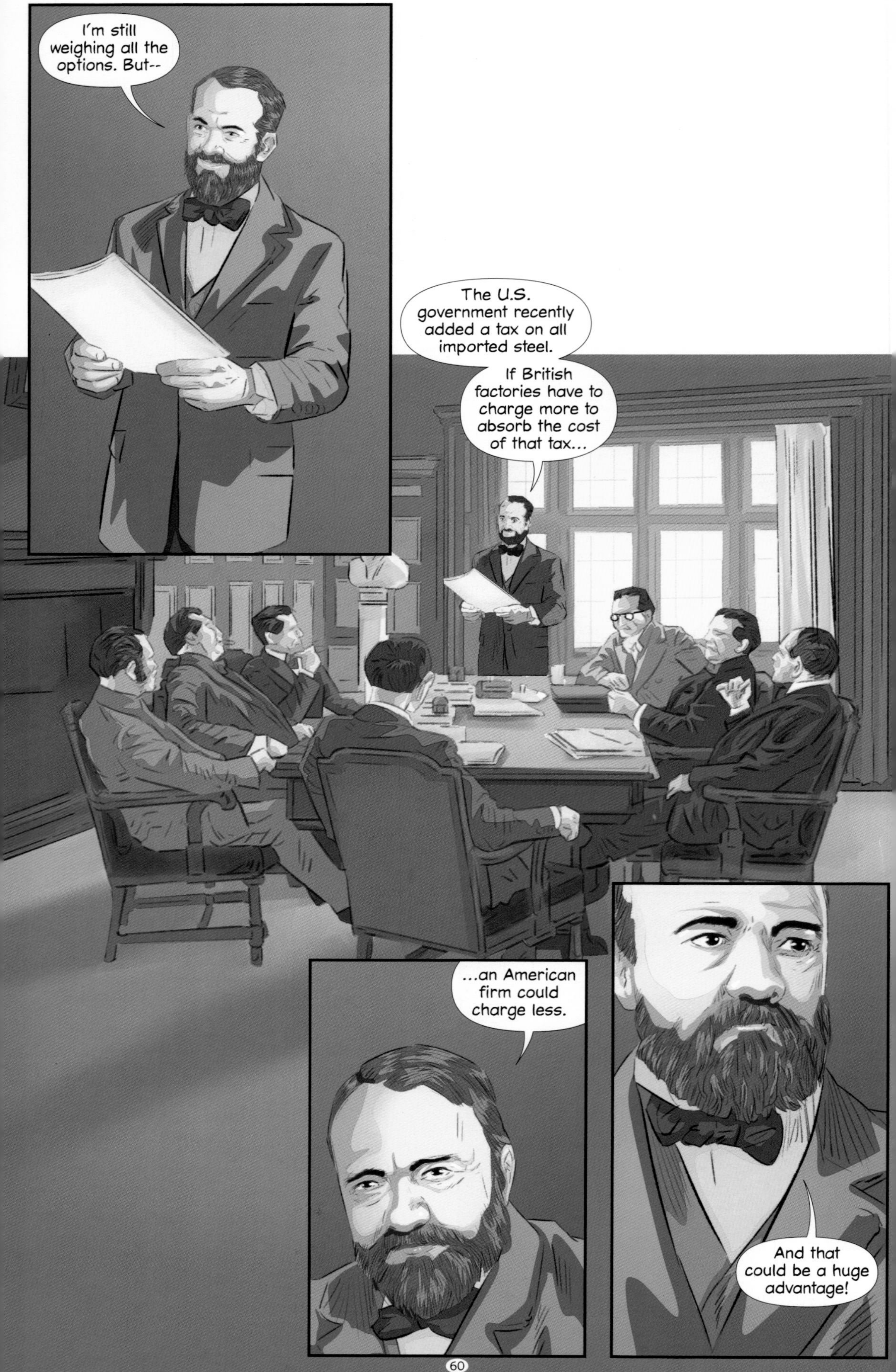
I'm still weighing all the options. But--
The U.S. government recently added a tax on all imported steel.
If British factories have to charge more to absorb the cost of that tax...
...an American firm could charge less.
And that could be a huge advantage!

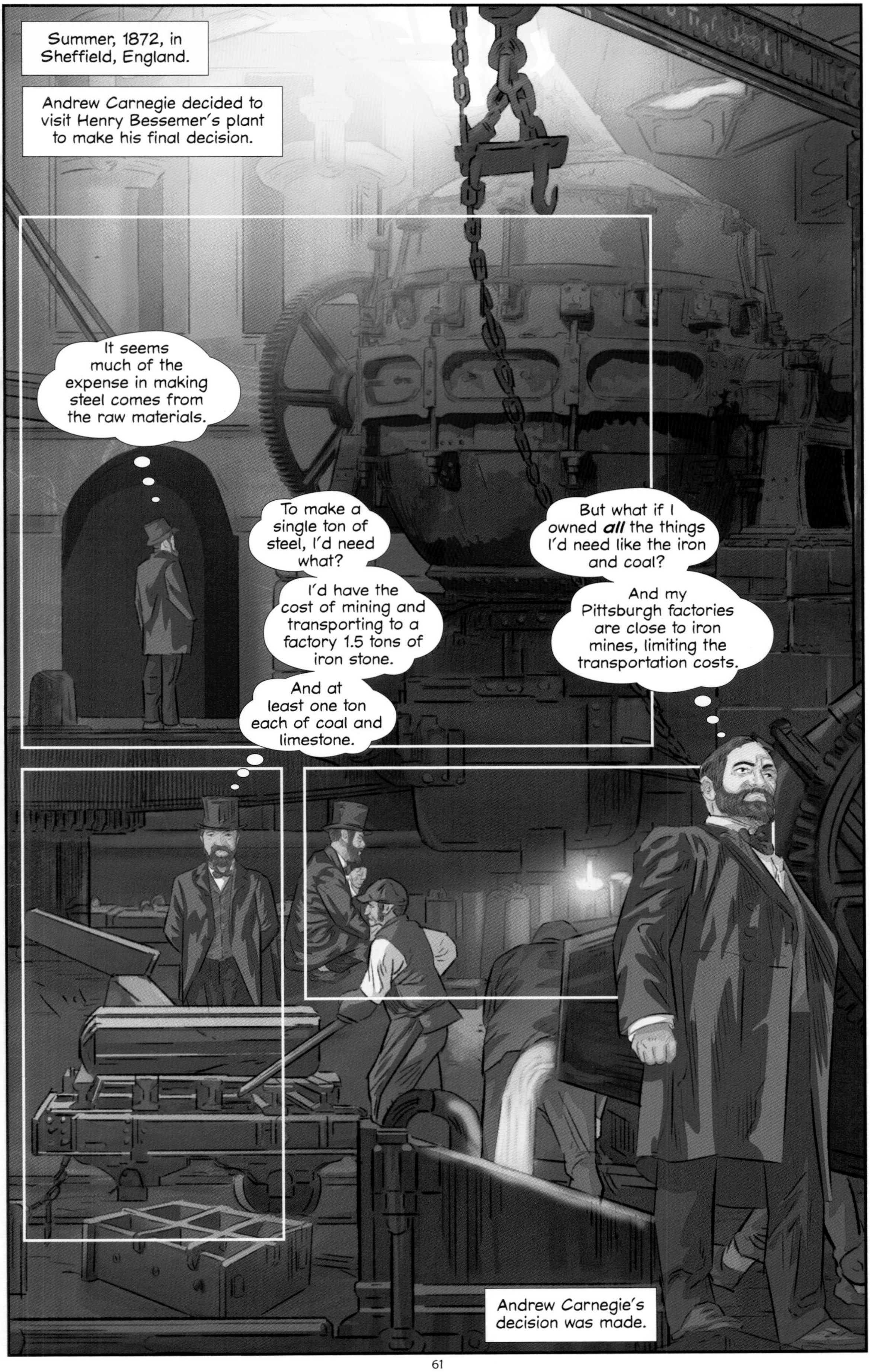

Summer, 1872, in Sheffield, England.
Andrew Carnegie decided to visit Henry Bessemer's plant to make his final decision.
It seems much of the expense in making steel comes from the raw materials.
To make a single ton of steel, I'd need what?
I'd have the cost of mining and transporting to a factory 1.5 tons of iron stone.
And at least one ton each of coal and limestone.
But what if I owned ***all*** the things I'd need like the iron and coal?
And my Pittsburgh factories are close to iron mines, limiting the transportation costs.
Andrew Carnegie's decision was made.

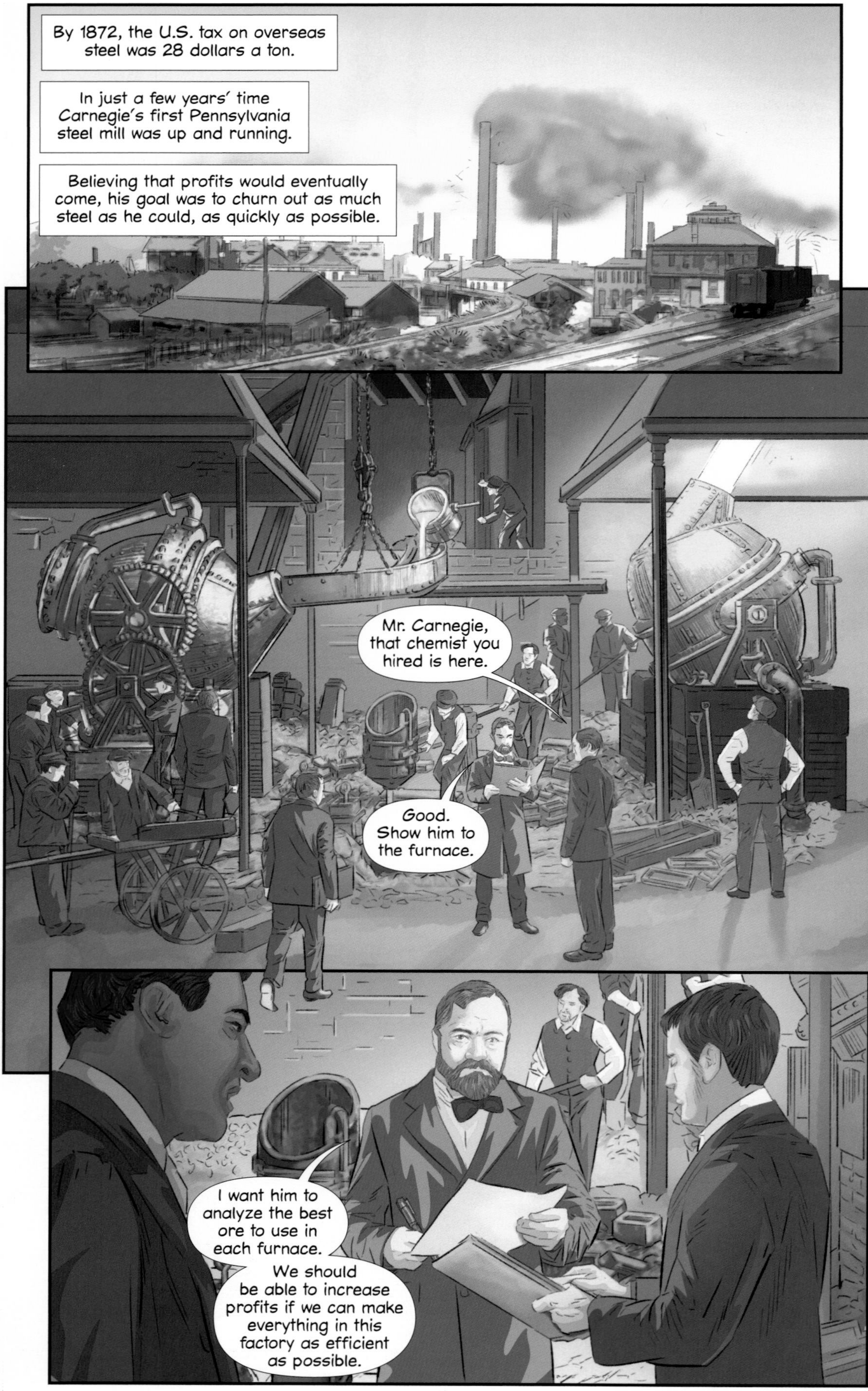
By 1872, the U.S. tax on overseas steel was 28 dollars a ton.
In just a few years' time Carnegie's first Pennsylvania steel mill was up and running.
Believing that profits would eventually come, his goal was to churn out as much steel as he could, as quickly as possible.
Mr. Carnegie, that chemist you hired is here.
Good. Show him to the furnace.
I want him to analyze the best ore to use in each furnace.
We should be able to increase profits if we can make everything in this factory as efficient as possible.

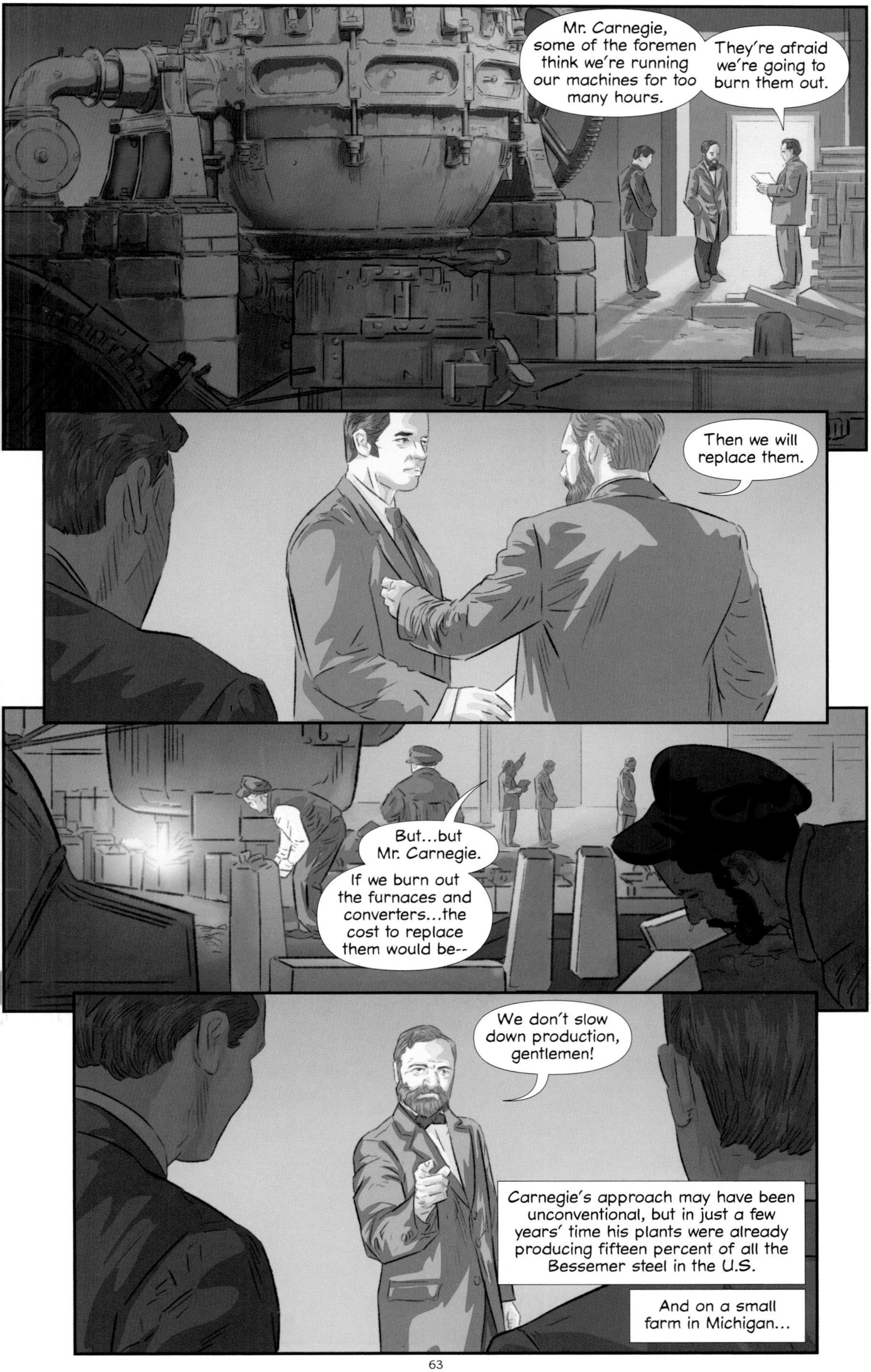
Mr. Carnegie, some of the foremen think we're running our machines for too many hours.
They're afraid we're going to burn them out.
Then we will replace them.
But...but Mr. Carnegie.
If we burn out the furnaces and converters...the cost to replace them would be--
We don't slow down production, gentlemen!
Carnegie's approach may have been unconventional, but in just a few years' time his plants were already producing fifteen percent of all the Bessemer steel in the U.S.
And on a small farm in Michigan...

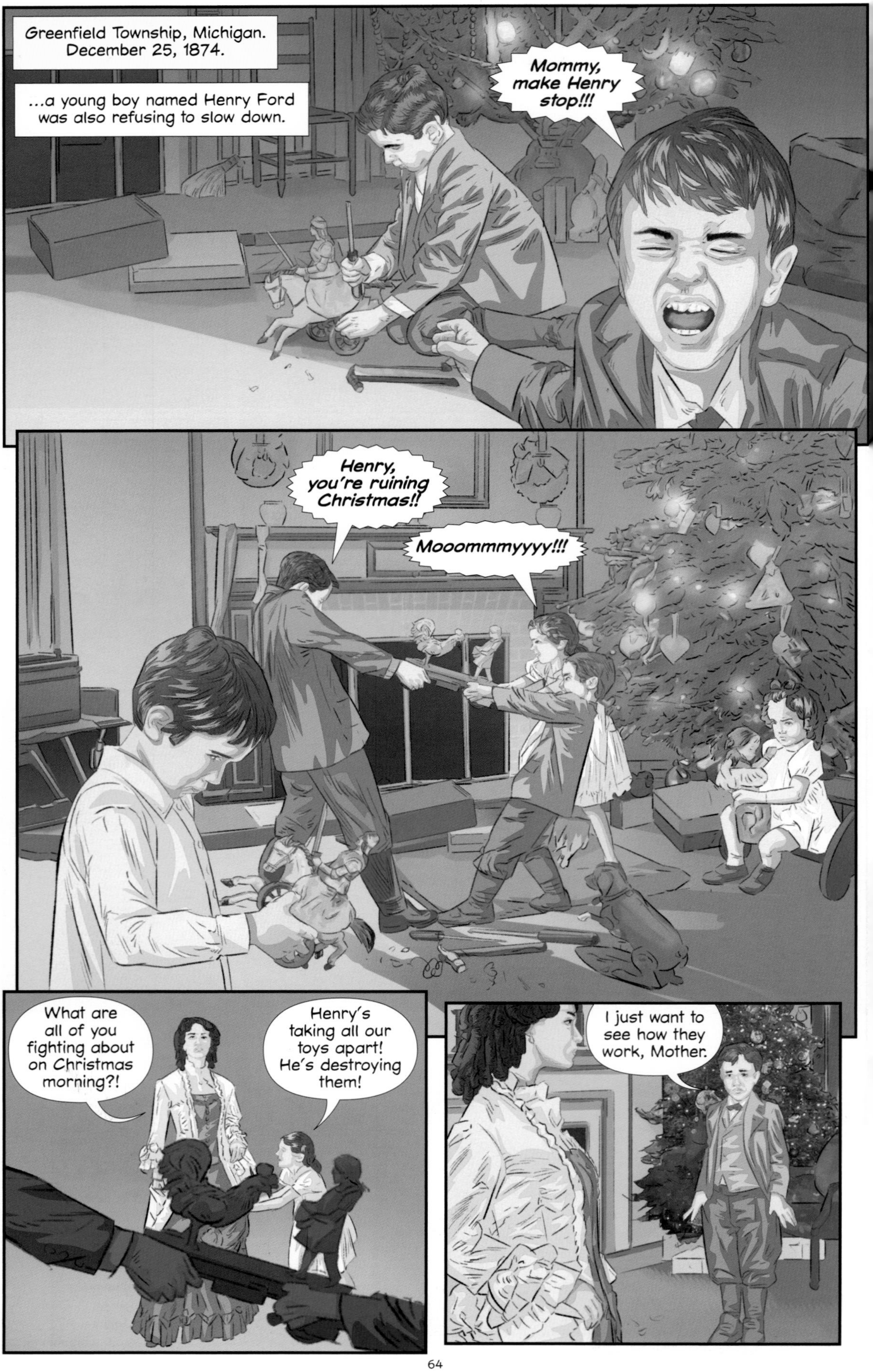

Greenfield Township, Michigan. December 25, 1874.
...a young boy named Henry Ford was also refusing to slow down.
Mommy, make Henry stop!!!
Henry, you're ruining Christmas!!
Mooommmyyyy!!!
What are all of you fighting about on Christmas morning?!
Henry's taking all our toys apart! He's destroying them!
I just want to see how they work, Mother.

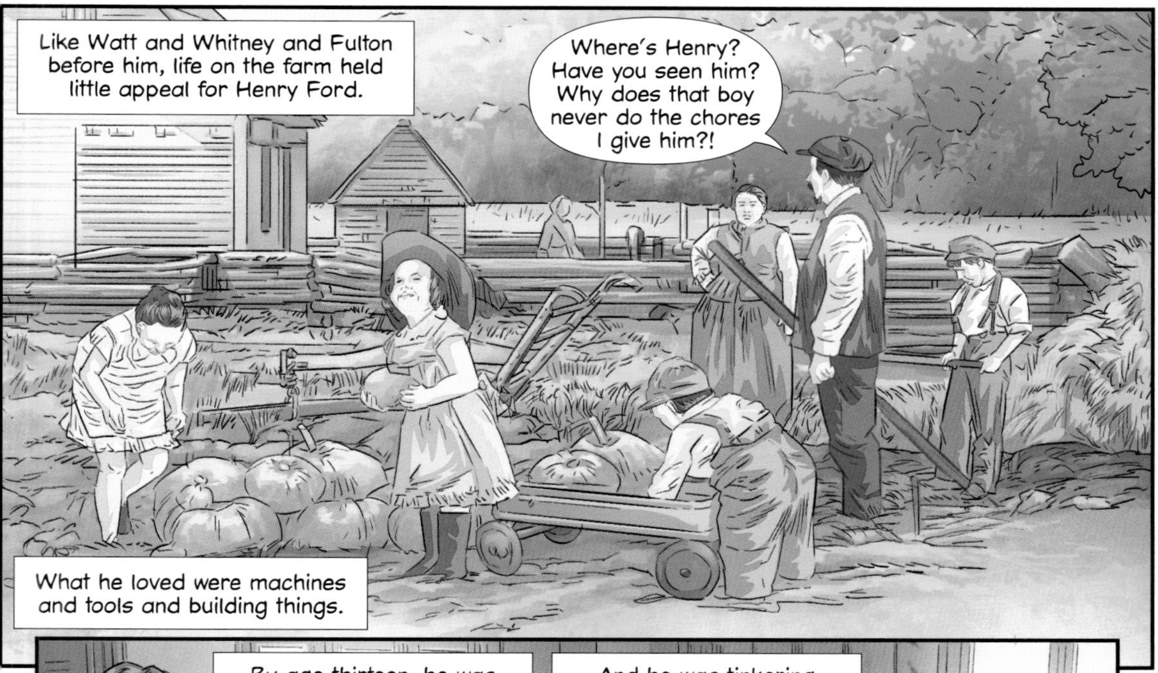
Like Watt and Whitney and Fulton before him, life on the farm held little appeal for Henry Ford.
Where's Henry? Have you seen him? Why does that boy never do the chores I give him?!
What he loved were machines and tools and building things.

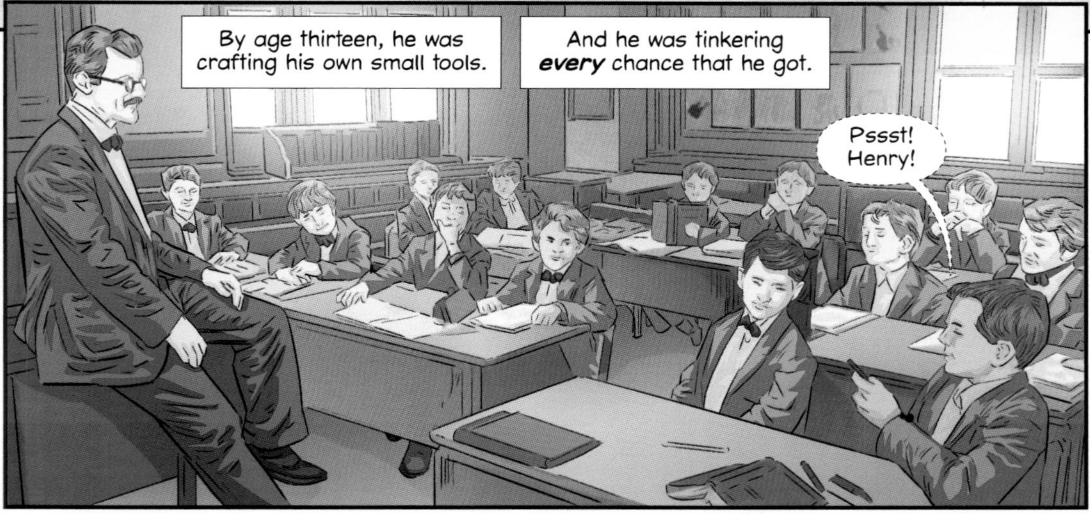
By age thirteen, he was crafting his own small tools.
And he was tinkering ***every*** chance that he got.
Pssst! Henry!

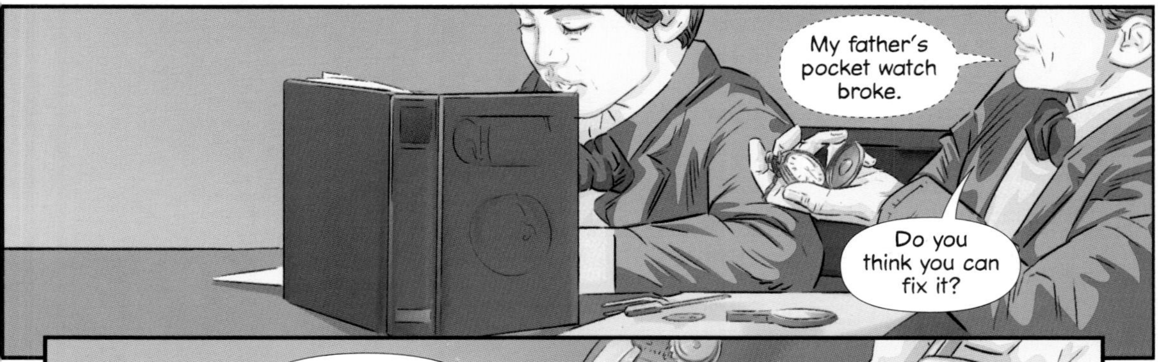
My father's pocket watch broke.
Do you think you can fix it?

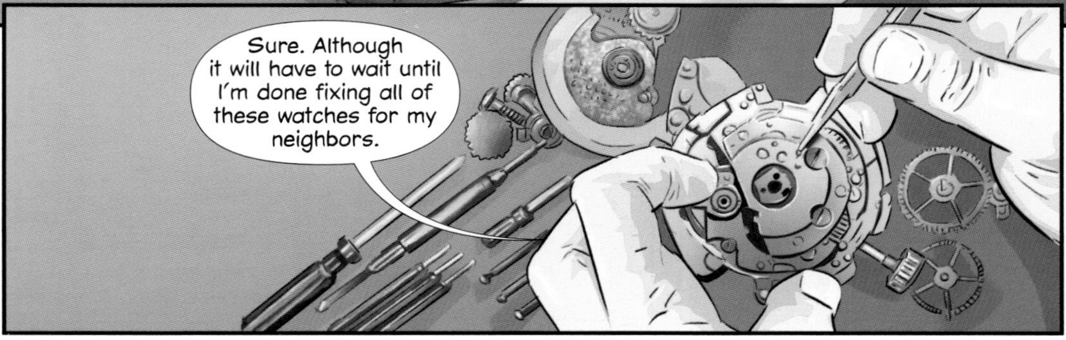
Sure. Although it will have to wait until I'm done fixing all of these watches for my neighbors.

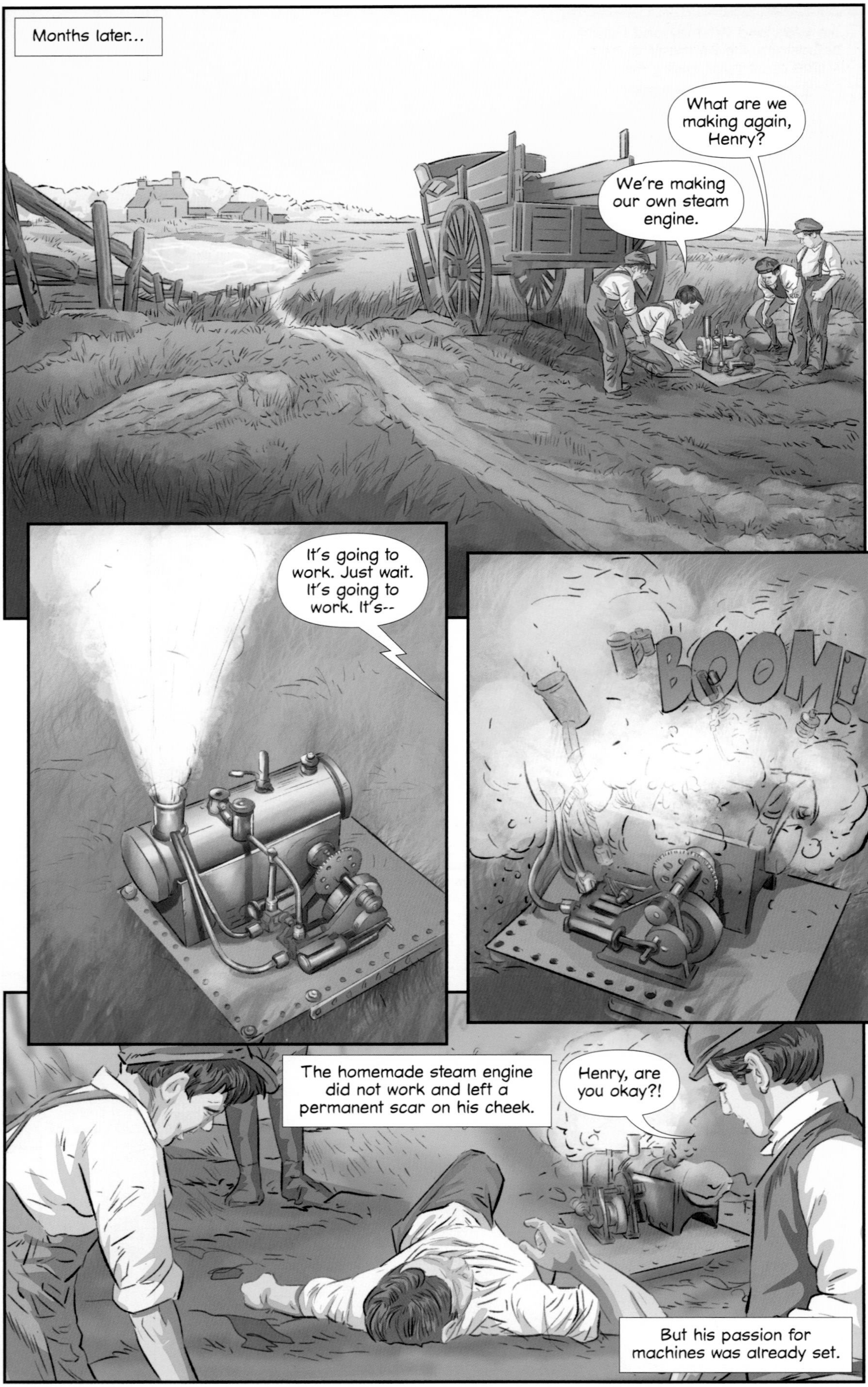
Months later...
What are we making again, Henry?
We're making our own steam engine.
It's going to work. Just wait. It's going to work. It's--
BOOM!
The homemade steam engine did not work and left a permanent scar on his cheek.
Henry, are you okay?!
But his passion for machines was already set.

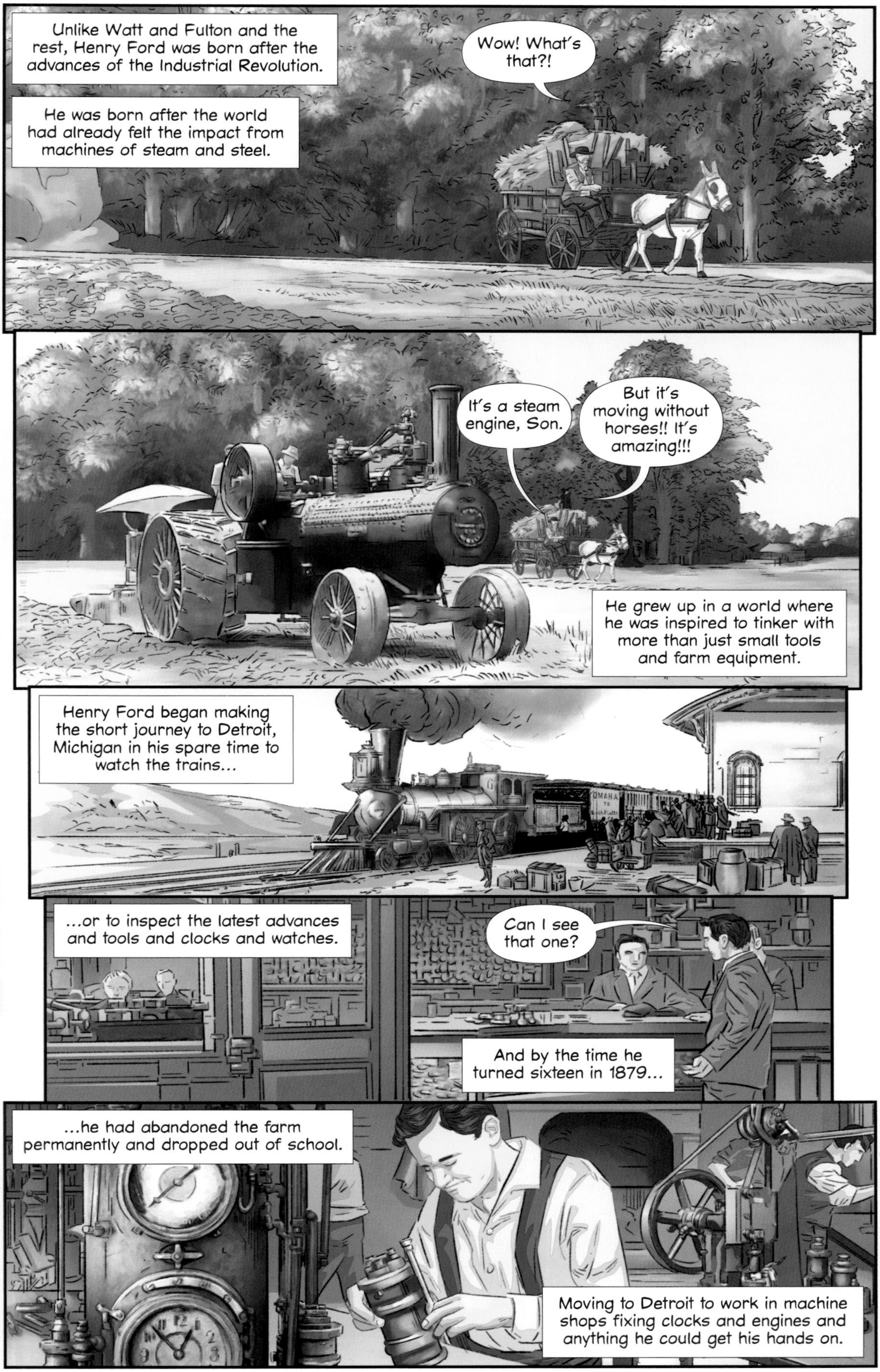
Unlike Watt and Fulton and the rest, Henry Ford was born after the advances of the Industrial Revolution.
He was born after the world had already felt the impact from machines of steam and steel.
Wow! What's that?!
It's a steam engine, Son.
But it's moving without horses!! It's amazing!!!
He grew up in a world where he was inspired to tinker with more than just small tools and farm equipment.
Henry Ford began making the short journey to Detroit, Michigan in his spare time to watch the trains...
OMAHA
...or to inspect the latest advances and tools and clocks and watches.
Can I see that one?
And by the time he turned sixteen in 1879...
...he had abandoned the farm permanently and dropped out of school.
Moving to Detroit to work in machine shops fixing clocks and engines and anything he could get his hands on.

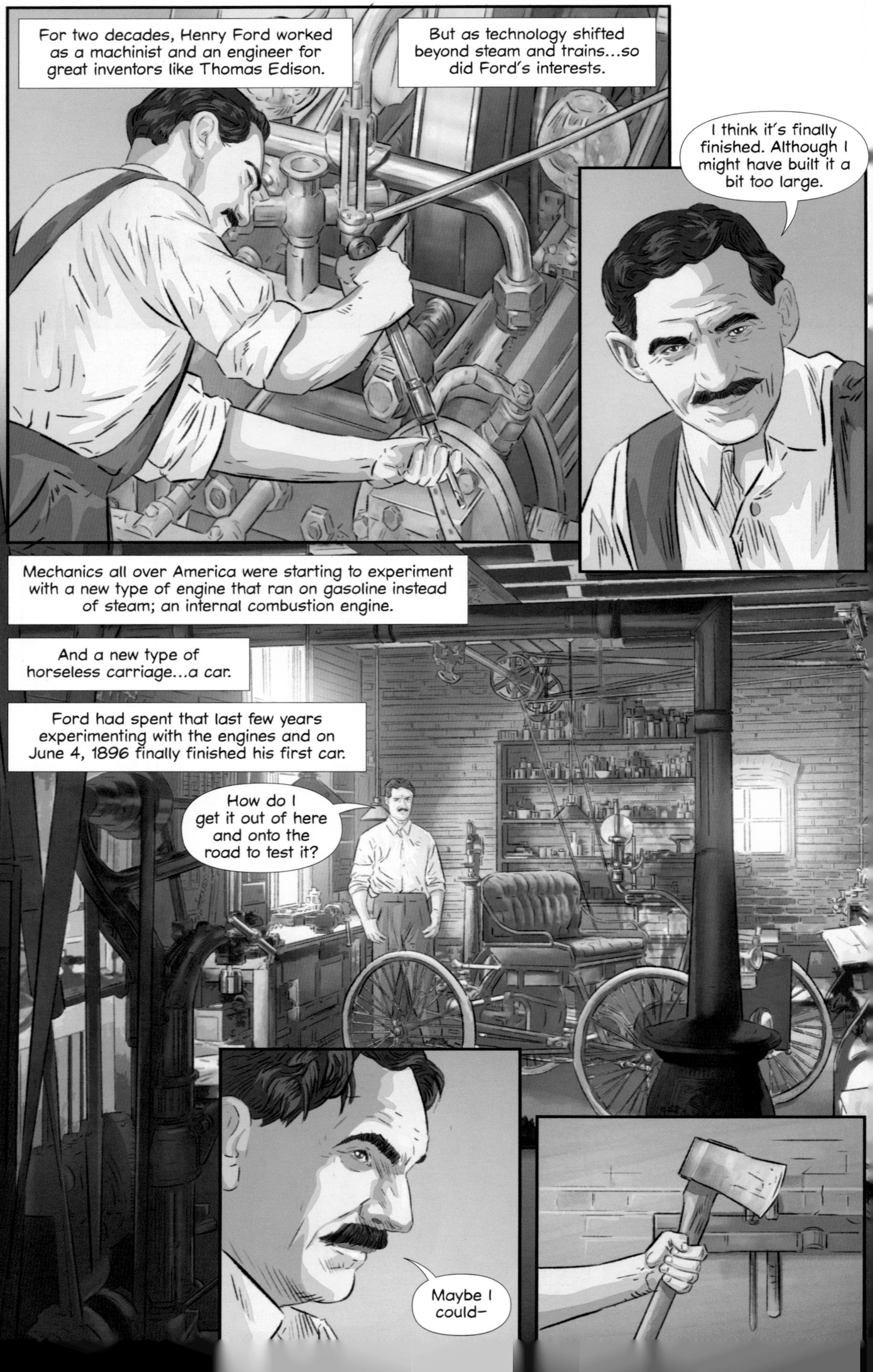

For two decades, Henry Ford worked as a machinist and an engineer for great inventors like Thomas Edison.
But as technology shifted beyond steam and trains...so did Ford's interests.
I think it's finally finished. Although I might have built it a bit too large.
Mechanics all over America were starting to experiment with a new type of engine that ran on gasoline instead of steam; an internal combustion engine.
And a new type of horseless carriage...a car.
Ford had spent that last few years experimenting with the engines and on June 4, 1896 finally finished his first car.
How do I get it out of here and onto the road to test it?
Maybe I could–

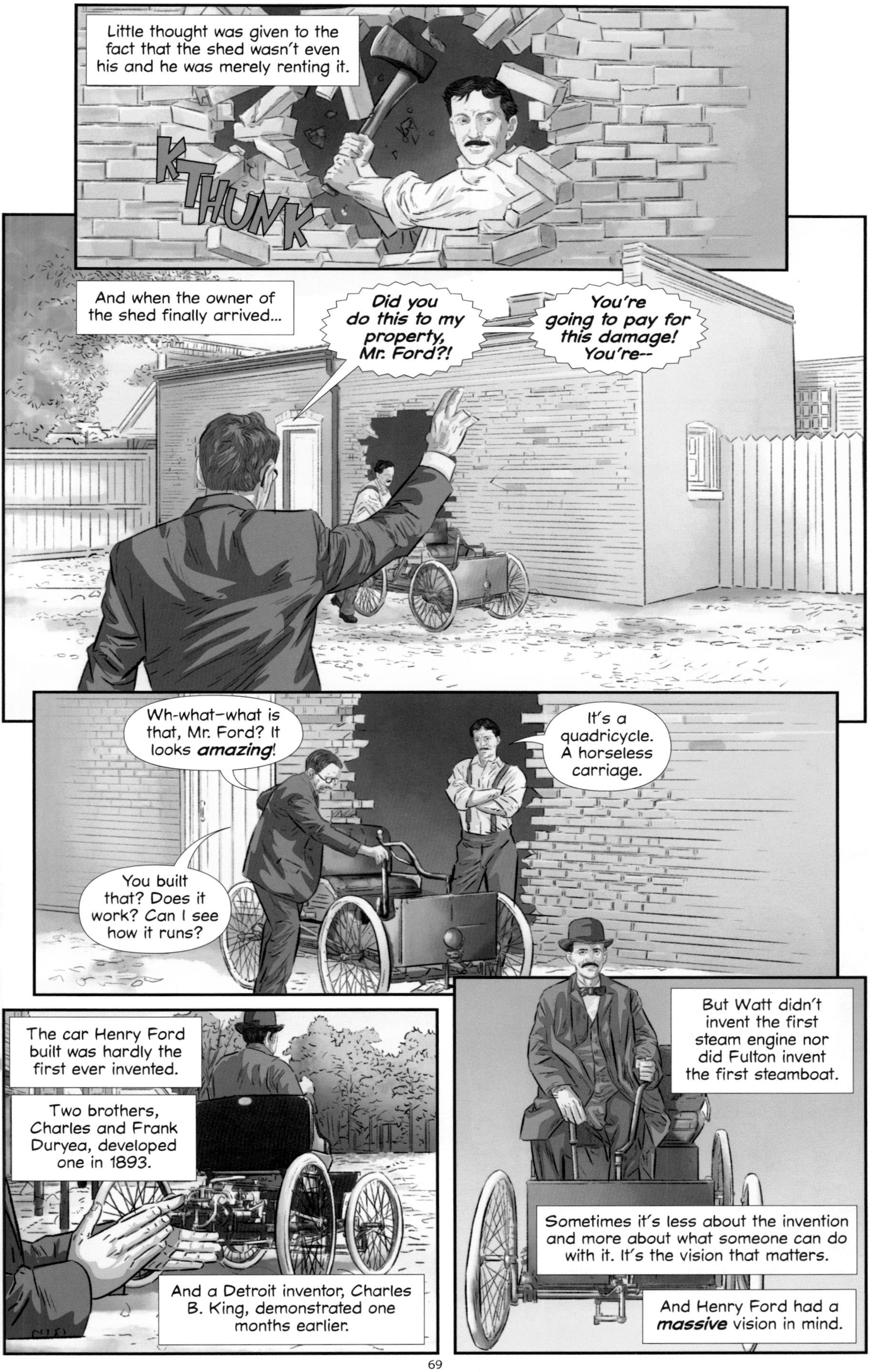
Little thought was given to the fact that the shed wasn't even his and he was merely renting it.
KTHUNK
And when the owner of the shed finally arrived...
Did you do this to my property, Mr. Ford?!
You're going to pay for this damage! You're--
Wh-what-what is that, Mr. Ford? It looks amazing!
It's a quadricycle. A horseless carriage.
You built that? Does it work? Can I see how it runs?
The car Henry Ford built was hardly the first ever invented.
Two brothers, Charles and Frank Duryea, developed one in 1893.
And a Detroit inventor, Charles B. King, demonstrated one months earlier.
But Watt didn't invent the first steam engine nor did Fulton invent the first steamboat.
Sometimes it's less about the invention and more about what someone can do with it. It's the vision that matters.
And Henry Ford had a massive vision in mind.

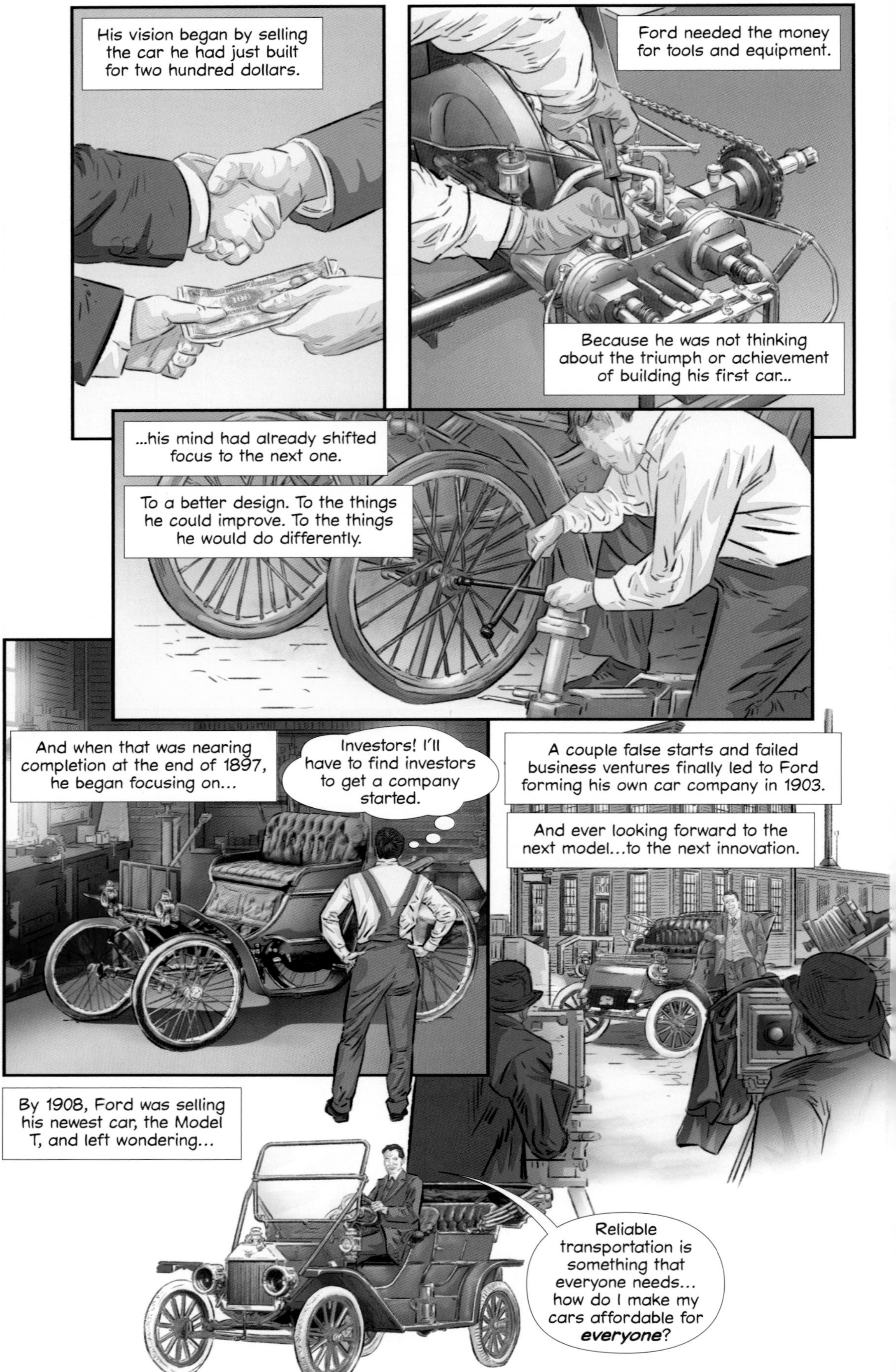
His vision began by selling the car he had just built for two hundred dollars.
Ford needed the money for tools and equipment.
Because he was not thinking about the triumph or achievement of building his first car...
...his mind had already shifted focus to the next one.
To a better design. To the things he could improve. To the things he would do differently.
And when that was nearing completion at the end of 1897, he began focusing on...
Investors! I'll have to find investors to get a company started.
A couple false starts and failed business ventures finally led to Ford forming his own car company in 1903.
And ever looking forward to the next model...to the next innovation.
By 1908, Ford was selling his newest car, the Model T, and left wondering...
Reliable transportation is something that everyone needs... how do I make my cars affordable for ***everyone***?

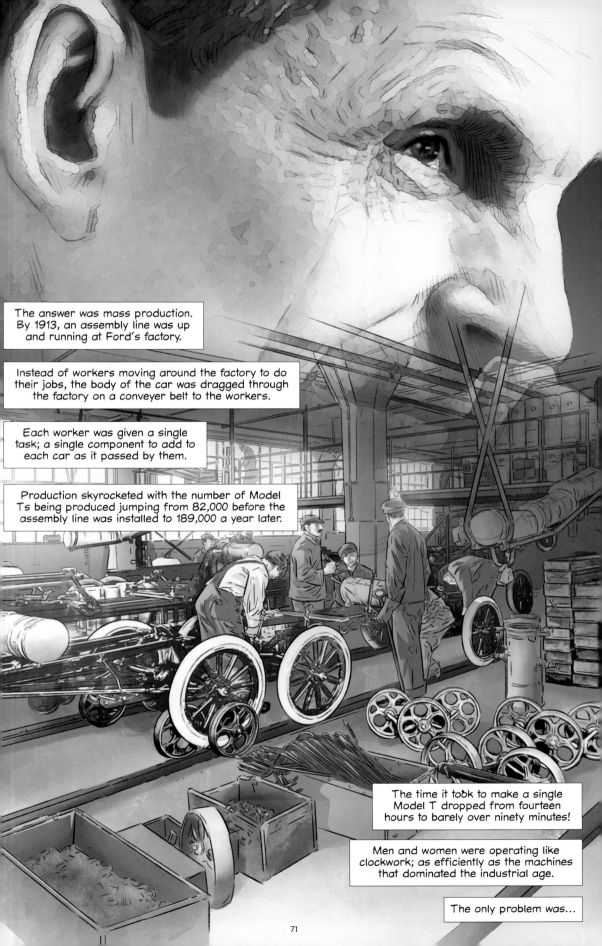

The answer was mass production. By 1913, an assembly line was up and running at Ford's factory.

Instead of workers moving around the factory to do their jobs, the body of the car was dragged through the factory on a conveyer belt to the workers.

Each worker was given a single task; a single component to add to each car as it passed by them.

Production skyrocketed with the number of Model Ts being produced jumping from 82,000 before the assembly line was installed to 189,000 a year later.

The time it took to make a single Model T dropped from fourteen hours to barely over ninety minutes!

Men and women were operating like clockwork; as efficiently as the machines that dominated the industrial age.

The only problem was...

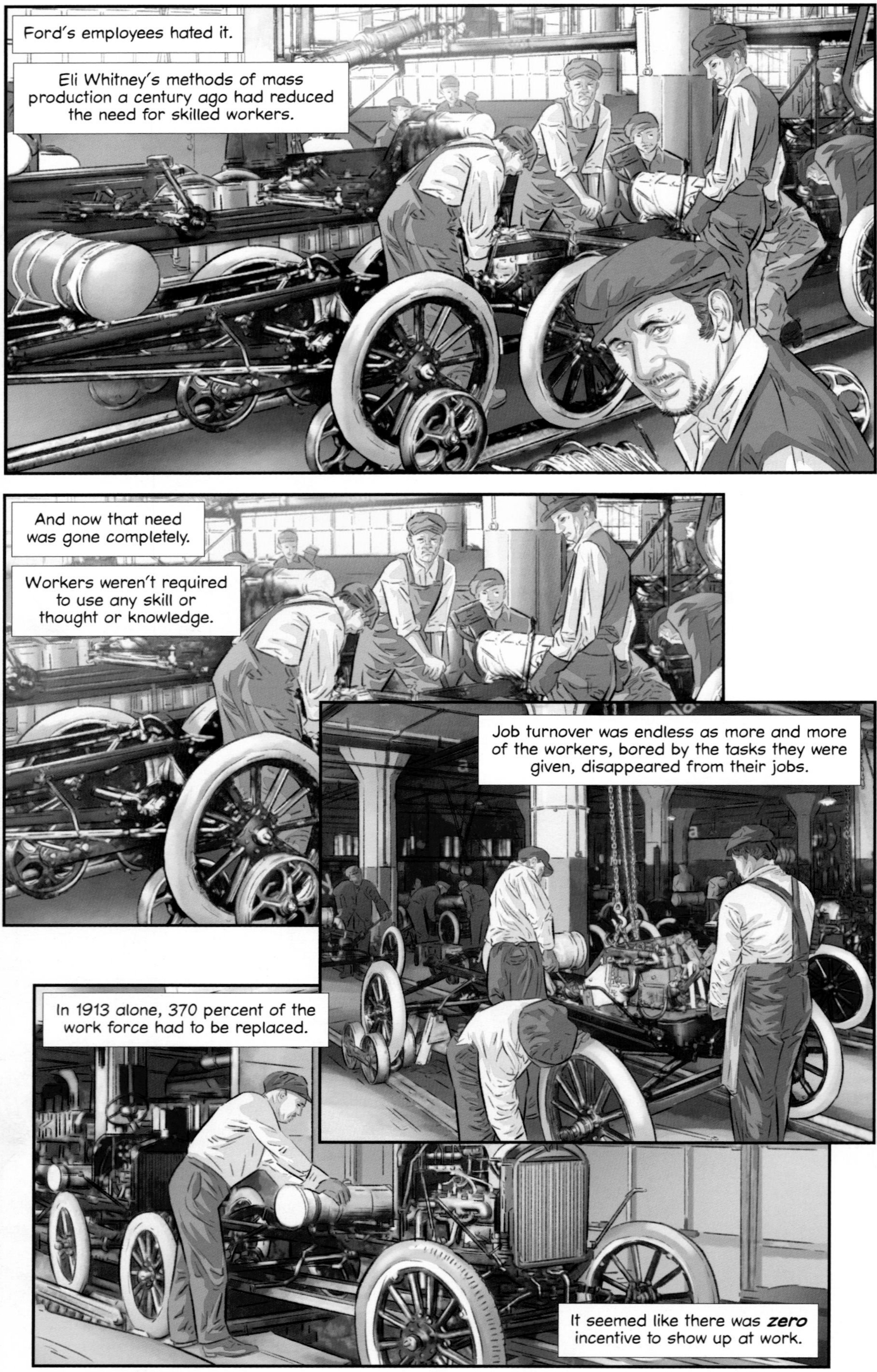
Ford's employees hated it.
Eli Whitney's methods of mass production a century ago had reduced the need for skilled workers.
And now that need was gone completely.
Workers weren't required to use any skill or thought or knowledge.
Job turnover was endless as more and more of the workers, bored by the tasks they were given, disappeared from their jobs.
In 1913 alone, 370 percent of the work force had to be replaced.
It seemed like there was ***zero*** incentive to show up at work.

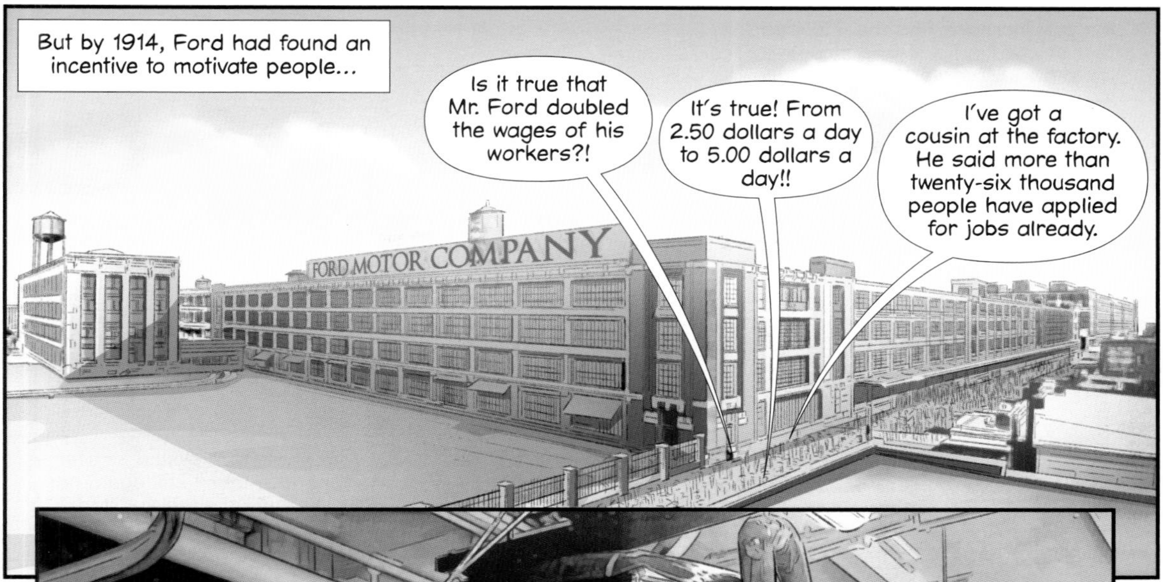
But by 1914, Ford had found an incentive to motivate people...
FORD MOTOR COMPANY
Is it true that Mr. Ford doubled the wages of his workers?!
It's true! From 2.50 dollars a day to 5.00 dollars a day!!
I've got a cousin at the factory. He said more than twenty-six thousand people have applied for jobs already.

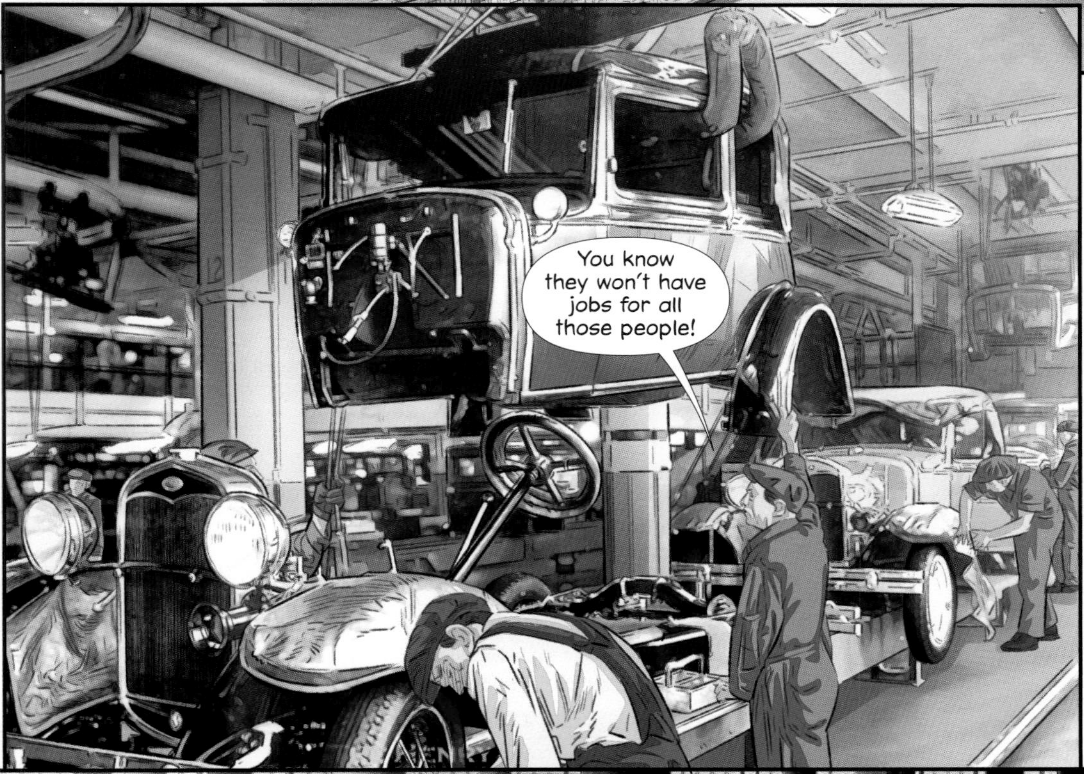
You know they won't have jobs for all those people!

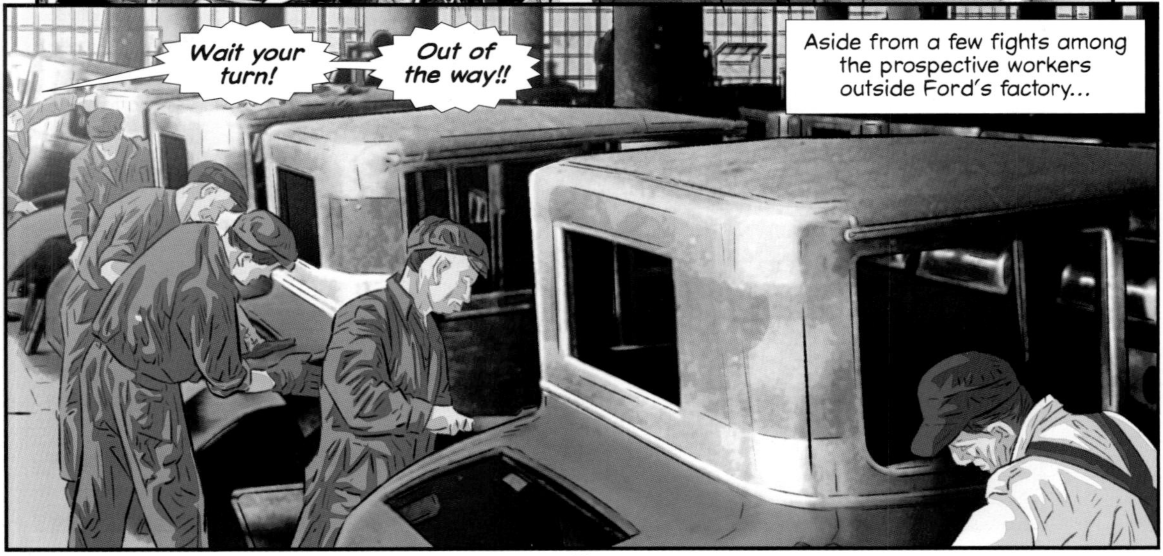
Wait your turn!
Out of the way!!
Aside from a few fights among the prospective workers outside Ford's factory...

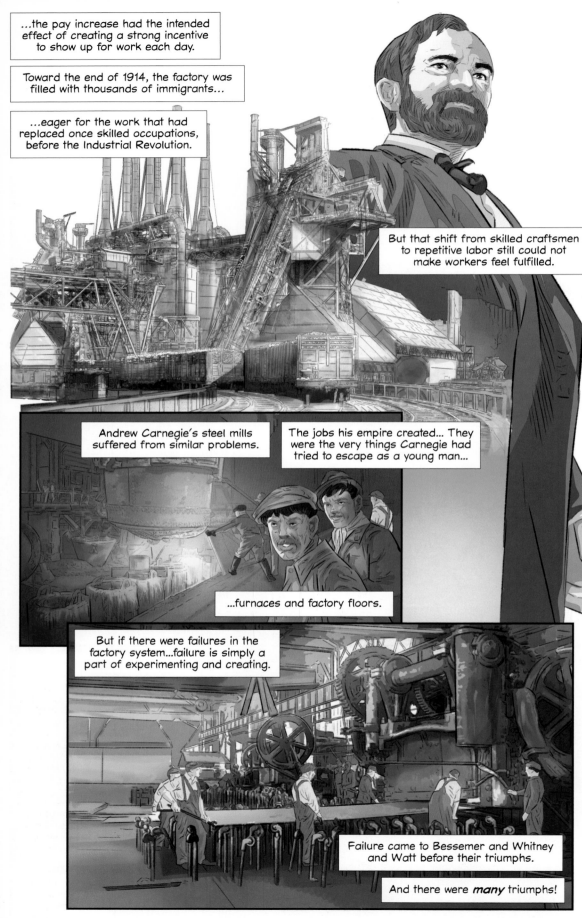

...the pay increase had the intended effect of creating a strong incentive to show up for work each day.

Toward the end of 1914, the factory was filled with thousands of immigrants...

...eager for the work that had replaced once skilled occupations, before the Industrial Revolution.

But that shift from skilled craftsmen to repetitive labor still could not make workers feel fulfilled.

Andrew Carnegie's steel mills suffered from similar problems.

The jobs his empire created... They were the very things Carnegie had tried to escape as a young man...

...furnaces and factory floors.

But if there were failures in the factory system...failure is simply a part of experimenting and creating.

Failure came to Bessemer and Whitney and Watt before their triumphs.

And there were *many* triumphs!

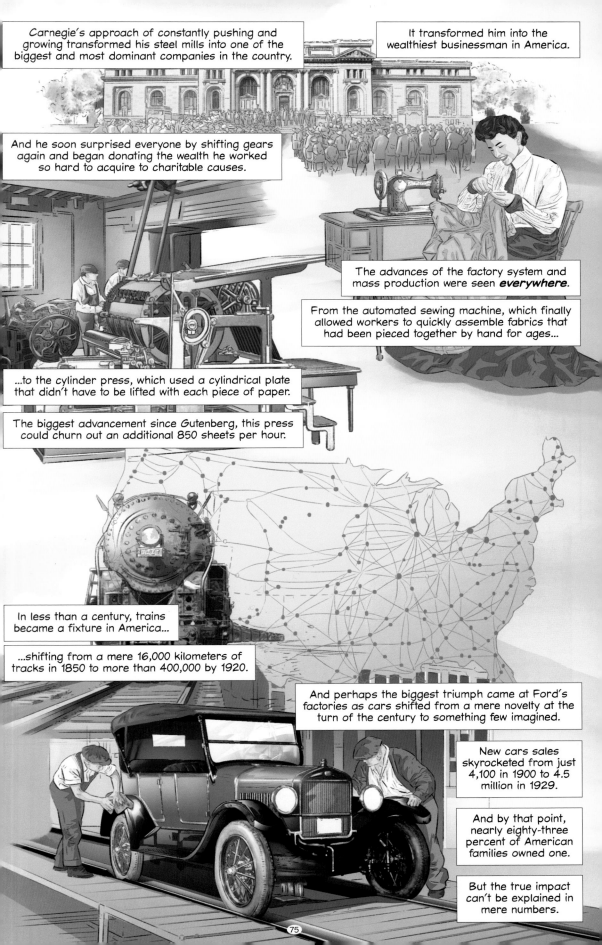

Carnegie's approach of constantly pushing and growing transformed his steel mills into one of the biggest and most dominant companies in the country.

It transformed him into the wealthiest businessman in America.

And he soon surprised everyone by shifting gears again and began donating the wealth he worked so hard to acquire to charitable causes.

The advances of the factory system and mass production were seen **everywhere**.

From the automated sewing machine, which finally allowed workers to quickly assemble fabrics that had been pieced together by hand for ages...

...to the cylinder press, which used a cylindrical plate that didn't have to be lifted with each piece of paper.

The biggest advancement since Gutenberg, this press could churn out an additional 850 sheets per hour.

In less than a century, trains became a fixture in America...

...shifting from a mere 16,000 kilometers of tracks in 1850 to more than 400,000 by 1920.

And perhaps the biggest triumph came at Ford's factories as cars shifted from a mere novelty at the turn of the century to something few imagined.

New cars sales skyrocketed from just 4,100 in 1900 to 4.5 million in 1929.

And by that point, nearly eighty-three percent of American families owned one.

But the true impact can't be explained in mere numbers.

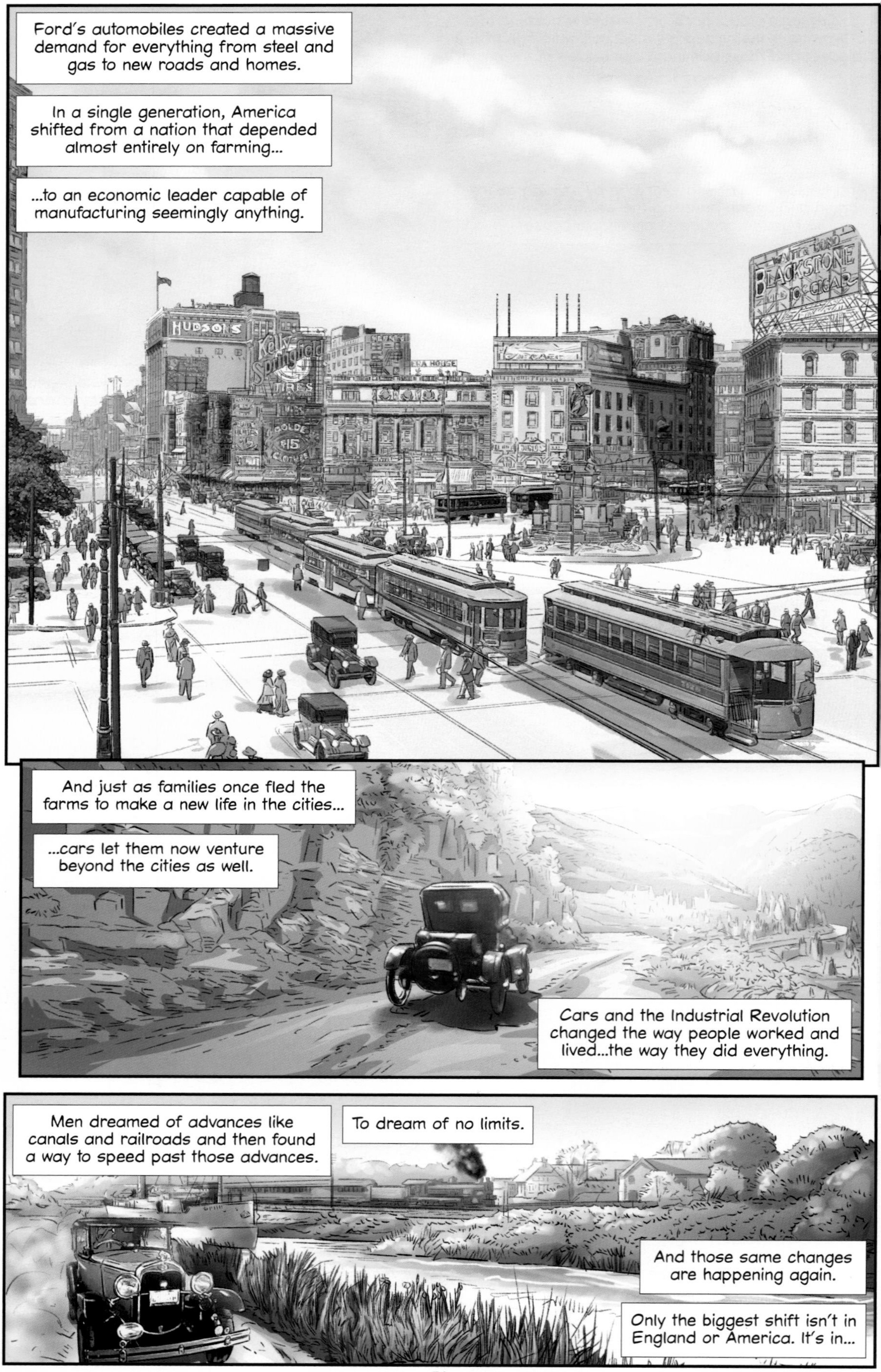
Ford's automobiles created a massive demand for everything from steel and gas to new roads and homes.
In a single generation, America shifted from a nation that depended almost entirely on farming...
...to an economic leader capable of manufacturing seemingly anything.
HUDSON'S
Kelly Springfield
TIRES
BLACKSTONE
And just as families once fled the farms to make a new life in the cities...
...cars let them now venture beyond the cities as well.
Cars and the Industrial Revolution changed the way people worked and lived...the way they did everything.
Men dreamed of advances like canals and railroads and then found a way to speed past those advances.
To dream of no limits.
And those same changes are happening again.
Only the biggest shift isn't in England or America. It's in...

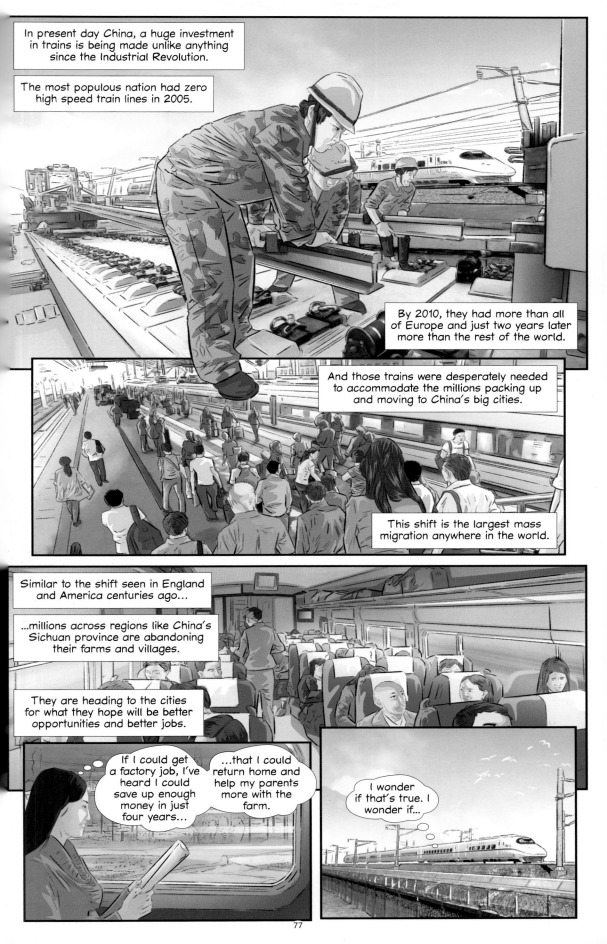

In present day China, a huge investment in trains is being made unlike anything since the Industrial Revolution.

The most populous nation had zero high speed train lines in 2005.

By 2010, they had more than all of Europe and just two years later more than the rest of the world.

And those trains were desperately needed to accommodate the millions packing up and moving to China's big cities.

This shift is the largest mass migration anywhere in the world.

Similar to the shift seen in England and America centuries ago...

...millions across regions like China's Sichuan province are abandoning their farms and villages.

They are heading to the cities for what they hope will be better opportunities and better jobs.

If I could get a factory job, I've heard I could save up enough money in just four years...

...that I could return home and help my parents more with the farm.

I wonder if that's true. I wonder if...

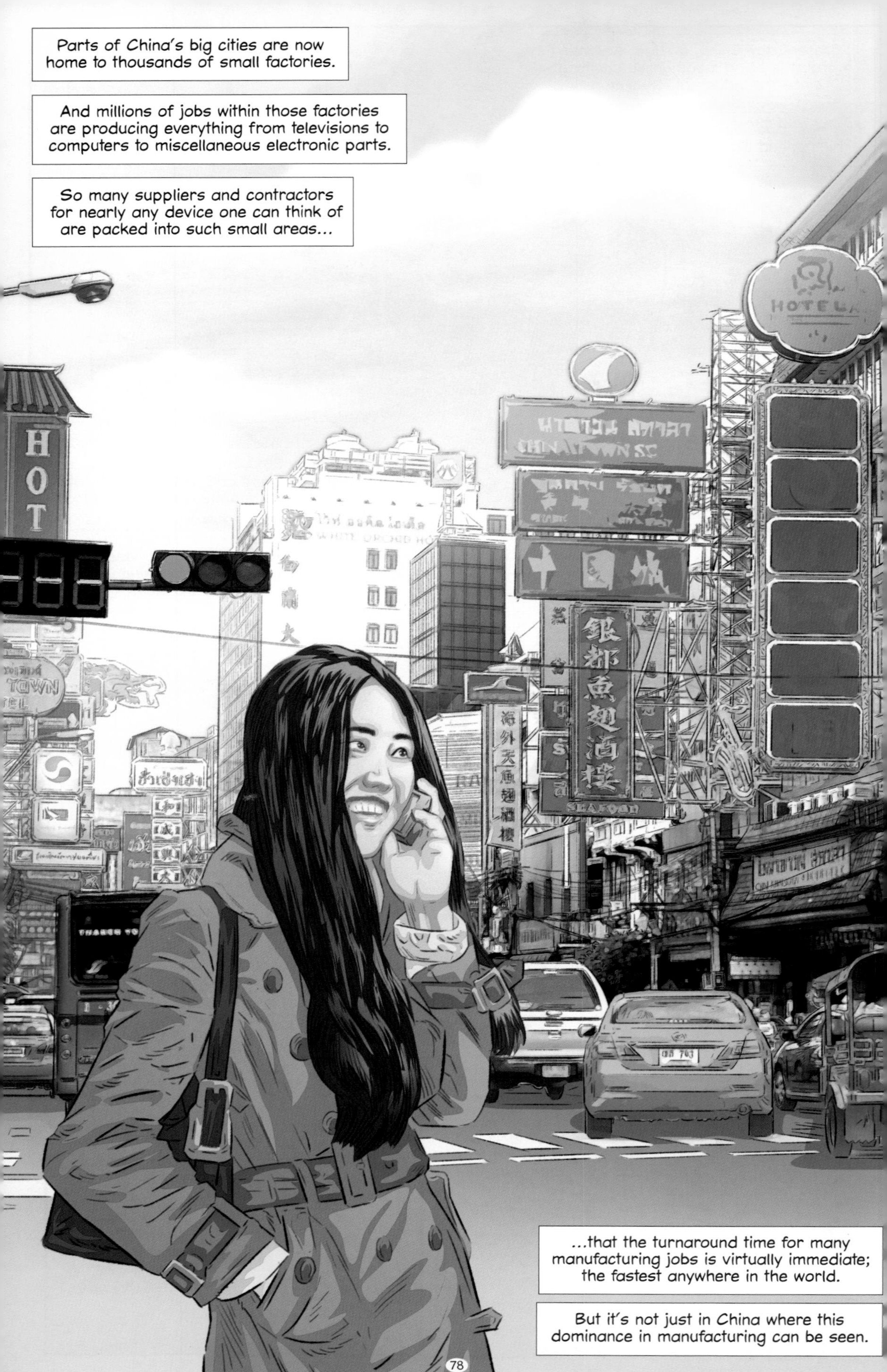
Parts of China's big cities are now home to thousands of small factories.
And millions of jobs within those factories are producing everything from televisions to computers to miscellaneous electronic parts.
So many suppliers and contractors for nearly any device one can think of are packed into such small areas...
HOT
銀都魚翅酒樓
SEAFOOD
...that the turnaround time for many manufacturing jobs is virtually immediate; the fastest anywhere in the world.
But it's not just in China where this dominance in manufacturing can be seen.

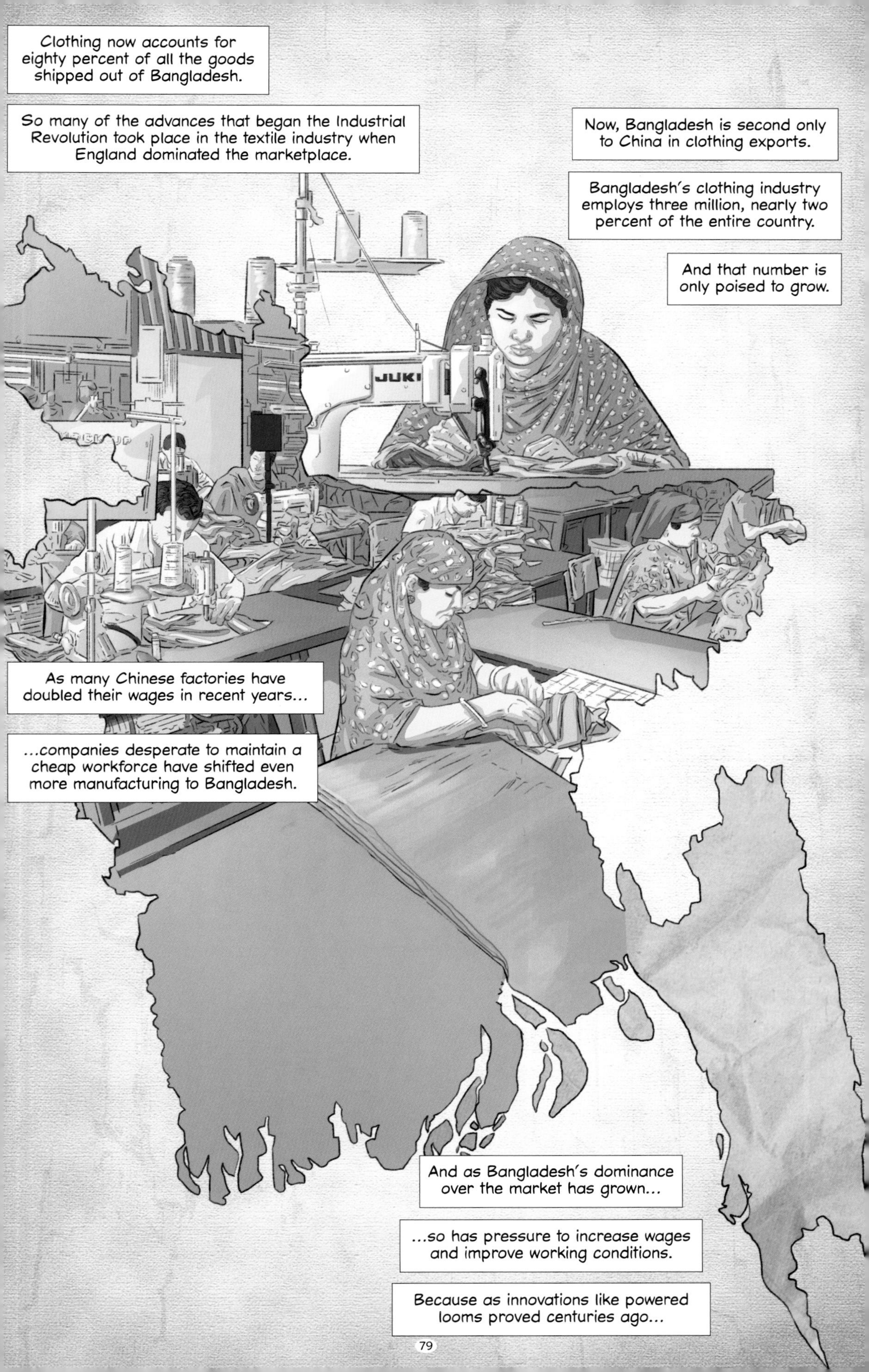
Clothing now accounts for eighty percent of all the goods shipped out of Bangladesh.
So many of the advances that began the Industrial Revolution took place in the textile industry when England dominated the marketplace.
Now, Bangladesh is second only to China in clothing exports.
Bangladesh's clothing industry employs three million, nearly two percent of the entire country.
And that number is only poised to grow.
JUKI
As many Chinese factories have doubled their wages in recent years...
...companies desperate to maintain a cheap workforce have shifted even more manufacturing to Bangladesh.
And as Bangladesh's dominance over the market has grown...
...so has pressure to increase wages and improve working conditions.
Because as innovations like powered looms proved centuries ago...

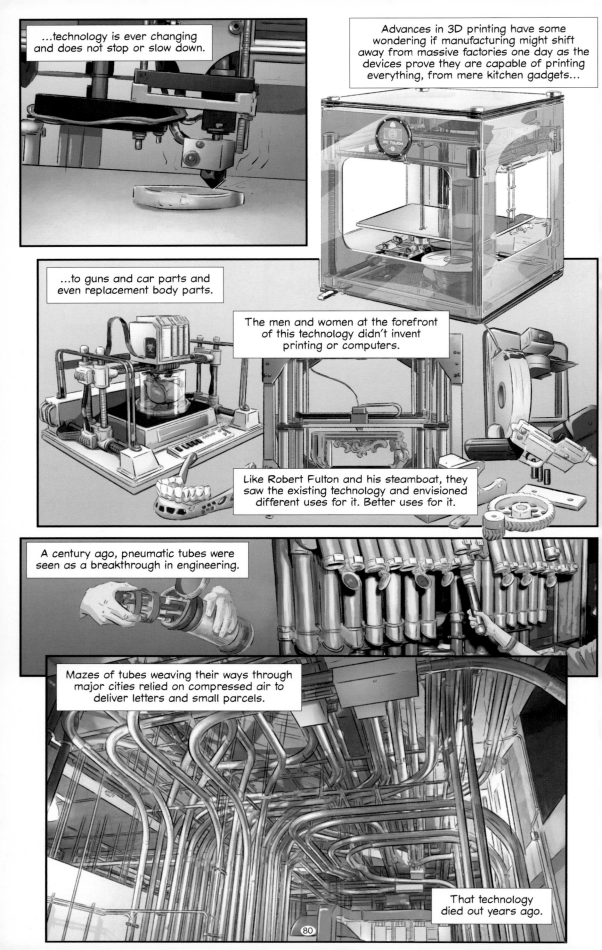

...technology is ever changing and does not stop or slow down.

Advances in 3D printing have some wondering if manufacturing might shift away from massive factories one day as the devices prove they are capable of printing everything, from mere kitchen gadgets...

...to guns and car parts and even replacement body parts.

The men and women at the forefront of this technology didn't invent printing or computers.

Like Robert Fulton and his steamboat, they saw the existing technology and envisioned different uses for it. Better uses for it.

A century ago, pneumatic tubes were seen as a breakthrough in engineering.

Mazes of tubes weaving their ways through major cities relied on compressed air to deliver letters and small parcels.

That technology died out years ago.

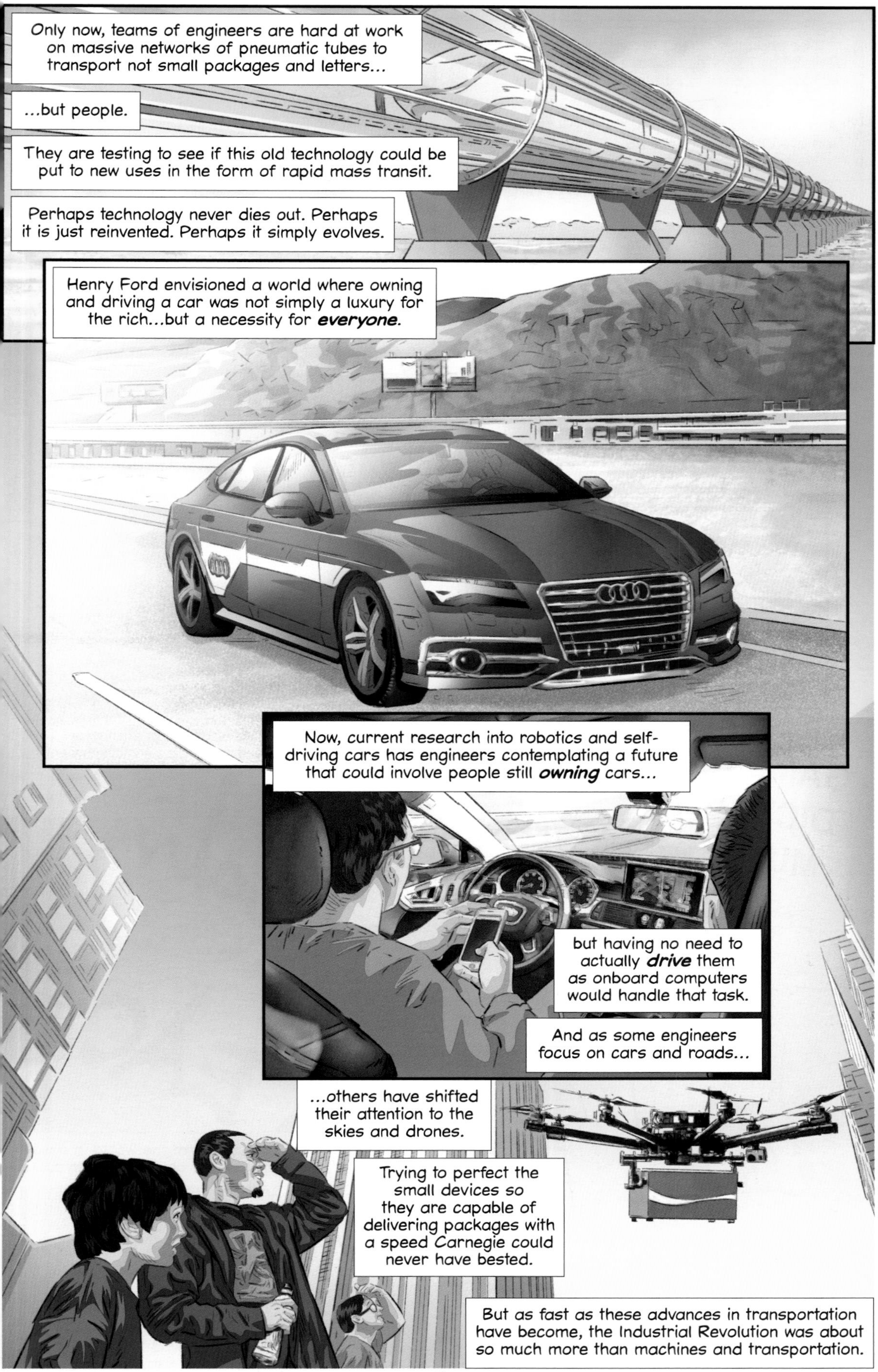
Only now, teams of engineers are hard at work on massive networks of pneumatic tubes to transport not small packages and letters...
...but people.
They are testing to see if this old technology could be put to new uses in the form of rapid mass transit.
Perhaps technology never dies out. Perhaps it is just reinvented. Perhaps it simply evolves.
Henry Ford envisioned a world where owning and driving a car was not simply a luxury for the rich...but a necessity for *everyone.*
Now, current research into robotics and self-driving cars has engineers contemplating a future that could involve people still *owning* cars...
but having no need to actually *drive* them as onboard computers would handle that task.
And as some engineers focus on cars and roads...
...others have shifted their attention to the skies and drones.
Trying to perfect the small devices so they are capable of delivering packages with a speed Carnegie could never have bested.
But as fast as these advances in transportation have become, the Industrial Revolution was about so much more than machines and transportation.

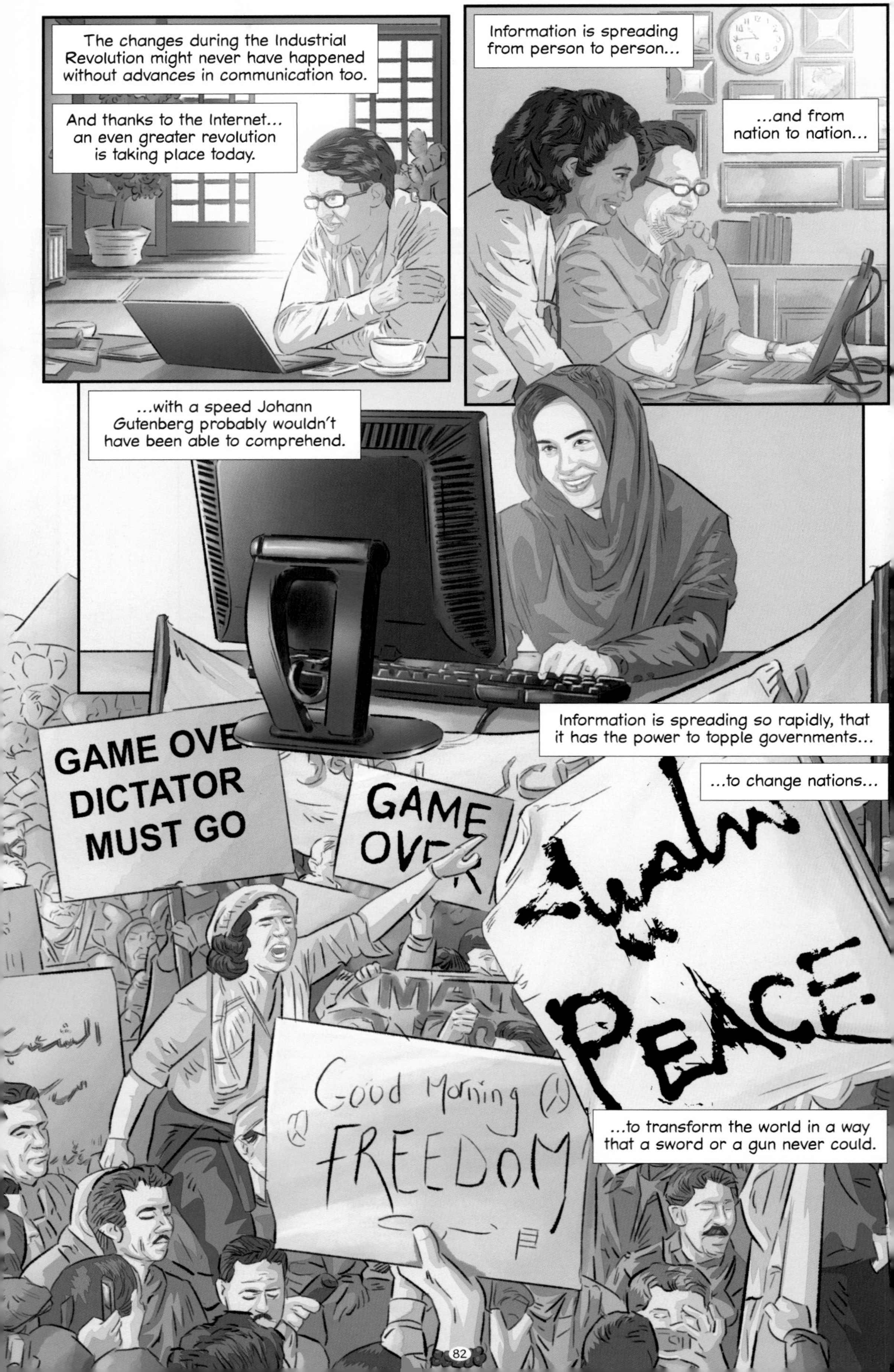

The changes during the Industrial Revolution might never have happened without advances in communication too.
And thanks to the Internet... an even greater revolution is taking place today.
Information is spreading from person to person...
...and from nation to nation...
...with a speed Johann Gutenberg probably wouldn't have been able to comprehend.
Information is spreading so rapidly, that it has the power to topple governments...
...to change nations...
GAME OVE
DICTATOR
MUST GO
GAME
OVE
PEACE
Good Morning
FREEDOM
...to transform the world in a way that a sword or a gun never could.

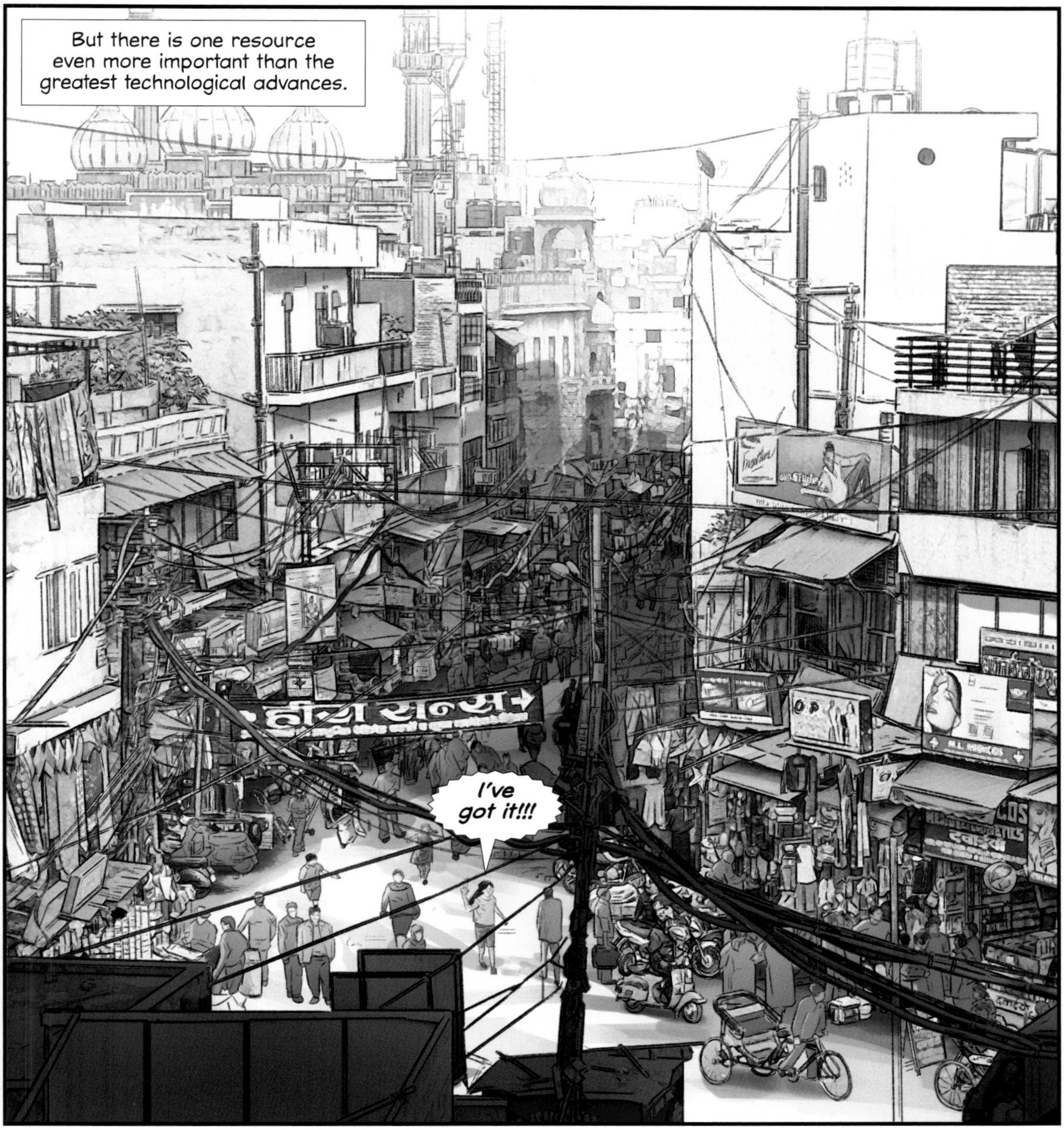
But there is one resource even more important than the greatest technological advances.
I've got it!!!

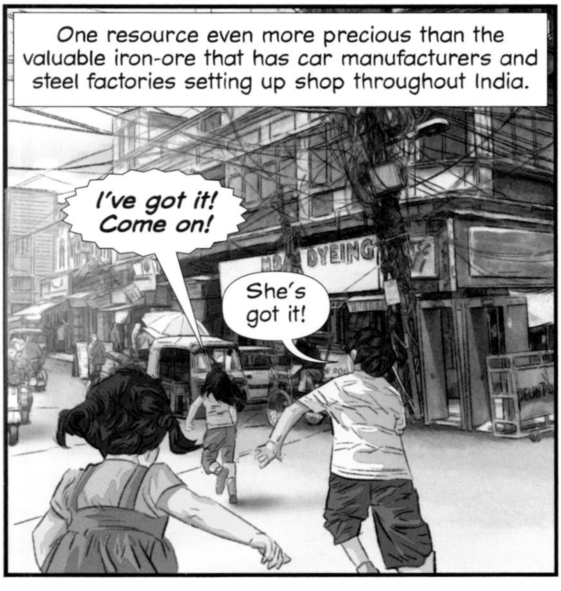
One resource even more precious than the valuable iron-ore that has car manufacturers and steel factories setting up shop throughout India.
I've got it! Come on!
She's got it!

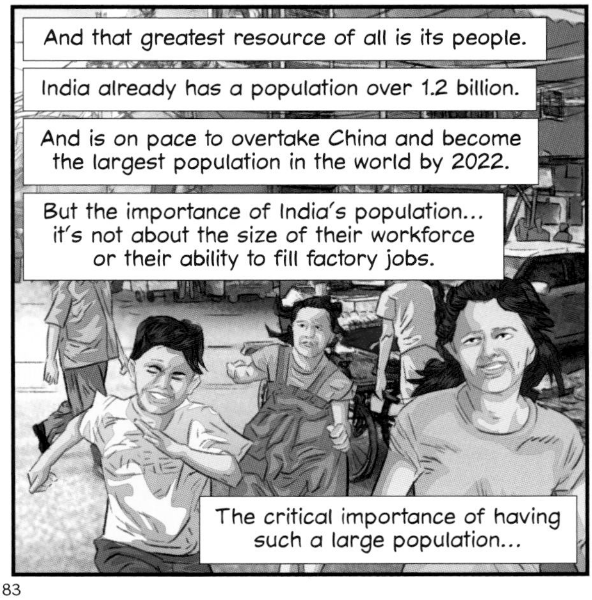
And that greatest resource of all is its people.
India already has a population over 1.2 billion.
And is on pace to overtake China and become the largest population in the world by 2022.
But the importance of India's population... it's not about the size of their workforce or their ability to fill factory jobs.
The critical importance of having such a large population...

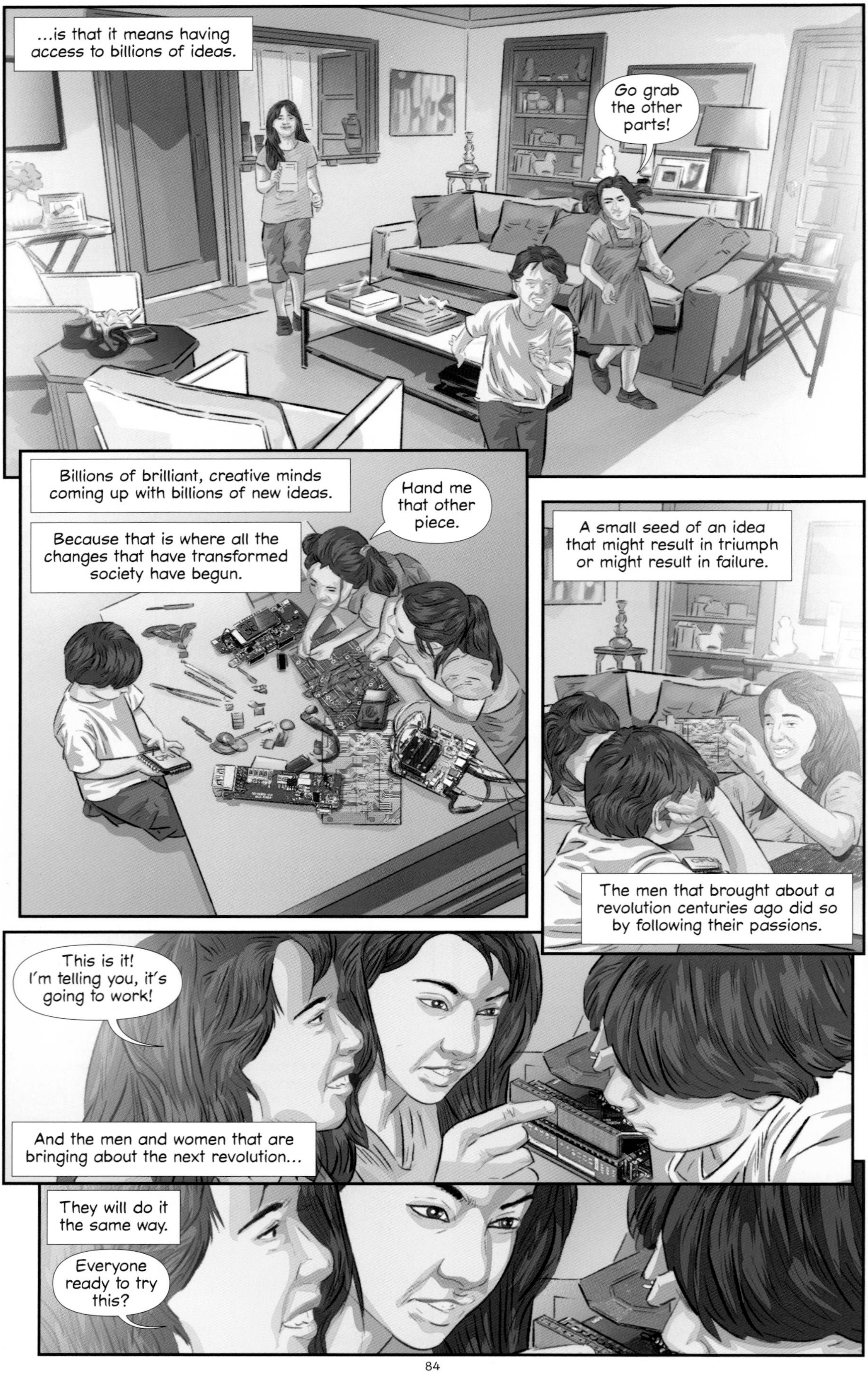
...is that it means having access to billions of ideas.
Go grab the other parts!
Billions of brilliant, creative minds coming up with billions of new ideas.
Because that is where all the changes that have transformed society have begun.
Hand me that other piece.
A small seed of an idea that might result in triumph or might result in failure.
The men that brought about a revolution centuries ago did so by following their passions.
This is it! I'm telling you, it's going to work!
And the men and women that are bringing about the next revolution...
They will do it the same way.
Everyone ready to try this?

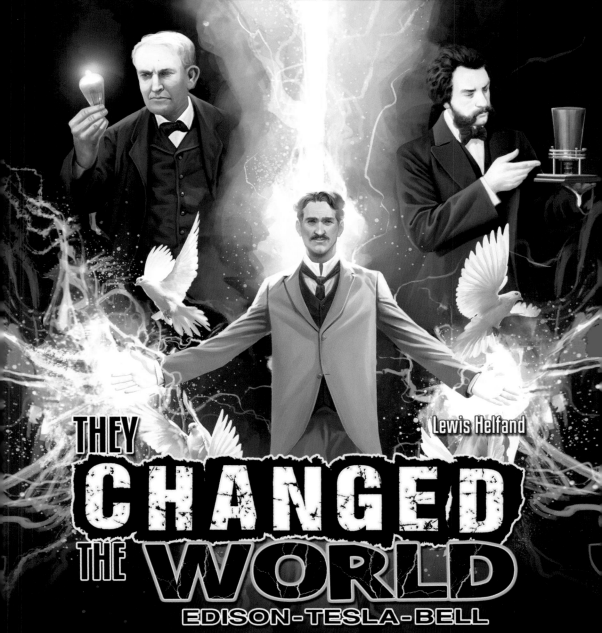

Industry 4.0 and after

Warfare without soldiers, cars that drive on their own, robots that can do all the housework – if you think these are snippets from a science fiction future, then the future is already here. We are in the middle of a new industrial revolution that is changing the way we work, communicate, entertain ourselves and even think. These drastic and far reaching changes have been termed the fourth industrial revolution or Industry 4.0. The term has been coined by Klaus Schwab, chairman of the World Economic Forum, in his book *The Fourth Industrial Revolution*.

The mainstay behind the fourth industrial revolution is cyber connectivity, enabling physical systems and operations to be remotely controlled through the internet. If you compare how life used to be as recently as ten years ago, you will notice the enormity of changes and developments that have taken place. None of us have stepped in a bank for a long time. Financial transactions are easily made at the click of a mouse or a swipe of a finger on a smartphone. You can shop for just about anything online. You can book a cab with an 'App' on your smartphone. No one ever buys DVDs, we watch movies or play games online. Lost on the road? Get your route with the help of GPS. These examples are just everyday low-end features of the fourth industrial revolution. When it comes to state-of-the-art technology, the fourth industrial revolution has the potential to unite all people and systems into one interconnected neural network, thereby changing life in ways we have never imagined possible.

But first, why is it called the fourth industrial revolution? What are the other three? As you have learned in this book, the Industrial Revolution began around the sixteenth century, with the onset of water and steam power. This was followed by the introduction of electricity and mass production in the late nineteenth century. The twentieth century saw the emergence of computers and automation. The twenty first century saw the rise of cyber-physical integration.

Industrial Revolution: The Four Stages

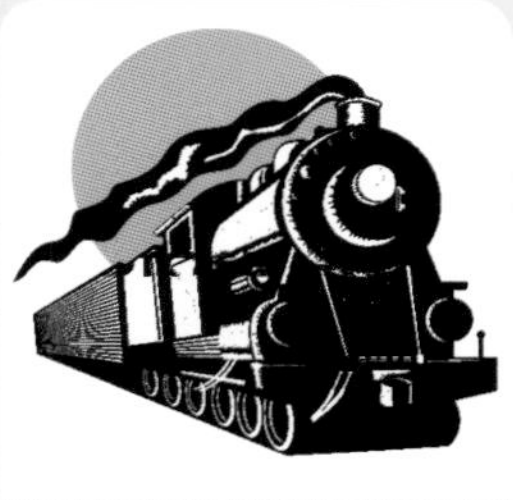

18th Century:
Steam power, water power

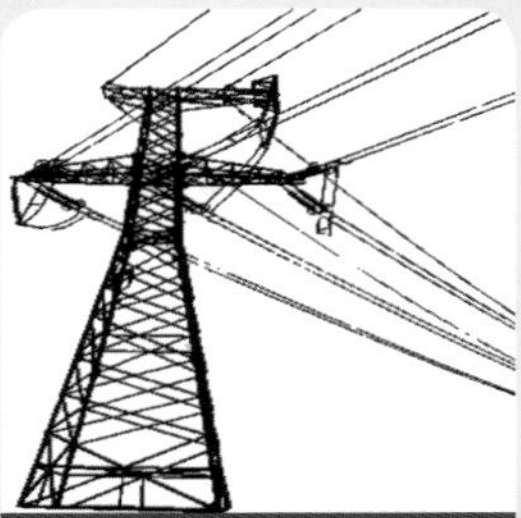

19th Century:
Electricity, mass production

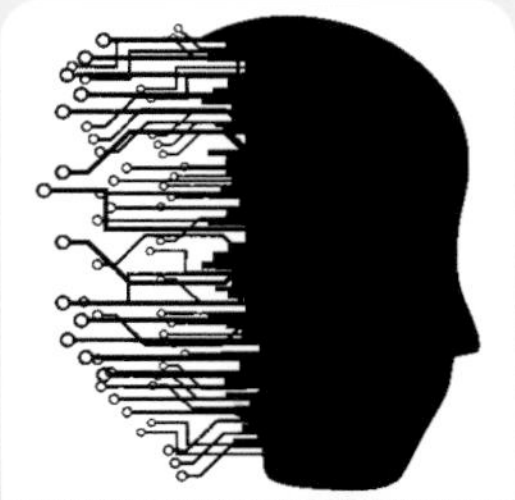

20th Century:
Electronics, information technology

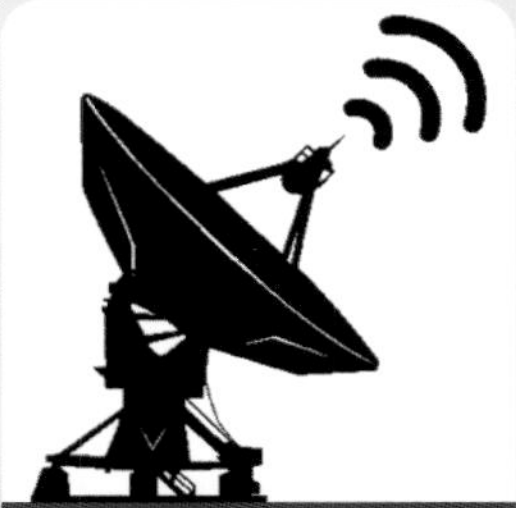

21st Century:
Cyber-physical integration

Thinking Computers

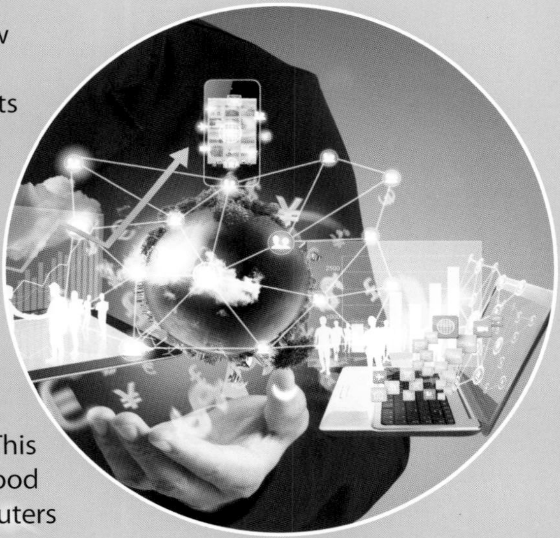

New applications are popping up every day now making computers incredibly smart. They beat grandmasters at chess. They translate documents in seconds. They extrapolate complex strategies by use of algorithms. They control and direct weaponry at long range. You can have a conversation with a computer without even knowing it. This has led some to fear a future where computers will control humans, and will no longer be slaves to do our bidding. This concept is known as the Technological Singularity, a possible scenario where artificial intelligence (AI) surpasses human intelligence. This futuristic possibility was foreseen in the Hollywood Terminator franchise, where a network of computers rules the world enslaving humans.

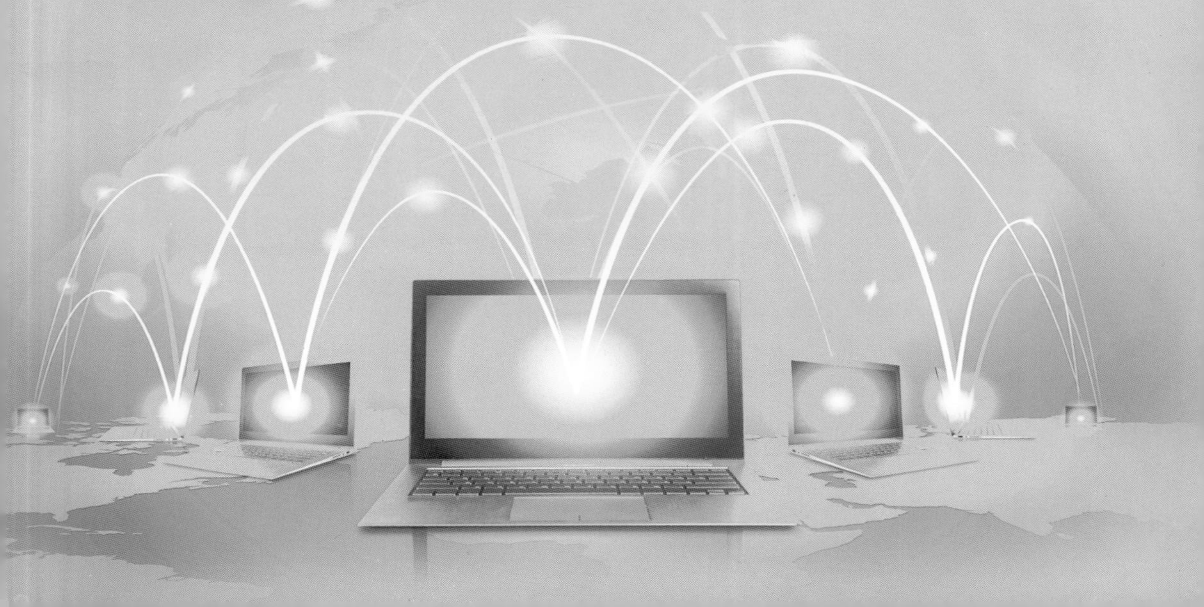

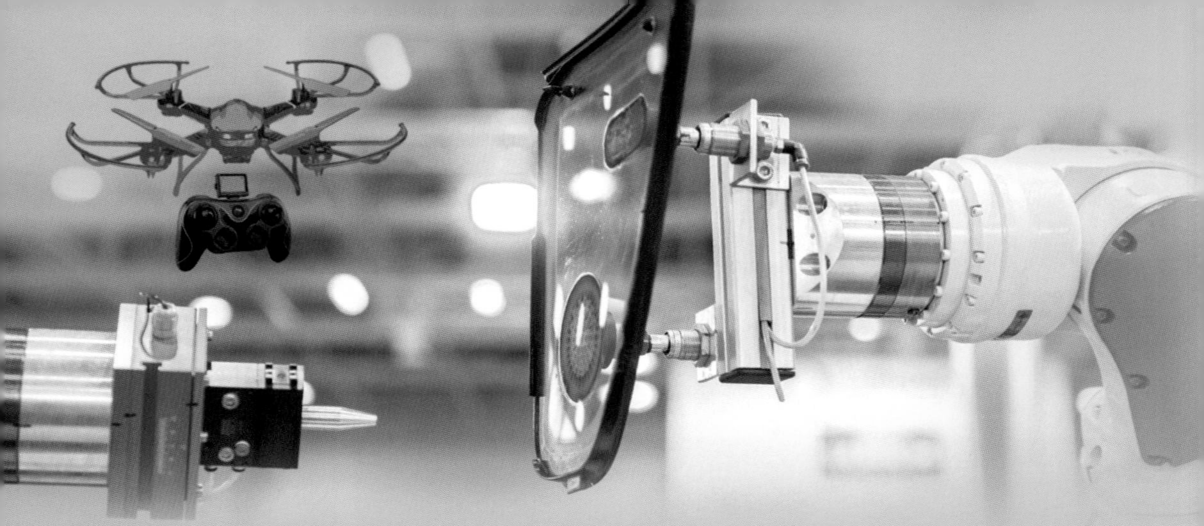

Living With Robots and Drones

Robots are autonomous machinery that can perform complex physical tasks. Computer and network-controlled robots have been used in industrial applications, warfare, exploration of hazardous environments, surgery and even space and extraterrestrial research. NASA's Mars Rover is controlled by scientists in NASA's control center, and on command explores the surface of Mars to send data back to Earth.

Remote controlled aircraft have been used by both militaries and hobbyists since the mid-twentieth century. Their latest manifestation, drones, are extremely powerful and versatile flying computers that do tasks that are dangerous or monotonous for piloted aircraft. Used extensively in modern warfare, drones have their peacetime uses as well.

There are far more civilian and commercial drones in operation today than in the military. Drones are used for high resolution aerial photography and live footage to assist in navigation, archeology, reconnaissance, disaster management, environmental protection, and crop data collection. Several innovative companies plan to use drones to deliver items ranging from pizzas to couriered packages to our homes.

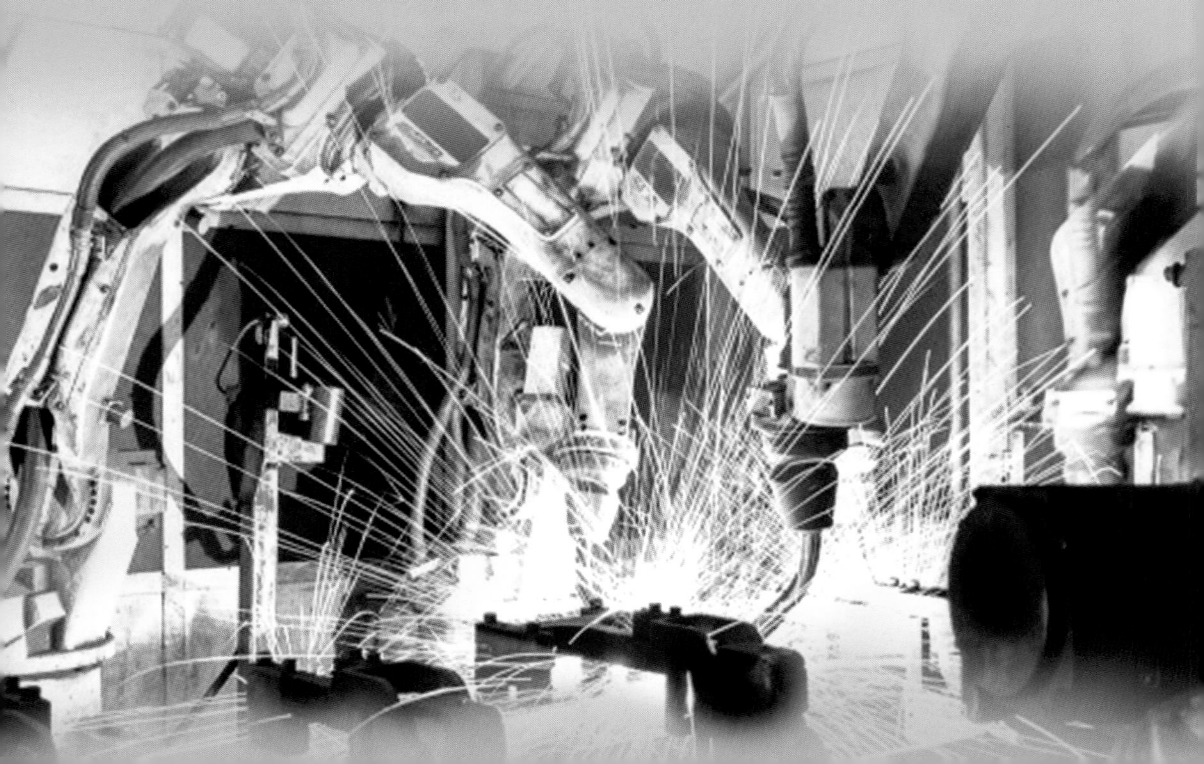

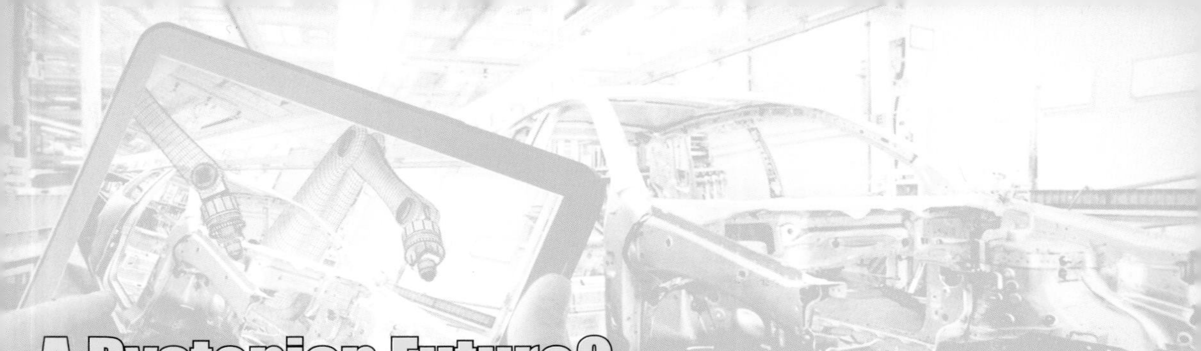

A Dystopian Future?

Robots are increasingly being used in agriculture for plowing, spraying, harvesting and picking, reducing the need for farm workers. Robots in both heavy and light industry have made labor almost redundant. A restaurant in China has been using 'Robot Waiters', a novelty that draws more customers. Employers find robots to be neither temperamental, nor prone to negotiate.

Economists and social scientists predict that the fourth industrial revolution will lead us to a Post-industrial age in which physical tasks can be programmed for computer operated machines. The only work left for humans will be the ones that require a significantly greater degree of intelligence and creativity. An obvious fear arising from this prospect is that a vast majority of what comprises the workforce today will become unemployed, leading to social unrest and widespread rebellion.

Contrary to this dismal outlook, optimists assert that the Post-industrial age will usher in an unprecedented era of prosperity and well being. With mundane work relegated to robots and machines, humans will be free to explore and achieve their fullest potential for creative work that is rewarding and a source of great self satisfaction.

The future, as always, remains hard to be foretold. Mankind has overcome the changes wrought by previous industrial revolutions, using every measure of progress to improve the lives of all members of society. The hope is that the challenges of the fourth industrial revolution will again call upon our ingenuity, and once again we shall emerge in triumph to create a better world with the advent of the fourth industrial revolution.

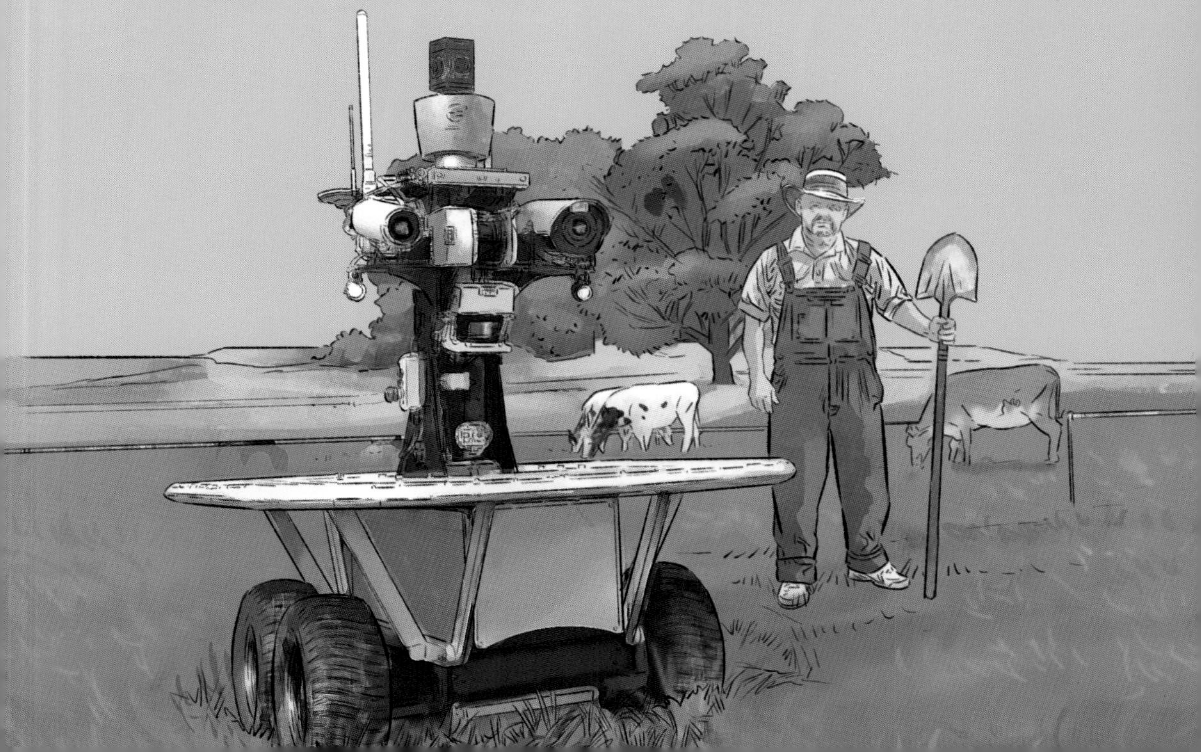

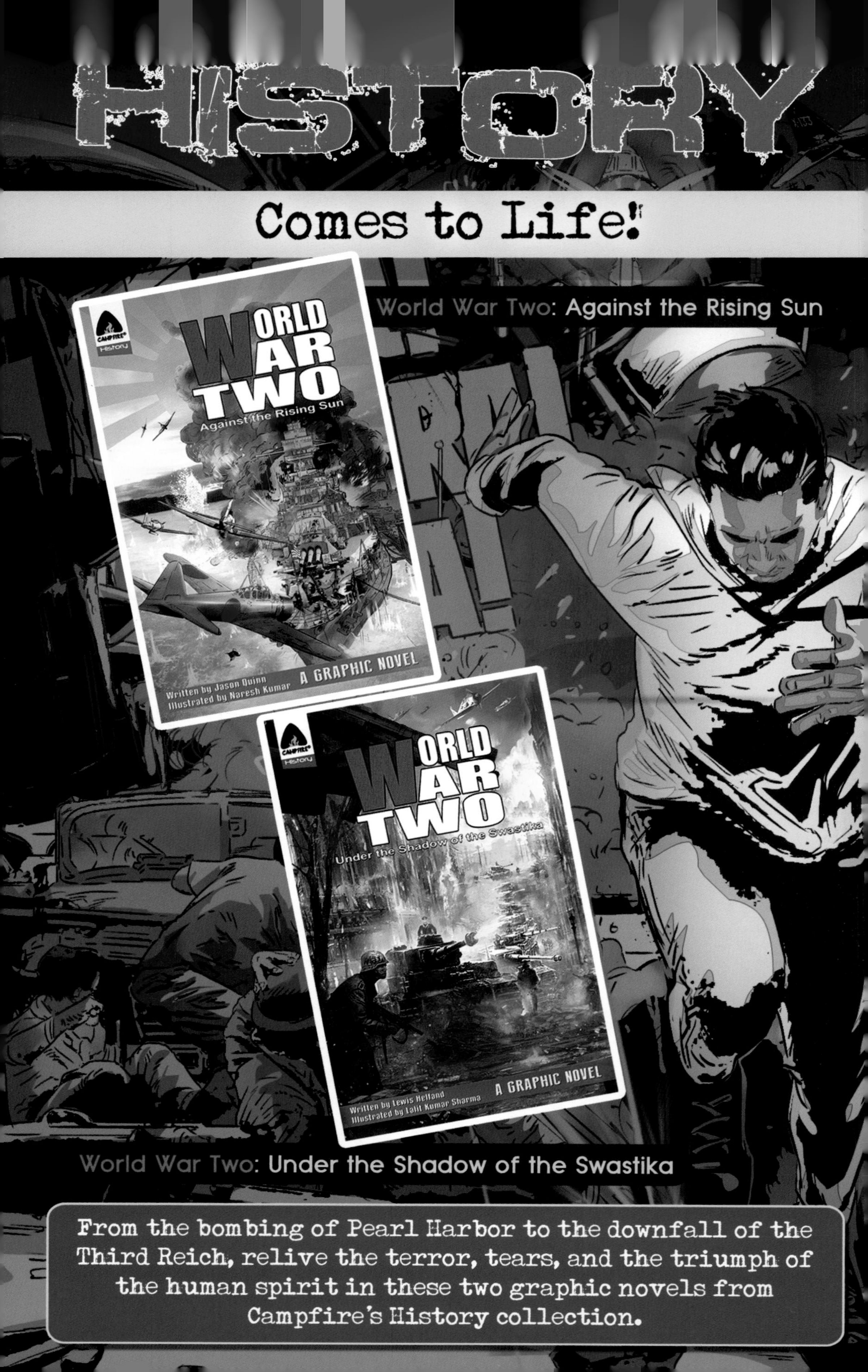
HISTORY
Comes to Life!
World War Two: Against the Rising Sun
WORLD WAR TWO
Against the Rising Sun
A GRAPHIC NOVEL
Written by Jason Quinn
Illustrated by Naresh Kumar
WORLD WAR TWO
Under the Shadow of the Swastika
A GRAPHIC NOVEL
Written by Lewis Helfand
Illustrated by Lalit Kumar Sharma
World War Two: Under the Shadow of the Swastika
From the bombing of Pearl Harbor to the downfall of the Third Reich, relive the terror, tears, and the triumph of the human spirit in these two graphic novels from Campfire's History collection.

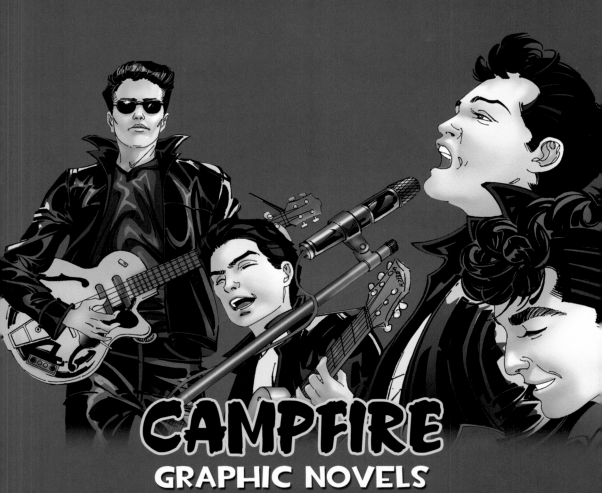
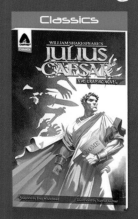

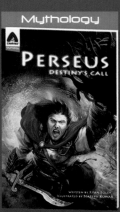

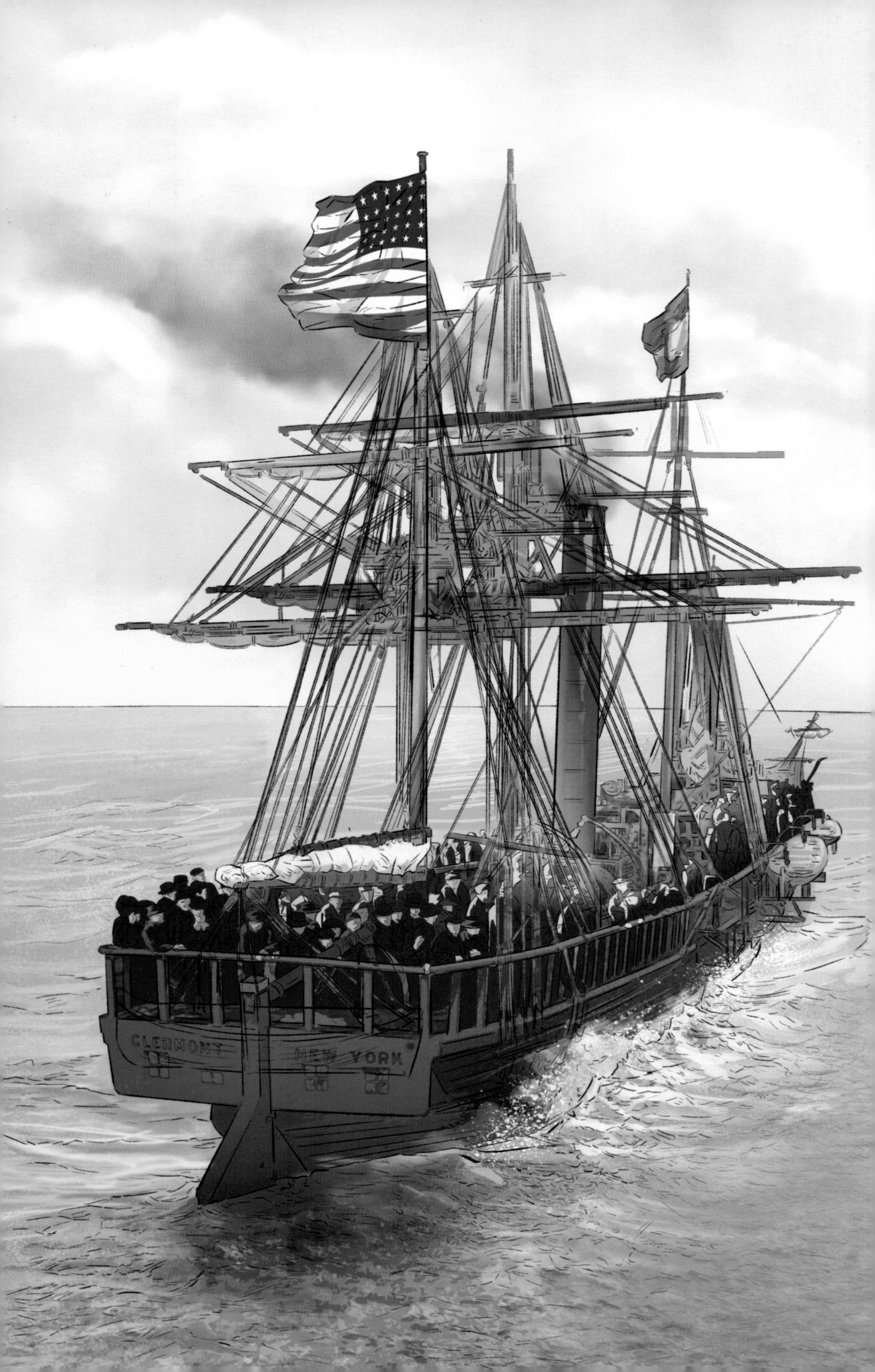
CLERMONT
NEW YORK